Author's National Edition

THE WRITINGS OF

MARK TWAIN

VOLUME I

This is the authorized Uniform Edition of all my books.

Mark Twain

1853.

1868.

EARLY PORTRAITS, 1853–1868

THE
INNOCENTS ABROAD

OR

THE NEW PILGRIMS' PROGRESS

BEING SOME ACCOUNT OF THE STEAMSHIP
QUAKER CITY'S PLEASURE EXCURSION
TO EUROPE AND THE HOLY LAND

BY

MARK TWAIN
(SAMUEL L. CLEMENS)

IN TWO VOLUMES
VOL. I

ILLUSTRATED

HARPER & BROTHERS PUBLISHERS
NEW YORK AND LONDON

To my most patient reader and most charitable critic, my aged Mother, this volume is affectionately inscribed.

BIOGRAPHICAL CRITICISM

By BRANDER MATTHEWS
Professor of Literature in Columbia University

IT is a common delusion of those who discuss con-
temporary literature that there is such an entity
as the "reading public," possessed of a certain uniformity of taste. There is not one public; there are
many publics,— as many in fact as there are different
kinds of taste; and the extent of an author's popularity is in proportion to the number of these separate
publics he may chance to please. Scott, for example, appealed not only to those who relished
romance and enjoyed excitement, but also to those
who appreciated his honest portrayal of sturdy characters. Thackeray is preferred by ambitious youth
who are insidiously flattered by his tacit compliments
to their knowledge of the world, by the disenchanted
who cannot help seeing the petty meannesses of society, and by the less sophisticated in whom sentiment

has not gone to seed in sentimentality. Dickens in
his own day bid for the approval of those who liked
broad caricature (and were therefore pleased with
Stiggins and Chadband), of those who fed greedily
on plentiful pathos (and were therefore delighted
with the deathbeds of Smike and Paul Dombey and
Little Nell) and also of those who asked for unex-
pected adventure (and were therefore glad to dis-
entangle the melodramatic intrigues of Ralph
Nickleby).

In like manner the American author who has
chosen to call himself Mark Twain has attained to an
immense popularity because the qualities he possesses in a high degree appeal to so many and so
widely varied publics,— first of all, no doubt, to the
public that revels in hearty and robust fun, but also
to the public which is glad to be swept along by the
full current of adventure, which is sincerely touched
by manly pathos, which is satisfied by vigorous and
exact portrayal of character, and which respects
shrewdness and wisdom and sanity and a healthy
hatred of pretense and affectation and sham. Perhaps no one book of Mark Twain's — with the possible exception of ' Huckleberry Finn ' — is equally a
favorite with all his readers; and perhaps some of
his best characteristics are absent from his earlier

books or but doubtfully latent in them.   Mark Twain is many-sided; and he has ripened in knowledge and in power since he first attracted attention as a wild Western funny man.   As he has grown older he has reflected more; he has both broadened and deepened.   The writer of " comic copy " for a mining-camp newspaper has developed into a liberal humorist, handling life seriously and making his readers think as he makes them laugh, until to-day Mark Twain has perhaps the largest audience of any author now using the English language.   To trace the stages of this evolution and to count the steps whereby the sage-brush reporter has risen to the rank of a writer of world-wide celebrity, is as interesting as it is instructive.

I.

Samuel Langhorne Clemens was born November 30, 1835, at Florida, Missouri.   His father was a merchant who had come from Tennessee and who removed soon after his son's birth to Hannibal, a little town on the Mississippi.   What Hannibal was like and what were the circumstances of Mr. Clemens's boyhood we can see for ourselves in the convincing pages of ' Tom Sawyer.'   Mr. Howells has called Hannibal " a loafing, out-at-elbows, down-at-the-heels, slave-holding Mississippi town; " and

Mr. Clemens was himself a slave owner, who silently abhorred slavery.

When the future author was but twelve his father died, and the son had to get his education as best he could. Of actual schooling he got little and of book-learning still less; but life itself is not a bad teacher for a boy who wants to study, and young Clemens did not waste his chances. He spent three years in the printing office of the little local paper, — for, like not a few others on the list of American authors that stretches from Benjamin Franklin to William Dean Howells, he began his connection with literature by setting type. As a journeyman printer the lad wandered from town to town and rambled even as far east as New York.

When he was seventeen he went back to the home of his boyhood resolved to become a pilot on the Mississippi. How he learnt the river he has told us in 'Life on the Mississippi,' wherein his adventures, his experiences, and his impressions while he was a cub-pilot are recorded with a combination of precise veracity and abundant humor which makes the earlier chapters of that marvelous book a most masterly fragment of autobiography. The life of a pilot was full of interest and excitement and opportunity, and what young Clemens saw and heard and

divined during the years when he was going up and
down the mighty river we may read in the pages of
'Huckleberry Finn' and 'Pudd'nhead Wilson.'
But toward the end of the fifties the railroads
began to rob the river of its supremacy as a carrier;
and in the beginning of the sixties the civil war broke
out and the Mississippi no longer went unvexed to
the sea. The skill, slowly and laboriously acquired,
was suddenly rendered useless, and at twenty-five the
young man found himself bereft of his calling. As a
border state, Missouri was sending her sons into the
armies of the Union and into the armies of the Con-
federacy, while many a man stood doubting, not
knowing which way to turn. The ex-pilot has given
us the record of his very brief and inglorious service
as a soldier of the South. When this escapade was
swiftly ended, he went to the Northwest with his
brother, who had been appointed Lieutenant-Gov-
ernor of Nevada. Thus the man who had been born
on the borderland of North and South, who had gone
East as a jour-printer, who had been again and again
up and down the Mississippi, now went West while he
was still plastic and impressionable; and he had thus
another chance to increase that intimate knowledge
of American life and American character which is
one of the most precious of his possessions.

While still on the river he had written a satiric
letter or two signed " Mark Twain "— taking the
name from a call of the man who heaves the
lead and who cries " By the mark, three," " Mark
twain," and so on. In Nevada he went to the
mines and lived the life he has described in ' Roughing It,' but when he failed to " strike it rich," he
naturally drifted into journalism and back into a
newspaper office again. The *Virginia City Enterprise* was not overmanned, and the newcomer did all
sorts of odd jobs, finding time now and then to write
a sketch which seemed important enough to permit
of his signature. The name of Mark Twain soon
began to be known to those who were curious in
newspaper humor. After a while he was drawn
across the mountains to San Francisco, where he
found casual employment on the *Morning Call*, and
where he joined himself to a little group of aspiring
literators which included Mr. Bret Harte, Mr. Noah
Brooks, Mr. Charles Henry Webb, and Mr. Charles
Warren Stoddard.

It was in 1867 that Mr. Webb published Mark
Twain's first book, ' The Celebrated Jumping Frog
of Calaveras '; and it was in 1867 that the proprietors of the *Alta California* supplied him with the
funds necessary to enable him to become one of the

passengers on the steamer *Quaker City*, which had
been chartered to take a select party on what is now
known as the Mediterranean trip. The weekly letters, in which he set forth what befel him on this
journey, were printed in the *Alta* Sunday after Sunday, and were copied freely by the other Californian
papers. These letters served as the foundation of a
book published in 1869 and called ' The Innocents
Abroad,' a book which instantly brought to the
author celebrity and cash.

Both of these valuable aids to ambition were in-
creased by his next step, his appearance on the
lecture platform. Mr. Noah Brooks, who was
present at his first attempt, has recorded that Mark
Twain's " method as a lecturer was distinctly unique
and novel. His slow, deliberate drawl, the anxious
and perturbed expression of his visage, the apparently painful effort with which he framed his sentences, the surprise that spread over his face when
the audience roared with delight or rapturously ap-
plauded the finer passages of his word-painting, were
unlike anything of the kind they had ever known."
In the thirty years since that first appearance the
method has not changed, although it has probably
matured. Mark Twain is one of the most effective
of platform-speakers and one of the most artistic,

with an art of his own which is very individual and
very elaborate in spite of its seeming simplicity.

Although he succeeded abundantly as a lecturer,
and although he was the author of the most widely-
circulated book of the decade, Mark Twain still
thought of himself only as a journalist; and when
he gave up the West for the East he became an
editor of the Buffalo *Express*, in which he had
bought an interest. In 1870 he married; and it is
perhaps not indiscreet to remark that his was
another of those happy unions of which there have
been so many in the annals of American authorship.
In 1871 he removed to Hartford, where his home
has been ever since; and at the same time he gave
up newspaper work.

In 1872 he wrote 'Roughing It,' and in the
following year came his first sustained attempt
at fiction, 'The Gilded Age,' written in collabora-
tion with Mr. Charles Dudley Warner. The character of *Colonel Mulberry Sellers* Mark Twain soon
took out of this book to make it the central figure
of a play, which the late John T. Raymond acted
hundreds of times throughout the United States, the
playgoing public pardoning the inexpertness of the
dramatist in favor of the delicious humor and the
compelling veracity with which the chief character

was presented. So universal was this type and so broadly recognizable its traits that there were few towns wherein the play was presented in which some-one did not accost the actor who impersonated the ever-hopeful schemer to declare, " I'm the original of *Sellers !* Didn't Mark ever tell you? Well, he took the *Colonel* from me ! "

Encouraged by the welcome accorded to this first attempt at fiction, Mark Twain turned to the days of his boyhood and wrote ' Tom Sawyer,' pub-lished in 1875. He also collected his sketches, scat-tered here and there in newspapers and magazines. Toward the end of the seventies he went to Europe again with his family; and the result of this journey is recorded in ' A Tramp Abroad,' published in 1880. Another volume of sketches, ' The Stolen White Elephant,' was put forth in 1882; and in the same year Mark Twain first came forward as a his-torical novelist— if 'The Prince and the Pauper' can fairly be called a historical novel. The year after, he sent forth the volume describing his ' Life on the Mississippi '; and in 1884 he followed this with the story in which that life has been crystallized forever, ' Huckleberry Finn,' the finest of his books, the deepest in its insight, and the widest in its appeal.

This Odyssey of the Mississippi was published by

a new firm, in which the author was a chief partner, just as Sir Walter Scott had been an associate of Ballantyne and Constable. There was at first a period of prosperity in which the house issued the 'Personal Memoirs' of Grant, giving his widow checks for $350,000 in 1886, and in which Mark Twain himself published 'A Connecticut Yankee at King Arthur's Court,' a volume of 'Merry Tales,' and a story called 'The American Claimant,' wherein *Colonel Sellers* reappears. Then there came a succession of hard years; and at last the publishing house in which Mark Twain was a partner failed, as the publishing house in which Walter Scott was a partner had formerly failed. The author of 'Huckleberry Finn' was past sixty when he found himself suddenly saddled with a load of debt, just as the author of 'Waverley' had been burdened full threescore years earlier; and Mark Twain stood up stoutly under it as Scott had done before him. More fortunate than the Scotchman, the American has lived to pay the debt in full.

Since the disheartening crash came, he has given to the public a third Mississippi River tale, 'Pudd'nhead Wilson,' issued in 1894; and a third historical novel 'Joan of Arc,' a reverent and sympathetic study of the bravest figure in all French

history, printed anonymously in *Harper's Magazine*
and then in a volume acknowledged by the author in
1896. As one of the results of a lecturing tour
around the world he has prepared another volume of
travels, 'Following the Equator,' published toward
the end of 1897. Mention must also be made of a
fantastic tale called 'Tom Sawyer Abroad,' sent
forth in 1894, of a volume of sketches, 'The Million Pound Bank-Note,' assembled in 1893, and also
of a collection of literary essays, 'How to Tell a
Story,' published in 1897.

This is but the barest outline of Mark Twain's life,
— such a brief summary as we must have before us
if we wish to consider the conditions under which the
author has developed and the stages of his growth.
It will serve, however, to show how various have
been his forms of activity — printer, pilot, miner,
journalist, traveler, lecturer, novelist, publisher —
and to suggest the width of his experience of life.

II.

A humorist is often without honor in his own
country. Perhaps this is partly because humor is
likely to be familiar, and familiarity breeds contempt.
Perhaps it is partly because (for some strange
reason) we tend to despise those who make us

2

laugh, while we respect those who make us weep —
forgetting that there are formulas for forcing tears
quite as facile as the formulas for forcing smiles.
Whatever the reason, the fact is indisputable that the
humorist must pay the penalty of his humor; he
must run the risk of being tolerated as a mere fun-
maker, not to be taken seriously, and unworthy of
critical consideration. This penalty is being paid
now by Mark Twain. In many of the discussions
of American literature he is dismissed as though
he were only a competitor of his predecessors,
Artemus Ward and John Phœnix, instead of being,
what he is really, a writer who is to be classed —
at whatever interval only time may decide — rather
with Cervantes and Molière.

Like the heroines of the problem-plays of the
modern theater, Mark Twain has had to live down
his past. His earlier writing gave but little promise
of the enduring qualities obvious enough in his later
works. Mr. Noah Brooks has told us how he was
advised if he wished to " see genuine specimens of
American humor, frolicsome, extravagant, and audacious," to look up the sketches which the then almost
unknown Mark Twain was printing in a Nevada newspaper. The humor of Mark Twain is still American,
still frolicsome, extravagant, and audacious; but it

is riper now and richer, and it has taken unto itself other qualities existing only in germ in these first-lings of his muse. The sketches in 'The Jumping Frog' and the letters which made up 'The Innocents Abroad' are "comic copy," as the phrase is in newspaper offices — comic copy not altogether unlike what John Phœnix had written and Artemus Ward, better indeed than the work of these newspaper humorists (for Mark Twain had it in him to develop as they did not), but not essentially dissimilar.

And in the eyes of many who do not think for themselves, Mark Twain is only the author of these genuine specimens of American humor. For when the public has once made up its mind about any man's work, it does not relish any attempt to force it to unmake this opinion and to remake it. Like other juries, it does not like to be ordered to reconsider its verdict as contrary to the facts of the case. It is always sluggish in beginning the necessary readjustment, and not only sluggish, but somewhat grudging. Naturally it cannot help seeing the later works of a popular writer from the point of view it had to take to enjoy his earlier writings. And thus the author of 'Huckleberry Finn' and 'Joan of Arc' is forced to pay a high price for the early and abundant popularity of 'The Innocents Abroad.'

No doubt, a few of his earlier sketches were inexpensive in their elements; made of materials worn threadbare by generations of earlier funny men, they were sometimes cut in the pattern of his predecessors. No doubt, some of the earliest of all were crude and highly colored, and may even be called forced, not to say violent. No doubt, also, they did not suggest the seriousness and the melancholy which always must underlie the deepest humor, as we find it in Cervantes and Molière, in Swift and in Lowell. But even a careless reader, skipping through the book in idle amusement, ought to have been able to see in ' The Innocents Abroad,' that the writer of that liveliest of books of travel was no mere merryandrew, grinning through a horse-collar to make sport for the groundlings; but a sincere observer of life, seeing through his own eyes and setting down what he saw with abundant humor, of course, but also with profound respect for the eternal verities.

George Eliot in one of her essays calls those who parody lofty themes " debasers of the moral currency." Mark Twain is always an advocate of the sterling ethical standard. He is ready to overwhelm an affectation with irresistible laughter, but he never lacks reverence for the things that really deserve reverence. It is not at the Old Masters that he scoffs in Italy, but rather at those who pay lip-service to things which they neither enjoy nor understand. For a ruin or a painting or a legend that does not seem to him to deserve the appreciation in which it is held he refuses to affect an admiration he does not feel; he cannot help being honest — he was born so. For meanness of all kinds he has a burning contempt; and on Abelard he pours out the vials of his wrath. He has a quick eye for all humbugs and a scorching scorn for them; but there is no attempt at being funny in the manner of the cockney comedians when he stands in the awful presence of the Sphinx. He is not taken in by the glamour of Palestine; he does not lose his head there; he keeps his feet; but he knows that he is standing on holy ground; and there is never a hint of irreverence in his attitude.

'A Tramp Abroad' is a better book than 'The Innocents Abroad'; it is quite as laughter-provoking, and its manner is far more restrained. Mark Twain was then master of his method, sure of himself, secure of his popularity; and he could do his best and spare no pains to be certain that it was his best. Perhaps there is a slight falling off in 'Following the Equator'; a trace of fatigue, of weari-

B*

ness, of disenchantment. But the last book of travels has passages as broadly humorous as any of the first; and it proves the author's possession of a pithy shrewdness not to be suspected from a perusal of its earliest predecessor. The first book was the work of a young fellow rejoicing in his own fun and resolved to make his readers laugh with him or at him; the latest book is the work of an older man, who has found that life is not all laughter, but whose eye is as clear as ever and whose tongue is as plain-spoken.

These three books of travel are like all other books of travel in that they relate in the first person what the author went forth to see. Autobiographic also are 'Roughing It' and 'Life on the Mississippi,' and they have always seemed to me better books than the more widely circulated travels. They are better because they are the result of a more intimate knowledge of the material dealt with. Every traveler is of necessity but a bird of passage; he is a mere carpet-bagger; his acquaintance with the countries he visits is external only; and this acquaintanceship is made only when he is a full-grown man. But Mark Twain's knowledge of the Mississippi was acquired in his youth; it was not purchased with a price; it was his birthright; and it was internal and complete. And his knowledge of the mining-camp was achieved in early manhood when the mind is open and sensitive to every new impression. There is in both these books a fidelity to the inner truth, a certainty of touch, a sweep of vision, not to be found in the three books of travels. For my own part I have long thought that Mark Twain could securely rest his right to survive as an author on those opening chapters in 'Life on the Mississippi' in which he makes clear the difficulties, the seeming impossibilities, that fronted those who wished to learn the river. These chapters are bold and brilliant; and they picture for us forever a period and a set of conditions, singularly interesting and splendidly varied, that otherwise would have had to forego all adequate record.

III.

It is highly probable that when an author reveals the power of evoking views of places and of calling up portraits of people such as Mark Twain showed in 'Life on the Mississippi,' and when he has the masculine grasp of reality Mark Twain made evident in 'Roughing It,' he must needs sooner or later turn from mere fact to avowed fiction and become a story-teller. The long stories which Mark Twain has written fall into two divisions,— first, those of which the scene is laid in the present, in reality, and mostly in the Mississippi Valley, and second, those of which the scene is laid in the past, in fantasy mostly, and in Europe.

As my own liking is a little less for the latter group, there is no need for me now to linger over them. In writing these tales of the past Mark Twain was making up stories in his head; personally I prefer the tales of his in which he has his foot firm on reality. 'The Prince and the Pauper' has the essence of boyhood in it; it has variety and vigor; it has abundant humor and plentiful pathos; and yet I for one would give the whole of it for the single chapter in which Tom Sawyer lets the contract for whitewashing his aunt's fence.

Mr. Howells has declared that there are two kinds of fiction he likes almost equally well,—"a real novel and a pure romance; " and he joyfully accepts 'A Connecticut Yankee at King Arthur's Court' as "one of the greatest romances ever imagined." It is a humorous romance overflowing with stalwart fun; and it is not irreverent but iconoclastic, in that it breaks not a few disestablished idols. It is intensely American and intensely nineteenth century and intensely democratic — in the best sense of that abused adjective. The British critics were greatly

displeased with the book;— and we are reminded of
the fact that the Spanish still somewhat resent 'Don
Quixote' because it brings out too truthfully the
fatal gap in the Spanish character between the ideal
and the real. So much of the feudal still survives in
British society that Mark Twain's merry and eluci-
dating assault on the past seemed to some almost an
insult to the present.

But no critic, British or American, has ventured to
discover any irreverence in 'Joan of Arc,' wherein
indeed the tone is almost devout and the humor
almost too much subdued. Perhaps it is my own
distrust of the so-called historical novel, my own dis-
belief that it can ever be anything but an inferior
form of art, which makes me care less for this worthy
effort to honor a noble figure. And elevated and
dignified as is the 'Joan of Arc,' I do not think
that it shows us Mark Twain at his best; although it
has many a passage that only he could have written,
it is perhaps the least characteristic of his works.
Yet it may well be that the certain measure of success
he has achieved in handling a subject so lofty and so
serious, will help to open the eyes of the public to
see the solid merits of his other stories, in which his
humor has fuller play and in which his natural gifts
are more abundantly displayed.

Of these other stories three are " real novels," to use Mr. Howells's phrase; they are novels as real as any in any literature. 'Tom Sawyer' and 'Huckleberry Finn' and 'Pudd'nhead Wilson' are invaluable contributions to American literature —for American literature is nothing if it is not a true picture of American life and if it does not help us to understand ourselves. 'Huckleberry Finn' is a very amusing volume, and a generation has read its pages and laughed over it immoderately; but it is very much more than a funny book; it is a marvelously accurate portrayal of a whole civilization. Mr. Ormsby, in an essay which accompanies his translation of 'Don Quixote,' has pointed out that for a full century after its publication that greatest of novels was enjoyed chiefly as a tale of humorous misadventure, and that three generations had laughed over it before anybody suspected that it was more than a mere funny book. It is perhaps rather with the picaresque romances of Spain that 'Huckleberry Finn' is to be compared than with the masterpiece of Cervantes; but I do not think it will be a century or take three generations before we Americans generally discover how great a book 'Huckleberry Finn' really is, how keen its vision of character, how close its observation of life, how sound its philosophy, and how it records for us once and for all certain phases of Southwestern society which it is most important for us to perceive and to understand. The influence of slavery, the prevalence of feuds, the conditions and the circumstances that make lynching possible — all these things are set before us clearly and without comment. It is for us to draw our own moral, each for himself, as we do when we see Shakespeare acted.

'Huckleberry Finn,' in its art, for one thing, and also in its broader range, is superior to 'Tom Sawyer' and to 'Pudd'nhead Wilson,' fine as both these are in their several ways. In no book in our language, to my mind, has the boy, simply as a boy, been better realized than in 'Tom Sawyer.' In some respects 'Pudd'nhead Wilson' is the most dramatic of Mark Twain's longer stories, and also the most ingenious; like 'Tom Sawyer' and 'Huckleberry Finn,' it has the full flavor of the Mississippi River, on which its author spent his own boyhood, and from contact with the soil of which he always rises reinvigorated.

It is by these three stories, and especially by 'Huckleberry Finn,' that Mark Twain is likely to live longest. Nowhere else is the life of the Mississippi Valley so truthfully recorded. Nowhere else

can we find a gallery of Southwestern characters as
varied and as veracious as those Huck Finn met in
his wanderings. The histories of literature all praise
the 'Gil Blas' of Le Sage for its amusing adventures, its natural characters, its pleasant humor, and
its insight into human frailty; and the praise is deserved. But in every one of these qualities ' Huckleberry Finn' is superior to 'Gil Blas.' Le Sage
set the model of the picaresque novel, and Mark
Twain followed his example; but the American
book is richer than the French — deeper, finer,
stronger. It would be hard to find in any language
better specimens of pure narrative, better examples
of the power of telling a story and of calling up
action so that the reader cannot help but see it, than
Mark Twain's account of the Shepherdson-Granger-
ford feud, and his description of the shooting of
Boggs by Sherburn and of the foiled attempt to
lynch Sherburn afterward.

These scenes, fine as they are, vivid, powerful,
and most artistic in their restraint, can be matched
in the two other books. In 'Tom Sawyer' they
can be paralleled by the chapter in which the boy and
the girl are lost in the cave, and Tom, seeing a gleam
of light in the distance, discovers that it is a candle
carried by Indian Joe, the one enemy he has in the

world. In ' Pudd'nhead Wilson ' the great passages
of ' Huckleberry Finn ' are rivaled by that most
pathetic account of the weak son willing to sell his
own mother as a slave " down the river."   Although
no one of the books is sustained throughout on this
high level, and although, in truth, there are in each of
them passages here and there that we could wish away
(because they are not worthy of the association in
which we find them), I have no hesitation in expressing here my own conviction that the man who has
given us four scenes like these is to be compared
with the masters of literature; and that he can abide
the comparison with equanimity.

IV.

Perhaps I myself prefer these three Mississippi
Valley books above all Mark Twain's other writings
(although with no lack of affection for those also)
partly because these have the most of the flavor of
the soil about them.   After veracity and the sense
of the universal, what I best relish in literature is this
native aroma, pungent, homely, and abiding.   Yet
I feel sure that I should not rate him so high if
he were the author of these three books only.   They
are the best of him, but the others are good also,
and good in a different way.   Other writers have

given us this local color more or less artistically, more or less convincingly: one New England and another New York, a third Virginia, and a fourth Georgia, and a fifth Wisconsin; but who so well as Mark Twain has given us the full spectrum of the Union? With all his exactness in reproducing the Mississippi Valley, Mark Twain is not sectional in his outlook; he is national always. He is not narrow; he is not Western or Eastern; he is American with a certain largeness and boldness and freedom and certainty that we like to think of as befitting a country so vast as ours and a people so independent.

In Mark Twain we have " the national spirit as seen with our own eyes," declared Mr. Howells; and, from more points of view than one, Mark Twain seems to me to be the very embodiment of Americanism. Self-educated in the hard school of life, he has gone on broadening his outlook as he has grown older. Spending many years abroad, he has come to understand other nationalities, without enfeebling his own native faith. Combining a mastery of the commonplace with an imaginative faculty, he is a practical idealist. No respecter of persons, he has a tender regard for his fellow man. Irreverent toward all outworn superstitions, he has ever revealed the deepest respect for all things truly worthy of reverence. Unwilling to take pay in words, he is impatient always to get at the root of the matter, to pierce to the center, to see the thing as it is. He has a habit of standing upright, of thinking for himself, and of hitting hard at whatsoever seems to him hateful and mean; but at the core of him there is genuine gentleness and honest sympathy, brave humanity and sweet kindliness. Perhaps it is boastful for us to think that these characteristics which we see in Mark Twain are characteristics also of the American people as a whole; but it is pleasant to think so.

Mark Twain has the very marrow of Americanism. He is as intensely and as typically American as Franklin or Emerson or Hawthorne. He has not a little of the shrewd common sense and the homely and unliterary directness of Franklin. He is not without a share of the aspiration and the elevation of Emerson; and he has a philosophy of his own as optimistic as Emerson's. He possesses also somewhat of Hawthorne's interest in ethical problems, with something of the same power of getting at the heart of them; he, too, has written his parables and apologues wherein the moral is obvious and unobtruded. He is uncompromisingly honest; and his conscience is as rugged as his style sometimes is.

3

No American author has to-day at his command a style more nervous, more varied, more flexible, or more various than Mark Twain's. His colloquial ease should not hide from us his mastery of all the devices of rhetoric. He may seem to disobey the letter of the law sometimes, but he is always obedient to the spirit. He never speaks unless he has something to say; and then he says it tersely, sharply, with a freshness of epithet and an individuality of phrase, always accurate however unacademic. His vocabulary is enormous, and it is deficient only in the dead words; his language is alive always, and actually tingling with vitality. He rejoices in the daring noun and in the audacious adjective. His instinct for the exact word is not always unerring, and now and again he has failed to exercise it; but there is in his prose none of the flatting and sharping he censured in Fenimore Cooper's. His style has none of the cold perfection of an antique statue; it is too modern and too American for that, and too completely the expression of the man himself, sincere and straightforward. It is not free from slang. although this is far less frequent than one might expect; but it does its work swiftly and cleanly. And it is capable of immense variety. Consider the tale of the Blue Jay in ' A Tramp Abroad,' wherein the humor is sustained by unstated pathos; what could be better told than this, with every word the right word and in the right place? And take Huck Finn's description of the storm when he was alone on the island, which is in dialect, which will not parse, which bristles with double negatives, but which none the less is one of the finest passages of descriptive prose in all American literature.

V.

After all, it is as a humorist pure and simple that Mark Twain is best known and best beloved. In the preceding pages I have tried to point out the several ways in which he transcends humor, as the word is commonly restricted, and to show that he is no mere fun-maker. But he is a fun-maker beyond all question, and he has made millions laugh as no other man of our century has done. The laughter he has aroused is wholesome and self-respecting; it clears the atmosphere. For this we cannot but be grateful. As Lowell said, "let us not be ashamed to confess that, if we find the tragedy a bore, we take the profoundest satisfaction in the farce. It is a mark of sanity." There is no laughter in *Don Quixote*, the noble enthusiast whose wits are unsettled; and there is little on the lips of *Alceste* the

3

misanthrope of Molière; but for both of them life would have been easier had they known how to laugh. Cervantes himself, and Molière also, found relief in laughter for their melancholy; and it was the sense of humor which kept them tolerantly interested in the spectacle of humanity, although life had pressed hardly on them both. On Mark Twain also life has left its scars; but he has bound up his wounds and battled forward with a stout heart, as Cervantes did, and Molière. It was Molière who declared that it was a strange business to undertake to make people laugh; but even now, after two centuries, when the best of Molière's plays are acted, mirth breaks out again and laughter overflows.

It would be doing Mark Twain a disservice to liken him to Molière, the greatest comic dramatist of all time; and yet there is more than one point of similarity. Just as Mark Twain began by writing comic copy which contained no prophecy of a masterpiece like 'Huckleberry Finn,' so Molière was at first the author only of semi-acrobatic farces on the Italian model in no wise presaging 'Tartuffe' and 'The Misanthrope.' Just as Molière succeeded first of all in pleasing the broad public that likes robust fun, and then slowly and step by step developed into a dramatist who set on the stage enduring figures plucked out of the abounding life about him, so also has Mark Twain grown, ascending from ' The Jumping Frog' to 'Huckleberry Finn,' as comic as its elder brother and as laughter-provoking, but charged also with meaning and with philosophy. And like Molière again, Mark Twain has kept solid hold of the material world; his doctrine is not of the earth earthy, but it is never sublimated into senti- mentality. He sympathizes with the spiritual side of humanity, while never ignoring the sensual. Like Molière, Mark Twain takes his stand on com- mon sense and thinks scorn of affectation of every sort. He understands sinners and strugglers and weaklings; and he is not harsh with them, reserving his scorching hatred for hypocrites and pretenders and frauds.

At how long an interval Mark Twain shall be rated after Molière and Cervantes it is for the future to declare. All that we can see clearly now is that it is with them that he is to be classed,— with Molière and Cervantes, with Chaucer and Fielding, humorists all of them, and all of them manly men.

PREFACE

TO

THE UNIFORM EDITION

---

*S*O FAR as I remember, I have never seen an Author's Preface which had any purpose but one — to furnish reasons for the publication of the book. Prefaces wear many disguises, call themselves by various names, and pretend to come on various businesses, but I think that upon examination we are quite sure to find that their errand is always the same : they are there to apologize for the book ; in other words, furnish reasons for its publication. This often insures brevity.

Upon these terms, if there is nothing to explain or nothing worth the explanation, there is no occasion for a Preface; there is nothing for it to do — except to explain its own presence, apologize for its intrusion. That is what this present Preface does.

When the books in this collection appeared in print originally, most of them had Prefaces which furnished reasons for publication. Those Introductions will be

3*

*found in their places, and need not be repeated here.
The jurisdiction of the present Preface is restricted to
furnishing reasons for the publication of the Collection
as a whole. This is not easy to do. Aside from the
ordinary commercial reasons I find none that I can offer
with dignity. I cannot say without immodesty that the
books have merit; I cannot say without immodesty that
the public want a Uniform Edition; I cannot say without immodesty that a Uniform Edition will turn the
nation toward high ideals and elevated thought; I cannot say without immodesty that a Uniform Edition will
eradicate crime. Though I think it will. I find no
reason which I can offer without immodesty except the
rather poor one that I should like to see a Uniform
Edition myself. It is nothing; a cat could say it about
her kittens. Still, I believe I will stand upon that.
I have to have a Preface and a reason, by law of custom, and the reason which I am putting forward is at
least without offense.*

MARK TWAIN.

Vienna, January, 1899.

PREFACE

THIS book is a record of a pleasure trip. If it were a record of a solemn scientific expedition, it would have about it that gravity, that profundity, and that impressive incomprehensibility which are so proper to works of that kind, and withal so attractive. Yet notwithstanding it is only a record of a picnic, it has a purpose, which is, to suggest to the reader how *he* would be likely to see Europe and the East if he looked at them with his own eyes instead of the eyes of those who traveled in those countries before him. I make small pretence of showing any one how he *ought* to look at objects of interest beyond the sea — other books do that, and therefore, even if I were competent to do it, there is no need.

I offer no apologies for any departures from the usual style of travel-writing that may be charged against me — for I think I have seen with impartial eyes, and I am sure I have written at least honestly, whether wisely or not.

In this volume I have used portions of letters which I wrote for the *Daily Alta California*, of San Francisco, the proprietors of that journal having waived their rights and given me the necessary permission.

I have also inserted portions of several letters written for the New York *Tribune* and the New York *Herald*.

THE AUTHOR.

SAN FRANCISCO.

ILLUSTRATIONS

CONTENTS.

(xli)

CHAPTER XV.

CHAPTER XVI.

CHAPTER XVII.

CHAPTER XVIII.

CHAPTER XIX.

CHAPTER XX.

CHAPTER XXI.

CHAPTER XXII.

THE INNOCENTS ABROAD

CHAPTER I.

FOR months the great Pleasure Excursion to Europe and the Holy Land was chatted about in the newspapers everywhere in America, and discussed at countless firesides. It was a novelty in the way of excursions — its like had not been thought of before, and it compelled that interest which attractive novelties always command. It was to be a picnic on a gigantic scale. The participants in it, instead of freighting an ungainly steam ferry-boat with youth and beauty and pies and doughnuts, and paddling up some obscure creek to disembark upon a grassy lawn and wear themselves out with a long summer day's laborious frolicking under the impression that it was fun, were to sail away in a great steamship with flags flying and cannon pealing, and take a royal holiday beyond the broad ocean, in many a strange clime and in many a land renowned in history! They were to sail for months over the breezy Atlantic and the sunny Mediterranean; they were to scamper about the decks by day, filling the ship with shouts and laughter — or read novels and poetry in the shade of the smoke-stacks, or watch

4

for the jelly-fish and the nautilus, over the side, and the shark, the whale, and other strange monsters of the deep; and at night they were to dance in the open air, on the upper deck, in the midst of a ball-room that stretched from horizon to horizon, and was domed by the bending heavens and lighted by no meaner lamps than the stars and the magnificent moon — dance, and promenade, and smoke, and sing, and make love, and search the skies for constellations that never associate with the "Big Dipper" they were so tired of: and they were to see the ships of twenty navies — the customs and costumes of twenty curious peoples — the great cities of half a world — they were to hobnob with nobility and hold friendly converse with kings and princes, Grand Moguls, and the anointed lords of mighty empires!

It was a brave conception; it was the offspring of a most ingenious brain. It was well advertised, but it hardly needed it: the bold originality, the extraordinary character, the seductive nature, and the vastness of the enterprise provoked comment everywhere and advertised it in every household in the land. Who could read the program of the excursion without longing to make one of the party? I will insert it here. It is almost as good as a map. As a text for this book, nothing could be better:

EXCURSION TO THE HOLY LAND, EGYPT, THE CRIMEA, GREECE, AND INTERMEDIATE POINTS OF INTEREST.

BROOKLYN, *February 1st, 1867.*

The undersigned will make an excursion as above during the coming season, and begs to submit to you the following programme:

A first-class steamer, to be under his own command, and capable of accommodating at least one hundred and fifty cabin passengers, will be selected, in which will be taken a select company, numbering not more than three-fourths of the ship's capacity. There is good reason to believe that this company can be easily made up in this immediate vicinity, of mutual friends and acquaintances.

The steamer will be provided with every necessary comfort, including library and musical instruments.

An experienced physician will be on board.

Leaving New York about June 1st, a middle and pleasant route will be taken across the Atlantic, and, passing through the group of Azores, St. Michael will be reached in about ten days. A day or two will be spent here, enjoying the fruit and wild scenery of these islands, and the voyage continued, and Gibraltar reached in three or four days.

A day or two will be spent here in looking over the wonderful subterraneous fortifications, permission to visit these galleries being readily obtained.

From Gibraltar, running along the coasts of Spain and France, Marseilles will be reached in three days. Here ample time will be given not only to look over the city, which was founded six hundred years before the Christian era, and its artificial port, the finest of the kind in the Mediterranean, but to visit Paris during the Great Exhibition; and the beautiful city of Lyons, lying intermediate, from the heights of which, on a clear day, Mont Blanc and the Alps can be distinctly seen. Passengers who may wish to extend the time at Paris can do so, and, passing down through Switzerland, rejoin the steamer at Genoa.

From Marseilles to Genoa is a run of one night. The excursionists will have an opportunity to look over this, the "magnificent city of palaces," and visit the birthplace of Columbus, twelve miles off, over a beautiful road built by Napoleon I. From this point, excursions may be made to Milan, Lakes Como and Maggiore, or to Milan, Verona (famous for its extraordinary fortifications), Padua, and Venice. Or, if passengers desire to visit Palma (famous for Correggio's frescoes) and

Bologna, they can by rail go on to Florence, and rejoin the steamer at Leghorn, thus spending about three weeks amid the cities most famous for art in Italy.

From Genoa the run to Leghorn will be made along the coast in one night, and time appropriated to this point in which to visit Florence, its palaces and galleries; Pisa, its Cathedral and "Leaning Tower," and Lucca and its baths and Roman amphitheater; Florence, the most remote, being distant by rail about sixty miles.

From Leghorn to Naples (calling at Civita Vecchia to land any who may prefer to go to Rome from that point) the distance will be made in about thirty-six hours; the route will lay along the coast of Italy, close by Caprera, Elba, and Corsica. Arrangements have been made to take on board at Leghorn a pilot for Caprera, and, if practicable, a call will be made there to visit the home of Garibaldi.

Rome (by rail), Herculaneum, Pompeii, Vesuvius, Virgil's tomb, and possibly, the ruins of Pæstum, can be visited, as well as the beautiful surroundings of Naples and its charming bay.

The next point of interest will be Palermo, the most beautiful city of Sicily, which will be reached in one night from Naples. A day will be spent here, and, leaving in the evening, the course will be taken towards Athens.

Skirting along the north coast of Sicily, passing through the group of Æolian Isles, in sight of Stromboli and Vulcania, both active volcanoes, through the Straits of Messina, with "Scylla" on the one hand and "Charybdis" on the other, along the east coast of Sicily, and in sight of Mount Ætna, along the south coast of Italy, the west and south coast of Greece, in sight of ancient Crete, up Athens Gulf, and into the Piræus, Athens will be reached in two and a half or three days. After tarrying here awhile, the Bay of Salamis will be crossed, and a day given to Corinth, whence the voyage will be continued to Constantinople, passing on the way through the Grecian Archipelago, the Dardanelles, the Sea of Marmora, and the mouth of the Golden Horn, and arriving in about forty-eight hours from Athens.

After leaving Constantinople, the way will be taken out through the beautiful Bosphorus, across the Black Sea to Sebastopol and Balaklava, a run of about twenty-four hours. Here it is proposed to remain two days, visiting the harbors, fortifications, and battlefields of the Crimea; thence back through the Bosphorus, touching at Constantinople to take in any who may have preferred to remain there; down through the Sea of Marmora and the Dardanelles, along the coasts of ancient Troy and Lydia in Asia, to Smyrna, which will be reached in two or two and a half days from Constantinople. A sufficient stay will be made here to give opportunity of visiting Ephesus, fifty miles distant by rail.

From Smyrna towards the Holy Land the course will lay through the Grecian Archipelago, close by the Isle of Patmos, along the coast of Asia, ancient Pamphylia, and the Isle of Cyprus. Beirout will be reached in three days. At Beirout time will be given to visit Damascus; after which the steamer will proceed to Joppa.

From Joppa, Jerusalem, the River Jordan, the Sea of Tiberias, Nazareth, Bethany, Bethlehem, and other points of interest in the Holy Land can be visited, and here those who may have preferred to make the journey from Beirout *through* the country, passing through Damascus, Galilee, Capernaum, Samaria, and by the River Jordan and Sea of Tiberias, can rejoin the steamer.

Leaving Joppa, the next point of interest to visit will be Alexandria, which will be reached in twenty-four hours. The ruins of Cæsar's Palace, Pompey's Pillar, Cleopatra's Needle, the Catacombs, and ruins of ancient Alexandria, will be found worth the visit. The journey to Cairo, one hundred and thirty miles by rail, can be made in a few hours, and from which can be visited the site of ancient Memphis, Joseph's Granaries, and the Pyramids.

From Alexandria the route will be taken homeward, calling at Malta, Cagliari (in Sardinia), and Palma (in Majorca), all magnificent harbors, with charming scenery, and abounding in fruits.

A day or two will be spent at each place, and leaving Palma in the evening, Valencia in Spain will be reached the next morning. A few days will be spent in this, the finest city of Spain.

From Valencia, the homeward course will be continued, skirting along the coast of Spain. Alicante, Carthagena, Palos, and Malaga will be passed but a mile or two distant, and Gibraltar reached in about twenty-four hours.

A stay of one day will be made here, and the voyage continued to Madeira, which will be reached in about three days. Captain Marryatt writes: "I do not know a spot on the globe which so much astonishes and delights upon first arrival as Madeira." A stay of one or two days will be made here, which, if time permits, may be extended, and passing on through the islands, and probably in sight of the Peak of Teneriffe, a southern track will be taken, and the Atlantic crossed within the latitudes

4*

of the Northeast trade winds, where mild and pleasant weather and a smooth sea can always be expected.

A call will be made at Bermuda, which lies directly in this route homeward, and will be reached in about ten days from Madeira, and after spending a short time with our friends the Bermudians, the final departure will be made for home, which will be reached in about three days.

Already, applications have been received from parties in Europe wishing to join the Excursion there.

The ship will at all times be a home, where the excursionists, if sick, will be surrounded by kind friends, and have all possible comfort and sympathy.

Should contagious sickness exist in any of the ports named in the programme, such ports will be passed, and others of interest substituted.

The price of passage is fixed at $1,250, currency, for each adult passenger. Choice of rooms and of seats at the tables apportioned in the order in which passages are engaged, and no passage considered engaged until ten per cent. of the passage money is deposited with the treasurer.

Passengers can remain on board of the steamer at all ports, if they desire, without additional expense, and all boating at the expense of the ship.

All passages must be paid for when taken, in order that the most perfect arrangements be made for starting at the appointed time.

Applications for passage must be approved by the committee before tickets are issued, and can be made to the undersigned.

Articles of interest or curiosity, procured by the passengers during the voyage, may be brought home in the steamer free of charge.

Five dollars per day, in gold, it is believed, will be a fair calculation to make for *all* traveling expenses on shore, and at the various points where passengers may wish to leave the steamer for days at a time.

The trip can be extended, and the route changed, by *unanimous* vote of the passengers.

CHAS. C. DUNCAN,

117 WALL STREET, NEW YORK.

R. R. G******, Treasurer.

COMMITTEE ON APPLICATIONS.

J. T. H******, Esq.,   R. R. G******, Esq.,   C. C. DUNCAN.

COMMITTEE ON SELECTING STEAMER.

CAPT. W. W. S******, *Surveyor for Board of Underwriters.*
C. W. C******, *Consulting Engineer for U. S. and Canada.*
J. T. H******, ESQ.
C. C. DUNCAN.

P. S. — The very beautiful and substantial side-wheel steamship "*Quaker City*" has been chartered for the occasion, and will leave New York, June 8th. Letters have been issued by the government commending the party to courtesies abroad.

What was there lacking about that program, to make it perfectly irresistible? Nothing, that any finite mind could discover. Paris, England, Scotland, Switzerland, Italy — Garibaldi! The Grecian archipelago! Vesuvius! Constantinople! Smyrna! The Holy Land! Egypt and "our friends the Bermudians"! People in Europe desiring to join the Excursion — contagious sickness to be avoided — boating at the expense of the ship — physician on board — the circuit of the globe to be made if the passengers unanimously desired it — the company to be rigidly selected by a pitiless "Committee on Applications" — the vessel to be as rigidly selected by as pitiless a "Committee on Selecting Steamer." Human nature could not withstand these bewildering temptations. I hurried to the Treasurer's office and deposited my ten per cent. I rejoiced to know that a few vacant staterooms were still left. I *did* avoid a critical personal examination into my character, by that bowelless committee, but I referred to all the people of high standing I could think of in the com-

D*

munity who would be least likely to know anything about me.

Shortly a supplementary program was issued which set forth that the Plymouth Collection of Hymns would be used on board the ship. I then paid the balance of my passage money.

I was provided with a receipt, and duly and officially accepted as an excursionist. There was happiness in that, but it was tame compared to the novelty of being "select."

This supplementary program also instructed the excursionists to provide themselves with light musical instruments for amusement in the ship; with saddles for Syrian travel; green spectacles and umbrellas; veils for Egypt; and substantial clothing to use in rough pilgrimizing in the Holy Land. Furthermore, it was suggested that although the ship's library would afford a fair amount of reading matter, it would still be well if each passenger would provide himself with a few guide-books, a Bible, and some standard works of travel. A list was appended, which consisted chiefly of books relating to the Holy Land, since the Holy Land was part of the excursion and seemed to be its main feature.

Rev. Henry Ward Beecher was to have accompanied the expedition, but urgent duties obliged him to give up the idea. There were other passengers who could have been spared better, and would have been spared more willingly. Lieutenant-General Sherman was to have been of the party, also, but the Indian war compelled his presence on the plains. A popular actress had entered her name on the ship's books, but something interfered, and *she* couldn't go. The " Drummer Boy of the Potomac " deserted, and lo, we had never a celebrity left!

However, we were to have a " battery of guns " from the Navy Department (as per advertisement), to be used in answering royal salutes; and the document furnished by the Secretary of the Navy, which was to make " General Sherman and party" welcome guests in the courts and camps of the old world, was still left to us, though both document and battery, I think, were shorn of somewhat of their original august proportions. However, had not we the seductive program, still, with its Paris, its Constantinople, Smyrna, Jerusalem, Jericho, and " our friends the Bermudians "? What did we care?

CHAPTER II.

OCCASIONALLY, during the following month, I dropped in at 117 Wall Street to inquire how the repairing and refurnishing of the vessel was coming on; how additions to the passenger list were averaging; how many people the committee were decreeing not "select," every day, and banishing in sorrow and tribulation. I was glad to know that we were to have a little printing-press on board and issue a daily newspaper of our own. I was glad to learn that our piano, our parlor organ, and our melodeon were to be the best instruments of the kind that could be had in the market. I was proud to observe that among our excursionists were three ministers of the gospel, eight doctors, sixteen or eighteen ladies, several military and naval chieftains with sounding titles, an ample crop of " Professors " of various kinds, and a gentleman who had " COMMISSIONER OF THE UNITED STATES OF AMERICA TO EUROPE, ASIA, AND AFRICA " thundering after his name in one awful blast! I had carefully prepared myself to take rather a back seat in that ship, because of the uncommonly select material that would

alone be permitted to pass through the camel's eye
of that committee on credentials; I had schooled
myself to expect an imposing array of military and
naval heroes, and to have to set that back seat still
further back in consequence of it, may be; but I
state frankly that I was all unprepared for *this*
crusher.

I fell under that titular avalanche a torn and
blighted thing. I said that if that potentate *must*
go over in our ship, why, I supposed he must — but
that to my thinking, when the United States considered it necessary to send a dignitary of that tonnage
across the ocean, it would be in better taste, and
safer, to take him apart and cart him over in sections,
in several ships.

Ah, if I had only known, then, that he was only
a common mortal, and that his mission had nothing
more overpowering about it than the collecting of
seeds, and uncommon yams and extraordinary cab-
bages and peculiar bullfrogs for that poor, useless,
innocent, mildewed old fossil, the Smithsonian In-
stitute, I would have felt *so* much relieved.

During that memorable month I basked in the happiness of being for once in my life drifting with the
tide of a great popular movement. Everybody was
going to Europe — I, too, was going to Europe.
Everybody was going to the famous Paris Exposition
— I, too, was going to the Paris Exposition. The
steamship lines were carrying Americans out of the
various ports of the country at the rate of four or

five thousand a week, in the aggregate. If I met a dozen individuals, during that month, who were not going to Europe shortly, I have no distinct remembrance of it now. I walked about the city a good deal with a young Mr. Blucher, who was booked for the excursion. He was confiding, good-natured, unsophisticated, companionable; but he was not a man to set the river on fire. He had the most extraordinary notions about this European exodus, and came at last to consider the whole nation as packing up for emigration to France. We stepped into a store in Broadway, one day, where he bought a handkerchief, and when the man could not make change, Mr. B. said:

"Never mind, I'll hand it to you in Paris."

"But I am not going to Paris."

"How is — what did I understand you to say?"

"I said I am not going to Paris."

"Not going to *Paris!* Not g— well then, where in the nation *are* you going to?"

"Nowhere at all."

"Not anywhere whatsoever? — not any place on earth but this?"

"Not any place at all but just this — stay here all summer."

My comrade took his purchase and walked out of the store without a word — walked out with an injured look upon his countenance. Up the street apiece he broke silence and said impressively: "It was a lie — that is my opinion of it!"

In the fullness of time the ship was ready to receive her passengers. I was introduced to the
young gentleman who was to be my room-mate, and
found him to be intelligent, cheerful of spirit, unselfish, full of generous impulses, patient, consider-
ate, and wonderfully good-natured. Not any
passenger that sailed in the *Quaker City* will withhold his endorsement of what I have just said. We
selected a stateroom forward of the wheel, on the
starboard side, " below decks." It had two berths
in it, a dismal dead-light, a sink with a wash-bowl in
it, and a long sumptuously cushioned locker, which
was to do service as a sofa — partly, and partly as a
hiding place for our things. Notwithstanding all this
furniture, there was still room to turn around in, but
not to swing a cat in, at least with entire security to
the cat. However, the room was large, for a ship's
stateroom, and was in every way satisfactory.

The vessel was appointed to sail on a certain Saturday early in June.

A little after noon, on that distinguished Saturday,
I reached the ship and went on board. All was
bustle and confusion. [I have seen that remark before, somewhere.] The pier was crowded with carriages and men ; passengers were arriving and hurrying on board ; the vessel's decks were encumbered
with trunks and valises ; groups of excursionists,
arrayed in unattractive traveling costumes, were
moping about in a drizzling rain and looking as
droopy and woe-begone as so many molting chick-

ens. The gallant flag was up, but it was under the spell, too, and hung limp and disheartened by the mast. Altogether, it was the bluest, bluest spectacle! It was a pleasure excursion — there was no gainsaying that, because the program said so — it was so nominated in the bond — but it surely hadn't the general aspect of one.

Finally, above the banging, and rumbling, and shouting and hissing of steam, rang the order to " cast off! "— a sudden rush to the gangways — a scampering ashore of visitors — a revolution of the wheels, and we were off — the picnic was begun! Two very mild cheers went up from the dripping crowd on the pier; we answered them gently from the slippery decks; the flag made an effort to wave, and failed; the " battery of guns " spake not — the ammunition was out.

We steamed down to the foot of the harbor and came to anchor. It was still raining. And not only raining, but storming. " Outside " we could see, ourselves, that there was a tremendous sea on. We must lie still, in the calm harbor, till the storm should abate. Our passengers hailed from fifteen states; only a few of them had ever been to sea before; manifestly it would not do to pit them against a fullblown tempest until they had got their sea-legs on. Towards evening the two steam tugs that had accompanied us with a rollicking champagne party of young New Yorkers on board who wished to bid farewell to one of our number in due and ancient form, departed, and we were alone on the deep. On deep five fathoms, and anchored fast to the bottom. And out in the solemn rain, at that. This was pleasuring with a vengeance.

It was an appropriate relief when the gong sounded for prayer-meeting. The first Saturday night of any other pleasure excursion might have been devoted to whist and dancing; but I submit it to the unprejudiced mind if it would have been in good taste for *us* to engage in such frivolities, considering what we had gone through and the frame of mind we were in. We would have shone at a wake, but not at anything more festive.

However, there is always a cheering influence about the sea; and in my berth, that night, rocked by the measured swell of the waves, and lulled by the murmur of the distant surf, I soon passed tranquilly out of all consciousness of the dreary experiences of the day and damaging premonitions of the future.

CHAPTER III.

ALL day Sunday at anchor. The storm had gone down a great deal, but the sea had not. It was still piling its frothy hills high in air "outside," as we could plainly see with the glasses. We could not properly begin a pleasure excursion on Sunday; we could not offer untried stomachs to so pitiless a sea as that. We must lie still till Monday. And we did. But we had repetitions of church and prayer-meetings; and so, of course, we were just as eligibly situated as we could have been anywhere.

I was up early that Sabbath morning, and was early to breakfast. I felt a perfectly natural desire to have a good, long, unprejudiced look at the passengers, at a time when they should be free from self-consciousness — which is at breakfast, when such a moment occurs in the lives of human beings at all.

I was greatly surprised to see so many elderly people — I might almost say, so many venerable people. A glance at the long lines of heads was apt to make one think it was *all* gray. But it was not. There was a tolerably fair sprinkling of young folks, and another fair sprinkling of gentlemen and ladies who were non-committal as to age, being neither actually old or absolutely young.

The next morning, we weighed anchor and went to sea. It was a great happiness to get away, after this dragging, dispiriting delay. I thought there never was such gladness in the air before, such brightness in the sun, such beauty in the sea. I was satisfied with the picnic, then, and with all its belongings. All my malicious instincts were dead within me; and as America faded out of sight, I think a spirit of charity rose up in their place that was as boundless, for the time being, as the broad ocean that was heaving its billows about us. I wished to express my feelings — I wished to lift up my voice and sing, but I did not know anything to sing, and so I was obliged to give up the idea. It was no loss to the ship though, perhaps.

It was breezy and pleasant, but the sea was still very rough. One could not promenade without risking his neck; at one moment the bowsprit was taking a deadly aim at the sun in mid-heaven, and at the next it was trying to harpoon a shark in the bottom of the ocean. What a weird sensation it is to feel the stern of a ship sinking swiftly from under you and see the bow climbing high away among the clouds! One's safest course, that day, was to clasp a railing and hang on; walking was too precarious a pastime.

By some happy fortune I was not seasick. That

s

was a thing to be proud of. I had not always escaped before. If there is one thing in the world that will make a man peculiarly and insufferably self-conceited, it is to have his stomach behave itself, the first day at sea, when nearly all his comrades are seasick. Soon, a venerable fossil, shawled to the chin and bandaged like a mummy, appeared at the door of the after deck-house, and the next lurch of the ship shot him into my arms. I said:

" Good morning, sir. It is a fine day."

He put his hand on his stomach and said, "*Oh, my!*" and then staggered away and fell over the coop of a skylight.

Presently another old gentleman was projected from the same door, with great violence. I said:

" Calm yourself, sir — There is no hurry. It is a fine day, sir."

He, also, put his hand on his stomach and said "*Oh, my!*" and reeled away.

In a little while another veteran was discharged abruptly from the same door, clawing at the air for a saving support. I said:

" Good morning, sir. It is a fine day for pleasuring. You were about to say——"

" *Oh, my!*"

I thought so. I anticipated *him*, anyhow. I stayed there and was bombarded with old gentlemen for an hour, perhaps; and all I got out of any of them was " *Oh, my!*"

I went away, then, in a thoughtful mood. I said, this is a good pleasure excursion. I like it. The passengers are not garrulous, but still they are sociable. I like those old people, but somehow they all seem to have the "Oh, my" rather bad.

I knew what was the matter with them. They were seasick. And I was glad of it. We all like to see people seasick when we are not, ourselves. Playing whist by the cabin lamps, when it is storming outside, is pleasant; walking the quarter-deck in the moonlight is pleasant; smoking in the breezy foretop is pleasant, when one is not afraid to go up there; but these are all feeble and commonplace compared with the joy of seeing people suffering the miseries of seasickness.

I picked up a good deal of information during the afternoon. At one time I was climbing up the quarter-deck when the vessel's stern was in the sky; I was smoking a cigar and feeling passably comfortable. Somebody ejaculated:

"Come, now, *that* won't answer. Read the sign up there—NO SMOKING ABAFT THE WHEEL!"

It was Captain Duncan, chief of the expedition. I went forward, of course. I saw a long spyglass lying on a desk in one of the upper-deck staterooms back of the pilot-house, and reached after it—there was a ship in the distance:

"Ah, ah—hands off! Come out of that!"

I came out of that. I said to a deck-sweep—but in a low voice:

"Who is that overgrown pirate with the whiskers and the discordant voice?"

"It's Captain Bursley — executive officer — sailing master."

I loitered about awhile, and then, for want of something better to do, fell to carving a railing with my knife. Somebody said, in an insinuating, admonitory voice:

"Now, *say* — my friend — don't you know any better than to be whittling the ship all to pieces that way? *You* ought to know better than that."

I went back and found the deck-sweep:

"Who is that smooth-faced animated outrage yonder in the fine clothes?"

"That's Captain L*****, the owner of the ship — he's one of the main bosses."

In the course of time I brought up on the starboard side of the pilot-house, and found a sextant lying on a bench. Now, I said, they "take the sun" through this thing; I should think I might see that vessel through it. I had hardly got it to my eye when some one touched me on the shoulder and said, deprecatingly:

"I'll have to get you to give that to me, sir. If there's anything you'd like to know about taking the sun, I'd as soon tell you as not — but I don't like to trust anybody with that instrument. If you want any figuring done — Aye-aye, sir!"

He was gone, to answer a call from the other side. I sought the deck-sweep:

"Who is that spider-legged gorilla yonder with the sanctimonious countenance?"

"It's Captain Jones, sir — the chief mate."

"Well. This goes clear away ahead of anything I ever heard of before. Do you — now I ask you as a man and a brother — *do* you think I could venture to throw a rock here in any given direction without hitting a captain of this ship?"

"Well, sir, I don't know — I think likely you'd fetch the captain of the watch, maybe, because he's a-standing right yonder in the way."

I went below — meditating, and a little downhearted. I thought, if five cooks can spoil a broth, what may not five captains do with a pleasure excursion.

CHAPTER IV.

WE plowed along bravely for a week or more, and without any conflict of jurisdiction among the captains worth mentioning. The passengers soon learned to accommodate themselves to their new circumstances, and life in the ship became nearly as systematically monotonous as the routine of a barrack. I do not mean that it was dull, for it was not entirely so by any means — but there was a good deal of sameness about it. As is always the fashion at sea, the passengers shortly began to pick up sailor terms — a sign that they were beginning to feel at home. Half-past six was no longer half-past six to these pilgrims from New England, the South, and the Mississippi Valley, it was "seven bells"; eight, twelve, and four o'clock were "eight bells"; the captain did not take the longitude at nine o'clock, but at "two bells." They spoke glibly of the "after cabin," the "for'rard cabin," "port and starboard" and the "fo'castle."

At seven bells the first gong rang; at eight there was breakfast, for such as were not too seasick to eat it. After that all the well people walked arm-

in-arm up and down the long promenade deck,
enjoying the fine summer mornings, and the seasick
ones crawled out and propped themselves up in the
lee of the paddle-boxes and ate their dismal tea and
toast, and looked wretched. From eleven o'clock
until luncheon, and from luncheon until dinner at
six in the evening, the employments and amusements
were various. Some reading was done; and much
smoking and sewing, though not by the same
parties; there were the monsters of the deep to be
looked after and wondered at; strange ships had to
be scrutinized through opera-glasses, and sage de-
cisions arrived at concerning them; and more than
that, everybody took a personal interest in seeing
that the flag was run up and politely dipped three
times in response to the salutes of those strangers;
in the smoking-room there were always parties of
gentlemen playing euchre, draughts, and dominoes,
especially dominoes, that delightfully harmless game;
and down on the main deck, "for'rard"—for'rard
of the chicken coops and the cattle—we had what
was called "horse-billiards." Horse-billiards is a
fine game. It affords good, active exercise, hilarity,
and consuming excitement. It is a mixture of
"hop-scotch" and shuffle-board played with a
crutch. A large hop-scotch diagram is marked out
on the deck with chalk, and each compartment numbered. You stand off three or four steps, with some
broad wooden disks before you on the deck, and
these you send forward with a vigorous thrust of a

E *

long crutch. If a disk stops on a chalk line, it does not count anything. If it stops in division No. 7, it counts 7; in 5, it counts 5, and so on. The game is 100, and four can play at a time. That game would be very simple, played on a stationary floor, but with us, to play it well required science. We had to allow for the reeling of the ship to the right or the left. Very often one made calculations for a heel to the right and the ship did not go that way. The consequence was that that disk missed the whole hop-scotch plan a yard or two, and then there was humiliation on one side and laughter on the other.

When it rained, the passengers had to stay in the house, of course — or at least the cabins — and amuse themselves with games, reading, looking out of the windows at the very familiar billows, and talking gossip.

By 7 o'clock in the evening, dinner was about over; an hour's promenade on the upper deck followed; then the gong sounded and a large majority of the party repaired to the after cabin (upper) a handsome saloon fifty or sixty feet long, for prayers. The unregenerated called this saloon the "Synagogue." The devotions consisted only of two hymns from the "Plymouth Collection," and a short prayer, and seldom occupied more than fifteen minutes. The hymns were accompanied by parlor organ music when the sea was smooth enough to allow a performer to sit at the instrument without being lashed to his chair.

After prayers the Synagogue shortly took the semblance of a writing-school. The like of that picture was never seen in a ship before. Behind the long dining-tables on either side of the saloon, and scattered from one end to the other of the latter, some twenty or thirty gentlemen and ladies sat them down under the swaying lamps, and for two or three hours wrote diligently in their journals. Alas! that journals so voluminously begun should come to so lame and impotent a conclusion as most of them did! I doubt if there is a single pilgrim of all that host but can show a hundred fair pages of journal concerning the first twenty days' voyaging in the *Quaker City;* and I am morally certain that not ten of the party can show twenty pages of journal for the succeeding twenty thousand miles of voyaging! At certain periods it becomes the dearest ambition of a man to keep a faithful record of his performances in a book; and he dashes at this work with an enthusiasm that imposes on him the notion that keeping a journal is the veriest pastime in the world, and the pleasantest. But if he only lives twenty-one days, he will find out that only those rare natures that are made up of pluck, endurance, devotion to duty for duty's sake, and invincible determination, may hope to venture upon so tremendous an enterprise as the keeping of a journal and not sustain a shameful defeat.

One of our favorite youths, Jack, a splendid young fellow with a head full of good sense, and a

pair of legs that were a wonder to look upon in the
way of length and straightness and slimness, used
to report progress every morning in the most glow-
ing and spirited way, and say:

"Oh, I'm coming along bully!" (he was a little
given to slang, in his happier moods) "I wrote ten
pages in my journal last night — and you know I
wrote nine the night before, and twelve the night
before that.   Why, it's only fun!"

"What do you find to put in it, Jack?"

"Oh, everything.   Latitude and longitude, noon
every day; and how many miles we made last
twenty-four hours; and all the domino games I beat,
and horse-billiards; and whales and sharks and
porpoises; and the text of the sermon, Sundays
(because that'll tell at home, you know); and the
ships we saluted and what nation they were; and
which way the wind was, and whether there was a
heavy sea, and what sail we carried, though we don't
ever carry *any*, principally, going against a head
wind always — wonder what is the reason of that? —
and how many lies Moult has told — Oh, everything!
I've got everything down.   My father told me to
keep that journal.   Father wouldn't take a thousand
dollars for it when I get it done."

"No, Jack; it will be worth more than a thousand dollars — when you get it done."

"Do you? — no, but do you think it will,
though?"

'Yes, it will be worth at least as much as a

thousand dollars — when you get it done. Maybe, more."

"Well, I about half think so, myself. It ain't no slouch of a journal."

But it shortly became a most lamentable "slouch of a journal." One night in Paris, after a hard day's toil in sight-seeing, I said:

"Now I'll go and stroll around the cafés awhile, Jack, and give you a chance to write up your journal, old fellow."

His countenance lost its fire. He said:

"Well, no, you needn't mind. I think I won't run that journal any more. It is awful tedious. Do you know — I reckon I'm as much as four thousand pages behindhand. I haven't got any France in it at all. First I thought I'd leave France out and start fresh. But that wouldn't do, *would* it? The gov ernor would say, 'Hello, here — didn't see anything in France?' *That* cat wouldn't fight, you know. First I thought I'd copy France out of the guide-book, like old Badger in the for'rard cabin who's writing a book, but there's more than three hundred pages of it. Oh, *I* don't think a journal's any use — do you? They're only a bother, *ain't* they?"

"Yes, a journal that is incomplete isn't of much use, but a journal properly kept is worth a thousand dollars,— when you've got it done."

"A thousand! — well, I should think so. *I* wouldn't finish it for a million."

His experience was only the experience of the

majority of that industrious night-school in the cabin. If you wish to inflict a heartless and malignant punishment upon a young person, pledge him to keep a journal a year.

A good many expedients were resorted to to keep the excursionists amused and satisfied. A club was formed, of all the passengers, which met in the writing-school after prayers and read aloud about the countries we were approaching, and discussed the information so obtained.

Several times the photographer of the expedition brought out his transparent pictures and gave us a handsome magic lantern exhibition. His views were nearly all of foreign scenes, but there were one or two home pictures among them. He advertised that he would " open his performance in the after cabin at ' two bells ' (9 p. m.), and show the passengers where they shall eventually arrive "— which was all very well, but by a funny accident the first picture that flamed out upon the canvas was a view of Greenwood Cemetery!

On several starlight nights we danced on the upper deck, under the awnings, and made something of a ball-room display of brilliancy by hanging a number of ship's lanterns to the stanchions. Our music consisted of the well-mixed strains of a melodeon which was a little asthmatic and apt to catch its breath where it ought to come out strong; a clarinet which was a little unreliable on the high keys and rather melancholy on the low ones; and a disreputable accordion that had a leak somewhere and breathed louder than it squawked — a more elegant term does not occur to me just now. However, the dancing was infinitely worse than the music. When the ship rolled to starboard the whole platoon of dancers came charging down to starboard with it, and brought up in mass at the rail; and when it rolled to port, they went floundering down to port with the same unanimity of sentiment. Waltzers spun around precariously for a matter of fifteen seconds and then went skurrying down to the rail as if they meant to go overboard. The Virginia reel, as performed on board the *Quaker City*, had more genuine reel about it than any reel I ever saw before, and was as full of interest to the spectator as it was full of desperate chances and hairbreadth escapes to the participant. We gave up dancing, finally.

We celebrated a lady's birthday anniversary, with toasts, speeches, a poem, and so forth. We also had a mock trial. No ship ever went to sea that hadn't a mock trial on board. The purser was accused of stealing an overcoat from stateroom No. 10. A judge was appointed; also clerks, a crier of the court, constables, sheriffs; counsel for the state and for the defendant; witnesses were subpœnaed, and a jury empaneled after much challenging. The witnesses were stupid and unreliable and contradictory, as witnesses always are. The counsel were eloquent, argumentative, and vindictively abusive of each other, as was characteristic and proper. The case was at last submitted, and duly finished by the judge with an absurd decision and a ridiculous sentence.

The acting of charades was tried, on several evenings, by the young gentlemen and ladies, in the cabins, and proved the most distinguished success of all the amusement experiments.

An attempt was made to organize a debating club, but it was a failure. There was no oratorical talent in the ship.

We all enjoyed ourselves — I think I can safely say that, but it was in a rather quiet way. We very, very seldom played the piano; we played the flute and the clarinet together, and made good music, too, what there was of it, but we always played the same old tune; it was a very pretty tune — how well I remember it — I wonder when I shall ever get rid of it. We never played either the melodeon or the organ, except at devotions — but I am too fast; young Albert *did* know part of a tune — something about " O Something-Or-Other How Sweet it is to Know that he's his What's-his-Name " (I do not remember the exact title of it, but it was very plaintive, and full of sentiment), Albert played that pretty much all the time, until we contracted with him to restrain himself. But nobody ever sang by moonlight on the upper deck, and the congregational singing at church and prayers was not of a superior order of architecture. I put up with it as long as I

could, and then joined in and tried to improve it,
but this encouraged young George to join in, too,
and that made a failure of it; because George's
voice was just "turning," and when he was singing
a dismal sort of bass, it was apt to fly off the handle
and startle everybody with a most discordant cackle
on the upper notes. George didn't know the tunes,
either, which was also a drawback to his performances. I said:

"Come, now, George, *don't* improvise. It looks
too egotistical. It will provoke remark. Just stick
to 'Coronation,' like the others. It is a good tune
—*you* can't improve it any, just off-hand, in this
way."

"Why, I'm not trying to improve it—and I *am*
singing like the others—just as it is in the notes."

And he honestly thought he was, too; and so he
had no one to blame but himself when his voice
caught on the center occasionally, and gave him the
lockjaw.

There were those among the unregenerated who
attributed the unceasing head winds to our distressing choir music. There were those who said openly
that it was taking chances enough to have such
ghastly music going on, even when it was at its best;
and that to exaggerate the crime by letting George
help, was simply flying in the face of Providence.
These said that the choir would keep up their lacerating attempts at melody until they would bring
down a storm some day that would sink the ship.

There were even grumblers at the prayers. The executive officer said the Pilgrims had no charity.

" There they are, down there every night at eight bells, praying for fair winds — when they know as well as I do that this is the only ship going east this time of the year, but there's a thousand coming west — what's a fair wind for us is a *head* wind to them — the Almighty's blowing a fair wind for a thousand vessels, and this tribe wants him to turn it clear around so as to accommodate *one*,— and she a steamship at that! It ain't good sense, it ain't good reason, it ain't good Christianity, it ain't common human charity. Avast with such nonsense!"

CHAPTER V.

TAKING it "by and large," as the sailors say, we had a pleasant ten days' run from New York to the Azores islands — not a fast run, for the distance is only twenty-four hundred miles — but a right pleasant one, in the main. True, we had head winds *all* the time, and several stormy experiences which sent fifty per cent. of the passengers to bed, sick, and made the ship look dismal and deserted — stormy experiences that all will remember who weathered them on the tumbling deck, and caught the vast sheets of spray that every now and then sprang high in air from the weather bow and swept the ship like a thunder shower; but for the most part we had balmy summer weather, and nights that were even finer than the days. We had the phenomenon of a full moon located just in the same spot in the heavens at the same hour every night. The reason of this singular conduct on the part of the moon did not occur to us at first, but it did afterward when we reflected that we were gaining about twenty minutes every day, because we were going east so fast — we gained just about enough

6

every day to keep along with the moon. It was becoming an old moon to the friends we had left behind us, but to us Joshuas it stood still in the same place, and remained always the same.

Young Mr. Blucher, who is from the Far West, and is on his first voyage, was a good deal worried by the constantly changing "ship time." He was proud of his new watch at first, and used to drag it out promptly when eight bells struck at noon, but he came to look after a while as if he were losing confidence in it. Seven days out from New York he came on deck, and said with great decision:

"This thing's a swindle!"

"What's a swindle?"

"Why, this watch. I bought her out in Illinois — gave $150 for her — and I thought she was good. And, by George, she *is* good on shore, but somehow she don't keep up her lick here on the water — gets seasick, maybe. She skips; she runs along regular enough till half-past eleven, and then, all of a sudden, she lets down. I've set that old regulator up faster and faster, till I've shoved it clear around, but it don't do any good; she just distances every watch in the ship, and clatters along in a way that's astonishing till it is noon, but them eight bells always gets in about ten minutes ahead of her, anyway. I don't know what to do with her now. She's doing all she can — she's going her best gait, but it won't save her. Now, don't you know, there ain't a watch in the ship that's making better time than she is;

but what does it signify? When you hear them
eight bells you'll find her just about ten minutes
short of her score, sure."

The ship was gaining a full hour every three days,
and this fellow was trying to make his watch go fast
enough to keep up to her. But, as he had said, he
had pushed the regulator up as far as it would go,
and the watch was "on its best gait," and so nothing was left him but to fold his hands and see the
ship beat the race. We sent him to the captain,
and he explained to him the mystery of "ship
time," and set his troubled mind at rest. This
young man asked a great many questions about
seasickness before we left, and wanted to know what
its characteristics were, and how he was to tell when
he had it. He found out.

We saw the usual sharks, blackfish, porpoises,
etc., of course, and by and by large schools of
Portuguese men-of-war were added to the regular
list of sea wonders. Some of them were white and
some of a brilliant carmine color. The nautilus is
nothing but a transparent web of jelly, that spreads
itself to catch the wind, and has fleshy-looking
strings a foot or two long dangling from it to keep
it steady in the water. It is an accomplished sailor,
and has good sailor judgment. It reefs its sail when
a storm threatens or the wind blows pretty hard, and
furls it entirely and goes down when a gale blows.
Ordinarily it keeps its sail wet and in good sailing
order by turning over and dipping it in the water for

a moment. Seamen say the nautilus is only found in these waters between the 35th and 45th parallels of latitude.

At three o'clock on the morning of the 21st of June we were awakened and notified that the Azores islands were in sight. I said I did not take any interest in islands at three o'clock in the morning. But another persecutor came, and then another and another, and finally believing that the general enthusiasm would permit no one to slumber in peace, I got up and went sleepily on deck. It was five and a half o'clock now, and a raw, blustering morning. The passengers were huddled about the smoke stacks and fortified behind ventilators, and all were wrapped in wintry costumes, and looking sleepy and unhappy in the pitiless gale and the drenching spray.

The island in sight was Flores. It seemed only a mountain of mud standing up out of the dull mists of the sea. But as we bore down upon it, the sun came out and made it a beautiful picture — a mass of green farms and meadows that swelled up to a height of fifteen hundred feet, and mingled its upper outlines with the clouds. It was ribbed with sharp, steep ridges, and cloven with narrow cañons, and here and there on the heights, rocky upheavals shaped themselves into mimic battlements and castles; and out of rifted clouds came broad shafts of sunlight, that painted summit and slope and glen with bands of fire, and left belts of somber shade between. It was the aurora borealis of the frozen pole exiled to a summer land!

We skirted around two-thirds of the island, four miles from shore, and all the opera-glasses in the ship were called into requisition to settle disputes as to whether mossy spots on the uplands were groves of trees or groves of weeds, or whether the white villages down by the sea were really villages or only the clustering tombstones of cemeteries. Finally, we stood to sea and bore away for San Miguel, and Flores shortly became a dome of mud again, and sank down among the mists and disappeared. But to many a seasick passenger it was good to see the green hills again, and all were more cheerful after this episode than anybody could have expected them to be, considering how sinfully early they had gotten up.

But we had to change our purpose about San Miguel, for a storm came up about noon that so tossed and pitched the vessel that common sense dictated a run for shelter. Therefore we steered for the nearest island of the group — Fayal (the people there pronounce it Fy-all, and put the accent on the first syllable). We anchored in the open roadstead of Horta, half a mile from the shore. The town has eight thousand to ten thousand inhabitants. Its snow-white houses nestle cosily in a sea of fresh green vegetation, and no village could look prettier or more attractive. It sits in the lap of an amphitheater of hills which are three hundred to seven

6.

hundred feet high, and carefully cultivated clear to
their summits — not a foot of soil left idle. Every
farm and every acre is cut up into little square in-
closures by stone walls, whose duty it is to protect
the growing products from the destructive gales that
blow there. These hundreds of green squares,
marked by their black lava walls, make the hills
look like vast checker-boards.

The islands belong to Portugal, and everything in
Fayal has Portuguese characteristics about it. But
more of that anon. A swarm of swarthy, noisy,
lying, shoulder-shrugging, gesticulating Portuguese
boatmen, with brass rings in their ears, and fraud in
their hearts, climbed the ship's sides, and various
parties of us contracted with them to take us ashore
at so much a head, silver coin of any country. We
landed under the walls of a little fort, armed with
batteries of twelve and thirty-two pounders, which
Horta considered a most formidable institution, but
if we were ever to get after it with one of our tur-
reted monitors, they would have to move it out in
the country if they wanted it where they could go
and find it again when they needed it. The group
on the pier was a rusty one — men and women,
and boys and girls, all ragged and barefoot, uncombed and unclean, and by instinct, education, and
profession, beggars. They trooped after us, and
never more, while we tarried in Fayal, did we get
rid of them. We walked up the middle of the principal street, and these vermin surrounded us on all

sides, and glared upon us; and every moment excited couples shot ahead of the procession to get a
good look back, just as village boys do when they
accompany the elephant on his advertising trip from
street to street. It was very flattering to me to be
part of the material for such a sensation. Here and
there in the doorways we saw women, with fashionable Portuguese hoods on. This hood is of thick
blue cloth, attached to a cloak of the same stuff, and
is a marvel of ugliness. It stands up high, and
spreads far abroad, and is unfathomably deep. It
fits like a circus tent, and a woman's head is hidden
away in it like the man's who prompts the singers
from his tin shed in the stage of an opera. There is
no particle of trimming about this monstrous *capote*,
as they call it — it is just a plain, ugly dead-blue
mass of sail, and a woman can't go within eight
points of the wind with one of them on; she has to
go before the wind or not at all. The general style
of the capote is the same in all the islands, and will
remain so for the next ten thousand years, but each
island shapes its capotes just enough differently from
the others to enable an observer to tell at a glance
what particular island a lady hails from.

The Portuguese pennies or *reis* (pronounced rays)
are prodigious. It takes one thousand reis to make
a dollar, and all financial estimates are made in reis.
We did not know this until after we had found it out
through Blucher. Blucher said he was so happy
and so grateful to be on solid land once more, that

F.

he wanted to give a feast — said he had heard it was a cheap land, and he was bound to have a grand banquet. He invited nine of us, and we ate an excellent dinner at the principal hotel. In the midst of the jollity produced by good cigars, good wine, and passable anecdotes, the landlord presented his bill. Blucher glanced at it and his countenance fell. He took another look to assure himself that his senses had not deceived him, and then read the items aloud, in a faltering voice, while the roses in his cheeks turned to ashes:

"'Ten dinners, at 600 reis, 6,000 reis!' Ruin and desolation!"

"'Twenty-five cigars, at 100 reis, 2,500 reis!' Oh, my sainted mother!"

"'Eleven bottles of wine, at 1,200 reis, 13,200 reis!' Be with us all!"

"'TOTAL, TWENTY-ONE THOUSAND SEVEN HUNDRED REIS!' The suffering Moses! — there ain't money enough in the ship to pay that bill! Go — leave me to my misery, boys, I am a ruined community."

I think it was the blankest looking party I ever saw. Nobody could say a word. It was as if every soul had been stricken dumb. Wine glasses descended slowly to the table, their contents untasted. Cigars dropped unnoticed from nerveless fingers. Each man sought his neighbor's eye, but found in it no ray of hope, no encouragement. At last the fearful silence was broken. The shadow of a des perate resolve settled upon Blucher's countenance like a cloud, and he rose up and said:

"Landlord, this is a low, mean swindle, and I'll never, never stand it. Here's a hundred and fifty dollars, sir, and it's all you'll get — I'll swim in blood, before I'll pay a cent more."

Our spirits rose and the landlord's fell — at least we thought so; he was confused at any rate, notwithstanding he had not understood a word that had been said. He glanced from the little pile of gold pieces to Blucher several times, and then went out. He must have visited an American, for, when he returned, he brought back his bill translated into a language that a Christian could understand — thus:

10 dinners, 6,000 reis, or • • • •	$6.00
25 cigars, 2,500 reis, or • • • •	2.50
11 bottles wine, 13,200 reis, or • • •	13.20
Total 21,700 reis, or . • • • •	$21.70

Happiness reigned once more in Blucher's dinner party. More refreshments were ordered.

CHAPTER VI.

I THINK the Azores must be very little known in America. Out of our whole ship's company there was not a solitary individual who knew anything whatever about them. Some of the party, well read concerning most other lands, had no other information about the Azores than that they were a group of nine or ten small islands far out in the Atlantic, something more than half way between New York and Gibraltar. That was all. These considerations move me to put in a paragraph of dry facts just here.

The community is eminently Portuguese — that is to say, it is slow, poor, shiftless, sleepy, and lazy. There is a civil governor, appointed by the King of Portugal; and also a military governor, who can assume supreme control and suspend the civil government at his pleasure. The islands contain a population of about 200,000, almost entirely Portuguese. Everything is staid and settled, for the country was one hundred years old when Columbus discovered America. The principal crop is corn, and they raise it and grind it just as their great-great-

great-grandfathers did. They plow with a board
slightly shod with iron; their trifling little harrows
are drawn by men and women; small windmills
grind the corn, ten bushels a day, and there is one
assistant superintendent to feed the mill and a general superintendent to stand by and keep him from
going to sleep. When the wind changes they hitch
on some donkeys, and actually turn the whole upper
half of the mill around until the sails are in proper
position, instead of fixing the concern so that the
sails could be moved instead of the mill. Oxen
tread the wheat from the ear, after the fashion pre-
valent in the time of Methuselah. There is not a
wheelbarrow in the land — they carry everything on
their heads, or on donkeys, or in a wicker-bodied
cart, whose wheels are solid blocks of wood and
whose axles turn with the wheel. There is not a
modern plow in the islands, or a threshing-machine.
All attempts to introduce them have failed. The
good Catholic Portuguese crossed himself and prayed
God to shield him from all blasphemous desire to
know more than his father did before him. The
climate is mild; they never have snow or ice, and I
saw no chimneys in the town. The donkeys and
the men, women, and children of a family, all eat
and sleep in the same room, and are unclean, are
ravaged by vermin, and are truly happy. The
people lie, and cheat the stranger, and are desper-
ately ignorant, and have hardly any reverence for
their dead. The latter trait shows how little better

they are than the donkeys they eat and sleep with.
The only well-dressed Portuguese in the camp are
the half a dozen well-to-do families, the Jesuit priests,
and the soldiers of the little garrison. The wages of
a laborer are twenty to twenty-four cents a day, and
those of a good mechanic about twice as much.
They count it in reis at a thousand to the dollar, and
this makes them rich and contented. Fine grapes
used to grow in the islands, and an excellent wine
was made and exported. But a disease killed all
the vines fifteen years ago, and since that time no
wine has been made. The islands being wholly of
volcanic origin, the soil is necessarily very rich.
Nearly every foot of ground is under cultivation,
and two or three crops a year of each article are
produced, but nothing is exported save a few
oranges — chiefly to England. Nobody comes here,
and nobody goes away. News is a thing unknown
in Fayal. A thirst for it is a passion equally unknown. A Portuguese of average intelligence inquired if our civil war was over? because, he said,
somebody had told him it was — or, at least, it ran
in his mind, that somebody had told him something
like that! And when a passenger gave an officer
of the garrison copies of the *Tribune*, the *Herald*,
and *Times*, he was surprised to find later news in
them from Lisbon than he had just received
by the little monthly steamer. He was told that
it came by cable. He said he knew they had
tried to lay a cable ten years ago, but it had

been in his mind, somehow, that they hadn't succeeded!

It is in communities like this that Jesuit humbuggery flourishes. We visited a Jesuit cathedral nearly two hundred years old, and found in it a piece of the veritable cross upon which our Saviour was crucified. It was polished and hard, and in as excellent a state of preservation as if the dread tragedy on Calvary had occurred yesterday instead of eighteen centuries ago. But these confiding people believe in that piece of wood unhesitatingly.

In a chapel of the cathedral is an altar with facings of solid silver — at least, they call it so, and I think myself it would go a couple of hundred to the ton (to speak after the fashion of the silver miners), and before it is kept forever burning a small lamp. A devout lady who died, left money and contracted for unlimited masses for the repose of her soul, and also stipulated that this lamp should be kept lighted always, day and night. She did all this before she died, you understand. It is a very small lamp, and a very dim one, and it could not work her much damage, I think, if it went out altogether.

The great altar of the cathedral, and also three or four minor ones, are a perfect mass of gilt gimcracks and gingerbread. And they have a swarm of rusty, dusty, battered apostles standing around the filigree work, some on one leg and some with one eye out but a gamey look in the other, and some with two

or three fingers gone, and some with not enough
nose left to blow — all of them crippled and dis-
couraged, and fitter subjects for the hospital than
the cathedral.

The walls of the chancel are of porcelain, all
pictured over with figures of almost life size, very
elegantly wrought, and dressed in the fanciful costumes of two centuries ago. The design was a history of something or somebody, but none of us were
learned enough to read the story. The old father,
reposing under a stone close by, dated 1686, might
have told us if he could have risen. But he didn't.

As we came down through the town, we encoun-
tered a squad of little donkeys ready saddled for
use. The saddles were peculiar, to say the least.
They consisted of a sort of saw-buck, with a small
mattress on it, and this furniture covered about half
the donkey. There were no stirrups, but really
such supports were not needed — to use such a
saddle was the next thing to riding a dinner table —
there was ample support clear out to one's knee
joints. A pack of ragged Portuguese muleteers
crowded around us, offering their beasts at half a
dollar an hour — more rascality to the stranger, for
the market price is sixteen cents. Half a dozen of
us mounted the ungainly affairs, and submitted to
the indignity of making a ridiculous spectacle of
ourselves through the principal streets of a town of
10,000 inhabitants.

We started. It was not a trot, a gallop, or a

canter, but a stampede, and made up of all possible
or conceivable gaits. No spurs were necessary.
There was a muleteer to every donkey and a dozen
volunteers beside, and they banged the donkeys
with their goad-sticks, and pricked them with their
spikes, and shouted something that sounded like
"*Sekki-yah!*" and kept up a din and a racket that
was worse than Bedlam itself. These rascals were
all on foot, but no matter, they were always up to
time — they can outrun and outlast a donkey.
Altogether ours was a lively and picturesque procession, and drew crowded audiences to the balconies
wherever we went.

Blucher could do nothing at all with his donkey.
The beast scampered zigzag across the road and the
others ran into him; he scraped Blucher against carts
and the corners of houses; the road was fenced in
with high stone walls, and the donkey gave him a
polishing first on one side and then on the other, but
never once took the middle; he finally came to the
house he was born in and darted into the parlor,
scraping Blucher off at the doorway. After re-
mounting, Blucher said to the muleteer, "Now,
that's enough, you know; you go slow hereafter."
But the fellow knew no English and did not understand, so he simply said, "*Sekki-yah!*" and the
donkey was off again like a shot. He turned a
corner suddenly, and Blucher went over his head.
And, to speak truly, every mule stumbled over the
two, and the whole cavalcade was piled up in a

heap. No harm done. A fall from one of those donkeys is of little more consequence than rolling off a sofa. The donkeys all stood still after the catastrophe, and waited for their dismembered saddles to be patched up and put on by the noisy muleteers. Blucher was pretty angry, and wanted to swear, but every time he opened his mouth his animal did so also, and let off a series of brays that drowned all other sounds.

It was fun, skurrying around the breezy hills and through the beautiful cañons. There was that rare thing, novelty, about it; it was a fresh, new, exhilarating sensation, this donkey riding, and worth a hundred worn and threadbare home pleasures.

The roads were a wonder, and well they might be. Here was an island with only a handful of people in it — 25,000 — and yet such fine roads do not exist in the United States outside of Central Park. Everywhere you go, in any direction, you find either a hard, smooth, level thoroughfare, just sprinkled with black lava sand, and bordered with little gutters neatly paved with small smooth pebbles, or compactly paved ones like Broadway. They talk much of the Russ pavement in New York, and call it a new invention — yet here they have been using it in this remote little isle of the sea for two hundred years! Every street in Horta is handsomely paved with the heavy Russ blocks, and the surface is neat and true as a floor — not marred by holes like Broadway. And every road is fenced in by tall, solid lava walls, which will last a thousand years in this land where frost is unknown. They are very thick, and are often plastered and whitewashed, and capped with projecting slabs of cut stone. Trees from gardens above hang their swaying tendrils down, and contrast their bright green with the white-wash or the black lava of the walls, and make them beautiful. The trees and vines stretch across these narrow roadways sometimes, and so shut out the sun that you seem to be riding through a tunnel. The pavements, the roads, and the bridges are all government work.

The bridges are of a single span — a single arch — of cut stone, without a support, and paved on top with flags of lava and ornamental pebble work. Everywhere are walls, walls, walls, — and all of them tasteful and handsome — and eternally substantial; and everywhere are those marvelous pavements, so neat, so smooth, and so indestructible. And if ever roads and streets, and the outsides of houses, were perfectly free from any sign or semblance of dirt or dust or mud, or uncleanliness of any kind, it is Horta, it is Fayal. The lower classes of the people, in their persons and their domiciles, are not clean — but there it stops — the town and the island are miracles of cleanliness.

We arrived home again finally, after a ten-mile excursion, and the irrepressible muleteers scampered at our heels through the main street, goading the donkeys, shouting the everlasting " *Sekki-yah*,"

7

and singing "John Brown's Body" in ruinous English.

When we were dismounted and it came to settling, the shouting and jawing and swearing and quarreling among the muleteers and with us, was nearly deafening. One fellow would demand a dollar an hour for the use of his donkey; another claimed half a dollar for pricking him up, another a quarter for helping in that service, and about fourteen guides presented bills for showing us the way through the town and its environs; and every vagrant of them was more vociferous, and more vehement, and more frantic in gesture than his neighbor. We paid one guide, and paid for cne muleteer to each donkey.

The mountains on some of the islands are very high. We sailed along the shore of the Island of Pico, under a stately green pyramid that rose up with one unbroken sweep from our very feet to an altitude of 7,613 feet, and thrust its summit above the white clouds like an island adrift in a fog!

We got plenty of fresh oranges, lemons, figs, apricots, etc., in these Azores, of course. But I will desist. I am not here to write patent office reports.

We are on our way to Gibraltar, and shall reach there five or six days out from the Azores.

CHAPTER VII.

A WEEK of buffeting a tempestuous and relent-
less sea; a week of seasickness and deserted
cabins; of lonely quarter-decks drenched with spray
— spray so ambitious that it even coated the smoke
stacks thick with a white crust of salt to their very
tops; a week of shivering in the shelter of the life-
boats and deck-houses by day, and blowing suffo-
cating "clouds" and boisterously performing at
dominoes in the smoking-room at night.

And the last night of the seven was the stormiest
of all. There was no thunder, no noise but the
pounding bows of the ship, the keen whistling of
the gale through the cordage, and the rush of the
seething waters. But the vessel climbed aloft as if
she would climb to heaven — then paused an instant
that seemed a century, and plunged headlong down
again, as from a precipice. The sheeted sprays
drenched the decks like rain. The blackness of
darkness was everywhere. At long intervals a flash
of lightning clove it with a quivering line of fire, that
revealed a heaving world of water where was nothing
before, kindled the dusky cordage to glittering silver,

(95)

and lit up the faces of the men with a ghastly luster!

Fear drove many on deck that were used to avoiding the night winds and the spray. Some thought the vessel could not live through the night, and it seemed less dreadful to stand out in the midst of the wild tempest and *see* the peril that threatened than to be shut up in the sepulchral cabins, under the dim lamps, and imagine the horrors that were abroad on the ocean. And once out — once where they could see the ship struggling in the strong grasp of the storm — once where they could hear the shriek of the winds, and face the driving spray and look out upon the majestic picture the lightnings disclosed, they were prisoners to a fierce fascination they could not resist, and so remained. It was a wild night — and a very, very long one.

Everybody was sent scampering to the deck at seven o'clock this lovely morning of the 30th of June with the glad news that land was in sight! It was a rare thing and a joyful, to see *all* the ship's family abroad once more, albeit the happiness that sat upon every countenance could only partly conceal the ravages which that long siege of storms had wrought there. But dull eyes soon sparkled with pleasure, pallid cheeks flushed again, and frames weakened by sickness gathered new life from the quickening influences of the bright, fresh morning. Yea, and from a still more potent influence: the worn castaways were to see the blessed land again!

— and to see it was to bring back that mother-land that was in all their thoughts.

Within the hour we were fairly within the Straits of Gibraltar, the tall yellow-splotched hills of Africa on our right, with their bases veiled in a blue haze and their summits swathed in clouds — the same being according to Scripture, which says that "clouds and darkness are over the land." The words were spoken of this particular portion of Africa, I believe. On our left were the granite-ribbed domes of old Spain. The Strait is only thirteen miles wide in its narrowest part.

At short intervals, along the Spanish shore, were quaint-looking old stone towers — Moorish, we thought — but learned better afterward. In former times the Morocco rascals used to coast along the Spanish Main in their boats till a safe opportunity seemed to present itself, and then dart in and capture a Spanish village, and carry off all the pretty women they could find. It was a pleasant business, and was very popular. The Spaniards built these watch towers on the hills to enable them to keep a sharper lookout on the Moroccan speculators.

The picture, on the other hand, was very beautiful to eyes weary of the changeless sea, and by and by the ship's company grew wonderfully cheerful. But while we stood admiring the cloud-capped peaks and the lowlands robed in misty gloom, a finer picture burst upon us and chained every eye like a magnet — a stately ship, with canvas piled on canvas

7*

till she was one towering mass of bellying sail! She came speeding over the sea like a great bird. Africa and Spain were forgotten. All homage was for the beautiful stranger. While everybody gazed, she swept superbly by and flung the Stars and Stripes to the breeze! Quicker than thought, hats and handkerchiefs flashed in the air, and a cheer went up! She was beautiful before — she was radiant now. Many a one on our decks knew then for the first time how tame a sight his country's flag is at home compared to what it is in a foreign land. To see it is to see a vision of home itself and all its idols, and feel a thrill that would stir a very river of sluggish blood!

We were approaching the famed Pillars of Hercules, and already the African one, "Ape's Hill," a grand old mountain with summit streaked with granite ledges, was in sight. The other, the great Rock of Gibraltar, was yet to come. The ancients considered the Pillars of Hercules the head of navigation and the end of the world. The information the ancients didn't have was very voluminous. Even the prophets wrote book after book and epistle after epistle, yet never once hinted at the existence of a great continent on our side of the water; yet they must have known it was there, I should think.

In a few moments a lonely and enormous mass of rock, standing seemingly in the center of the wide strait and apparently washed on all sides by the sea, swung magnificently into view, and we needed no

tedious traveled parrot to tell us it was Gibraltar.
There could not be two rocks like that in one king-
dom.

The Rock of Gibraltar is about a mile and a half
long, I should say, by 1,400 to 1,500 feet high, and
a quarter of a mile wide at its base. One side and
one end of it come about as straight up out of the
sea as the side of a house, the other end is irregular
and the other side is a steep slant which an army
would find very difficult to climb. At the foot of
this slant is the walled town of Gibraltar — or rather
the town occupies part of the slant. Everywhere —
on hillside, in the precipice, by the sea, on the
heights,— everywhere you choose to look, Gibraltar
is clad with masonry and bristling with guns. It
makes a striking and lively picture, from whatsoever
point you contemplate it. It is pushed out into the
sea on the end of a flat, narrow strip of land, and is
suggestive of a "gob" of mud on the end of a
shingle. A few hundred yards of this flat ground at
its base belongs to the English, and then, extending
across the strip from the Atlantic to the Mediterranean, a distance of a quarter of a mile, comes the
"Neutral Ground," a space two or three hundred
yards wide, which is free to both parties.

"Are you going through Spain to Paris?" That
question was bandied about the ship day and night
from Fayal to Gibraltar, and I thought I never could
get so tired of hearing any one combination of words
again, or more tired of answering, "I don't know."

G*

At the last moment six or seven had sufficient
decision of character to make up their minds to go,
and did go, and I felt a sense of relief at once — it
was forever too late, now, and I could make up my
mind at my leisure, not to go. I must have a prodigious quantity of mind; it takes me as much as a
week, sometimes, to make it up.

But behold how annoyances repeat themselves.
We had no sooner gotten rid of the Spain distress
than the Gibraltar guides started another — a tiresome repetition of a legend that had nothing very
astonishing about it, even in the first place: "That
high hill yonder is called the Queen's Chair; it is
because one of the queens of Spain placed her chair
there when the French and Spanish troops were besieging Gibraltar, and said she would never move
from the spot till the English flag was lowered from
the fortresses. If the English hadn't been gallant
enough to lower the flag for a few hours one day,
she'd have had to break her oath or die up there."

We rode on asses and mules up the steep, narrow
streets and entered the subterranean galleries the
English have blasted out in the rock. These galleries are like spacious railway tunnels, and at short
intervals in them great guns frown out upon sea and
town through portholes five or six hundred feet
above the ocean. There is a mile or so of this
subterranean work, and it must have cost a vast deal
of money and labor. The gallery guns command
the peninsula and the harbors of both oceans, but

they might as well not be there, I should think, for
an army could hardly climb the perpendicular wall
of the rock anyhow. Those lofty portholes afford
superb views of the sea, though. At one place,
where a jutting crag was hollowed out into a great
chamber whose furniture was huge cannon and
whose windows were portholes, a glimpse was
caught of a hill not far away, and a soldier said:

"That high hill yonder is called the Queen's
Chair; it is because a queen of Spain placed her
chair there once, when the French and Spanish
troops were besieging Gibraltar, and said she would
never move from the spot till the English flag was
lowered from the fortresses. If the English hadn't
been gallant enough to lower the flag for a few
hours, one day, she'd have had to break her oath
or die up there."

On the topmost pinnacle of Gibraltar we halted a
good while, and no doubt the mules were tired.
They had a right to be. The military road was
good, but rather steep, and there was a good deal
of it. The view from the narrow ledge was magnificent; from it vessels seeming like the tiniest little
toy boats, were turned into noble ships by the telescopes; and other vessels that were fifty miles away,
and even sixty, they said, and invisible to the naked
eye, could be clearly distinguished through those
same telescopes. Below, on one side, we looked
down upon an endless mass of batteries, and on the
other straight down to the sea.

While I was resting ever so comfortably on a rampart, and cooling my baking head in the delicious breeze, an officious guide belonging to another party came up and said:

"Senor, that high hill yonder is called the Queen's Chair——"

"Sir, I am a helpless orphan in a foreign land. Have pity on me. Don't—now *don't* inflict that most in-FERNAL old legend on me any more to-day!"

There—I had used strong language, after promising I would never do so again; but the provocation was more than human nature could bear. If you had been bored so, when you had the noble panorama of Spain and Africa and the blue Mediterranean spread abroad at your feet, and wanted to gaze, and enjoy, and surfeit yourself with its beauty in silence, you might have even burst into stronger language than I did.

Gibraltar has stood several protracted sieges, one of them of nearly four years' duration (it failed), and the English only captured it by stratagem. The wonder is that anybody should ever dream of trying so impossible a project as the taking it by assault— and yet it has been tried more than once.

The Moors held the place twelve hundred years ago, and a staunch old castle of theirs of that date still frowns from the middle of the town, with moss-grown battlements and sides well scarred by shots fired in battles and sieges that are forgotten now.

A secret chamber, in the rock behind it, was discovered some time ago, which contained a sword of
exquisite workmanship, and some quaint old armor
of a fashion that antiquaries are not acquainted with,
though it is supposed to be Roman. Roman armor
and Roman relics, of various kinds, have been found
in a cave in the sea extremity of Gibraltar; history
says Rome held this part of the country about the
Christian era, and these things seem to confirm the
statement.

In that cave, also, are found human bones, crusted
with a very thick, stony coating, and wise men have
ventured to say that those men not only lived before
the flood, but as much as ten thousand years before
it. It may be true — it looks reasonable enough —
but as long as those parties can't vote any more,
the matter can be of no great public interest. In
this cave, likewise, are found skeletons and fossils
of animals that exist in every part of Africa, yet
within memory and tradition have never existed in
any portion of Spain save this lone peak of Gibraltar!
So the theory is that the channel between Gibraltar
and Africa was once dry land, and that the low, neutral
neck between Gibraltar and the Spanish hills behind
it was once ocean, and, of course, that these African
animals, being over at Gibraltar (after rock, perhaps — there is plenty there), got closed out when
the great change occurred. The hills in Africa,
across the channel, are full of apes, and there are
now, and always have been, apes on the rock of

Gibraltar — but not elsewhere in Spain! The subject is an interesting one.

There is an English garrison at Gibraltar of 6,000 or 7,000 men, and so uniforms of flaming red are plenty; and red and blue, and undress costumes of snowy white, and also the queer uniform of the bare-kneed Highlander; and one sees soft-eyed Spanish girls from San Roque, and veiled Moorish beauties (I suppose they are beauties) from Tarifa, and turbaned, sashed, and trowsered Moorish merchants from Fez, and long-robed, bare-legged, ragged Mohammedan vagabonds from Tetouan and Tangier, some brown, some yellow, and some as black as virgin ink — and Jews from all around, in gaberdine, skull-cap, and slippers, just as they are in pictures and theaters, and just as they were three thousand years ago, no doubt. You can easily understand that a tribe (somehow our pilgrims suggest that expression, because they march in a straggling procession through these foreign places with such an Indian-like air of complacency and independence about them) like ours, made up from fifteen or sixteen states of the Union, found enough to stare at in this shifting panorama of fashion to-day.

Speaking of our pilgrims reminds me that we have one or two people among us who are sometimes an annoyance. However, I do not count the Oracle in that list. I will explain that the Oracle is an innocent old ass who eats for four and looks wiser than the whole Academy of France would have any right to look, and never uses a one-syllable word when he can think of a longer one, and never by any possible chance knows the meaning of any long word he uses, or ever gets it in the right place; yet he will serenely venture an opinion on the most abstruse subject, and back it up complacently with quotations from authors who never existed, and finally when cornered will slide to the other side of the question, say he has been there all the time, and come back at you with your own spoken arguments, only with the big words all tangled, and play them in your very teeth as original with himself. He reads a chapter in the guide books, mixes the facts all up, with his bad memory, and then goes off to inflict the whole mess on somebody as wisdom which has been festering in his brain for years, and which he gathered in college from erudite authors who are dead now and out of print. This morning at breakfast he pointed out of the window, and said:

"Do you see that there hill out there on that African coast? It's one of them Pillows of Herkewls, I should say — and there's the ultimate one alongside of it."

"The ultimate one — that is a good word — but the Pillars are not both on the same side of the strait." (I saw he had been deceived by a carelessly written sentence in the Guide Book.)

"Well, it ain't for you to say, nor for me. Some authors states it that way, and some states it different. Old Gibbons don't say nothing about it,— just shirks it complete — Gibbons always done that when he got stuck — but there is Rolampton, what does *he* say? Why, he says that they was both on the same side, and Trinculian, and Sobaster, and Syraccus, and Langomarganbl ——''

"Oh, that will do — that's enough. If you have got your hand in for inventing authors and testimony, I have nothing more to say — let them *be* on the same side."

We don't mind the Oracle. We rather like him. We can tolerate the Oracle very easily; but we have a poet and a good-natured, enterprising idiot on board, and they *do* distress the company. The one gives copies of his verses to consuls, commanders, hotel keepers, Arabs, Dutch, — to anybody, in fact, who will submit to a grievous infliction most kindly meant. His poetry is all very well on shipboard, notwithstanding when he wrote an "Ode to the Ocean in a Storm" in one half-hour, and an "Apostrophe to the Rooster in the Waist of the Ship" in the next, the transition was considered to be rather abrupt; but when he sends an invoice of rhymes to the governor of Fayal and another to the commander-in-chief and other dignitaries in Gibraltar, with the compliments of the Laureate of the Ship, it is not popular with the passengers.

The other personage I have mentioned is young and green, and not bright, not learned, and not wise. He will be, though, some day, if he recollects the answers to all his questions. He is known about the ship as the "Interrogation Point," and this by constant use has become shortened to "Interrogation." He has distinguished himself twice already. In Fayal they pointed out a hill and told him it was eight hundred feet high and eleven hundred feet long. And they told him there was a tunnel two thousand feet long and one thousand feet high running through the hill, from end to end. He believed it. He repeated it to everybody, discussed it, and read it from his notes. Finally, he took a useful hint from this remark which a thoughtful old pilgrim made:

"Well, yes, it *is* a little remarkable — singular tunnel altogether — stands up out of the top of the hill about two hundred feet, and one end of it sticks out of the hill about nine hundred!"

Here in Gibraltar he corners these educated British officers and badgers them with braggadocio about America and the wonders she can perform. He told one of them a couple of our gunboats could come here and knock Gibraltar into the Mediterranean sea!

At this present moment, half a dozen of us are taking a private pleasure excursion of our own devising. We form rather more than half the list of white passengers on board a small steamer bound for the venerable Moorish town of Tangier, Africa. Nothing could be more absolutely certain than that we are enjoying ourselves. One cannot do otherwise who speeds over these sparkling waters, and breathes the soft atmosphere of this sunny land. Care cannot assail us here. We are out of its jurisdiction.

We even steamed recklessly by the frowning fortress of Malabat (a stronghold of the Emperor of Morocco), without a twinge of fear. The whole garrison turned out under arms, and assumed a threatening attitude — yet still we did not fear. The entire garrison marched and counter-marched, within the rampart, in full view — yet notwithstanding even this, we never flinched.

I suppose we really do not know what fear is. I inquired the name of the garrison of the fortress of Malabat, and they said it was Mehemet Ali Ben Sancom. I said it would be a good idea to get some more garrisons to help him; but they said no; he had nothing to do but hold the place, and he was competent to do that; had done it two years already. That was evidence which one could not well refute. There is nothing like reputation.

Every now and then, my glove purchase in Gibraltar last night intrudes itself upon me. Dan and the ship's surgeon and I had been up to the great square, listening to the music of the fine military bands, and contemplating English and Spanish female loveliness and fashion, and, at 9 o'clock, were on our way to the theater, when we met the General, the Judge, the Commodore, the Colonel, and the Commissioner of the United States of America to Europe, Asia, and Africa, who had been

to the Club House, to register their several titles
and impoverish the bill of fare; and they told us to
go over to the little variety store, near the Hall of
Justice, and buy some kid gloves. They said they
were elegant, and very moderate in price. It seemed
a stylish thing to go to the theater in kid gloves,
and we acted upon the hint. A very handsome
young lady in the store offered me a pair of blue
gloves. I did not want blue, but she said they
would look very pretty on a hand like mine. The
remark touched me tenderly. I glanced furtively at
my hand, and somehow it did seem rather a comely
member. I tried a glove on my left, and blushed a
little. Manifestly the size was too small for me.
But I felt gratified when she said:

"Oh, it is just right!" — yet I knew it was no
such thing.

I tugged at it diligently, but it was discouraging
work. She said:

"Ah! I see *you* are accustomed to wearing kid
gloves — but some gentlemen are *so* awkward about
putting them on."

It was the last compliment I had expected. I
only understand putting on the buckskin article
perfectly. I made another effort, and tore the glove
from the base of the thumb into the palm of the
hand — and tried to hide the rent. She kept up her
compliments, and I kept up my determination to
deserve them or die:

"Ah, you have had experience!" [A rip down

8

the back of the hand.] "They are just right for you — your hand is very small — if they tear you need not pay for them." [A rent across the middle.] "I can always tell when a gentleman understands putting on kid gloves. There is a grace about it that only comes with long practice." [The whole after guard of the glove "fetched away," as the sailors say, the fabric parted across the knuckles, and nothing was left but a melancholy ruin.]

I was too much flattered to make an exposure, and throw the merchandise on the angel's hands. I was hot, vexed, confused, but still happy; but I hated the other boys for taking such an absorbing interest in the proceedings. I wished they were in Jericho. I felt exquisitely mean when I said cheerfully:

"This one does very well; it fits elegantly. I like a glove that fits. No, never mind, ma'am, never mind; I'll put the other on in the street. It is warm here."

It *was* warm. It was the warmest place I ever was in. I paid the bill, and as I passed out with a fascinating bow, I thought I detected a light in the woman's eye that was gently ironical; and when I looked back from the street, and she was laughing all to herself about something or other, I said to myself, with withering sarcasm, "Oh, certainly; *you* know how to put on kid gloves, don't you? — a self-complacent ass, ready to be flattered out of your senses by every petticoat that chooses to take the trouble to do it!''

The silence of the boys annoyed me. Finally, Dan said, musingly:

"Some gentlemen don't know how to put on kid gloves at all; but some do."

And the doctor said (to the moon, I thought):

"But it is always easy to tell when a gentleman is used to putting on kid gloves."

Dan soliloquized, after a pause:

"Ah, yes; there is a grace about it that only comes with long, very long practice."

"Yes, indeed, I've noticed that when a man hauls on a kid glove like he was dragging a cat out of an ash-hole by the tail, *he* understands putting on kid gloves; *he's* had ex——"

"Boys, enough of a thing's enough! You think you are very smart, I suppose, but I don't. And if you go and tell any of those old gossips in the ship about this thing, I'll never forgive you for it; that's all."

They let me alone then, for the time being. We always let each other alone in time to prevent ill feeling from spoiling a joke. But they had bought gloves, too, as I did. We threw all the purchases away together this morning. They were coarse, unsubstantial, freckled all over with broad yellow splotches, and could neither stand wear nor public exhibition. We had entertained an angel unawares, but we did not take her in. She did that for us.

Tangier! A tribe of stalwart Moors are wading into the sea to carry us ashore on their backs from the small boats.

CHAPTER VIII.

THIS is royal! Let those who went up through Spain make the best of it — these dominions of the Emperor of Morocco suit our little party well enough. We have had enough of Spain at Gibraltar for the present. Tangier is the spot we have been longing for all the time. Elsewhere we have found foreign-looking things and foreign-looking people, but always with things and people intermixed that we were familiar with before, and so the novelty of the situation lost a deal of its force. We wanted something thoroughly and uncompromisingly foreign — foreign from top to bottom — foreign from center to circumference — foreign inside and outside and all around — nothing anywhere about it to dilute its foreignness — nothing to remind us of any other people or any other land under the sun. And lo! in Tangier we have found it. Here is not the slightest thing that ever we have seen save in pictures — and we always mistrusted the pictures before. We can not any more. The pictures used to seem exaggerations — they seemed too weird and fanciful for reality. But behold, they were not wild enough —

8.

they were not fanciful enough — they have not told
half the story. Tangier is a foreign land if ever
there was one; and the true spirit of it can never
be found in any book save the Arabian Nights.
Here are no white men visible, yet swarms of
humanity are all about us. Here is a packed and
jammed city inclosed in a massive stone wall which
is more than a thousand years old. All the houses
nearly are one and two story; made of thick walls
of stone; plastered outside; square as a dry-goods
box; flat as a floor on top; no cornices; whitewashed all over — a crowded city of snowy tombs!
And the doors are arched with a peculiar arch we
see in Moorish pictures; the floors are laid in vari-
colored diamond flags; in tessellated many-colored
porcelain squares wrought in the furnaces of Fez;
in red tiles and broad bricks that time cannot wear;
there is no furniture in the rooms (of Jewish dwellings) save divans — what there is in Moorish ones
no man may know; within their sacred walls no
Christian dog can enter. And the streets are oriental — some of them three feet wide, some six, but
only two that are over a dozen; a man can blockade
the most of them by extending his body across them.
Isn't it an oriental picture?

There are stalwart Bedouins of the desert here, and
stately Moors, proud of a history that goes back to
the night of time; and Jews, whose fathers fled
hither centuries upon centuries ago ; and swarthy
Riffians from the mountains — born cutthroats — and

original, genuine negroes, as black as Moses; and howling dervishes, and a hundred breeds of Arabs — all sorts and descriptions of people that are foreign and curious to look upon.

And their dresses are strange beyond all description. Here is a bronzed Moor in a prodigious white turban, curiously embroidered jacket, gold and crimson sash of many folds, wrapped round and round his waist, trowsers that only come a little below his knee, and yet have twenty yards of stuff in them, ornamented scimetar, bare shins, stockingless feet, yellow slippers, and gun of preposterous length — a mere soldier! — I thought he was the Emperor at least. And here are aged Moors with flowing white beards, and long white robes with vast cowls; and Bedouins with long, cowled, striped cloaks, and negroes and Riffians with heads clean-shaven, except a kinky scalp-lock back of the ear, or rather up on the after corner of the skull, and all sorts of barbarians in all sorts of weird costumes, and all more or less ragged. And here are Moorish women who are enveloped from head to foot in coarse white robes and whose sex can only be determined by the fact that they only leave one eye visible, and never look at men of their own race, or are looked at by them in public. Here are five thousand Jews in blue gaberdines, sashes about their waists, slippers upon their feet, little skull-caps upon the backs of their heads, hair combed down on the forehead, and cut straight across the middle of it from side to side —

H.

the self-same fashion their Tangier ancestors have worn for I don't know how many bewildering centuries. Their feet and ankles are bare. Their noses are all hooked, and hooked alike. They all resemble each other so much that one could almost believe they were of one family. Their women are plump and pretty, and do smile upon a Christian in a way which is in the last degree comforting.

What a funny old town it is! It seems like profanation to laugh and jest and bandy the frivolous chat of our day amid its hoary relics. Only the stately phraseology and the measured speech of the sons of the Prophet are suited to a venerable antiquity like this. Here is a crumbling wall that was old when Columbus discovered America; was old when Peter the Hermit roused the knightly men of the Middle Ages to arm for the first Crusade; was old when Charlemagne and his paladins beleaguered enchanted castles and battled with giants and genii in the fabled days of the olden time; was old when Christ and his disciples walked the earth; stood where it stands to-day when the lips of Memnon were vocal, and men bought and sold in the streets of ancient Thebes!

The Phœnicians, the Carthaginians, the English, Moors, Romans, all have battled for Tangier — all have won it and lost it. Here is a ragged, oriental-looking negro from some desert place in interior Africa, filling his goat-skin with water from a stained and battered fountain built by the Romans twelve hundred years ago. Yonder is a ruined arch of a bridge built by Julius Cæsar nineteen hundred years ago. Men who had seen the infant Saviour in the Virgin's arms have stood upon it, may be.

Near it are the ruins of a dockyard where Cæsar repaired his ships and loaded them with grain when he invaded Britain, fifty years before the Christian era.

Here, under the quiet stars, these old streets seemed thronged with the phantoms of forgotten ages. My eyes are resting upon a spot where stood a monument which was seen and described by Roman historians less than two thousand years ago, whereon was inscribed:

"WE ARE THE CANAANITES. WE ARE THEY THAT HAVE BEEN DRIVEN OUT OF THE LAND OF CANAAN BY THE JEWISH ROBBER, JOSHUA."

Joshua drove them out, and they came here. Not many leagues from here is a tribe of Jews whose ancestors fled thither after an unsuccessful revolt against King David, and these their descendants are still under a ban and keep to themselves.

Tangier has been mentioned in history for three thousand years. And it was a town, though a queer one, when Hercules, clad in his lion-skin, landed here, four thousand years ago. In these streets he met Anytus, the king of the country, and brained him with his club, which was the fashion among gentlemen in those days. The people of Tangier (called

Tingis, then) lived in the rudest possible huts, and dressed in skins and carried clubs, and were as savage as the wild beasts they were constantly obliged to war with. But they were a gentlemanly race, and did no work. They lived on the natural products of the land. Their king's country residence was at the famous Garden of Hesperides, seventy miles down the coast from here. The garden, with its golden apples (oranges), is gone now — no vestige of it remains. Antiquarians concede that such a personage as Hercules did exist in ancient times, and agree that he was an enterprising and energetic man, but decline to believe him a good, bona fide god, because that would be unconstitutional.

Down here at Cape Spartel is the celebrated cave of Hercules, where that hero took refuge when he was vanquished and driven out of the Tangier country. It is full of inscriptions in the dead languages, which fact makes me think Hercules could not have traveled much, else he would not have kept a journal.

Five days' journey from here — say two hundred miles — are the ruins of an ancient city, of whose history there is neither record nor tradition. And yet its arches, its columns, and its statues, proclaim it to have been built by an enlightened race.

The general size of a store in Tangier is about that of an ordinary shower-bath in a civilized land. The Mohammedan merchant, tinman, shoemaker, or vender of trifles, sits cross-legged on the floor, and

reaches after any article you may want to buy.   You
can rent a whole block of these pigeon-holes for fifty
dollars a month.   The market people crowd the
market-place with their baskets of figs, dates, melons,
apricots, etc., and among them file trains of laden
asses, not much larger, if any, than a Newfoundland
dog.   The scene is lively, is picturesque, and smells
like a police court.   The Jewish money-changers
have their dens close at hand; and all day long are
counting bronze coins and transferring them from
one bushel basket to another.   They don't coin
much money now-a-days, I think.   I saw none but
what was dated four or five hundred years back, and
was badly worn and battered.   These coins are not
very valuable.   Jack went out to get a napoleon
changed, so as to have money suited to the general
cheapness of things, and came back and said he had
" swamped the bank; had bought eleven quarts of
coin, and the head of the firm had gone on the street
to negotiate for the balance of the change."   I
bought nearly half a pint of their money for a shil-
ling myself.   I am not proud on account of having
so much money, though.   I care nothing for wealth.
The Moors have some small silver coins, and also
some silver slugs worth a dollar each.   The latter
are exceedingly scarce — so much so that when poor
ragged Arabs see one they beg to be allowed to kiss it.
   They have also a small gold coin worth two dollars.   And that reminds me of something.   When
Morocco is in a state of war, Arab couriers carry

letters through the country, and charge a liberal postage. Every now and then they fall into the hands of marauding bands and get robbed. Therefore, warned by experience, as soon as they have collected two dollars' worth of money they exchange it for one of those little gold pieces, and when robbers come upon them, swallow it. The stratagem was good while it was unsuspected, but after that the marauders simply gave the sagacious United States mail an emetic and sat down to wait.

The Emperor of Morocco is a soulless despot, and the great officers under him are despots on a smaller scale. There is no regular system of taxation, but when the Emperor or the Bashaw want money, they levy on some rich man, and he has to furnish the cash or go to prison. Therefore, few men in Morocco dare to be rich. It is too dangerous a luxury. Vanity occasionally leads a man to display wealth, but sooner or later the Emperor trumps up a charge against him — any sort of one will do — and confiscates his property. Of course, there are many rich men in the empire, but their money is buried, and they dress in rags and counterfeit poverty. Every now and then the Emperor imprisons a man who is suspected of the crime of being rich, and makes things so uncomfortable for him that he is forced to discover where he has hidden his money.

Moors and Jews sometimes place themselves under the protection of the foreign consuls, and then they can flout their riches in the Emperor's face with impunity.

CHAPTER IX.

ABOUT the first adventure we had yesterday afternoon, after landing here, came near finishing
that heedless Blucher. We had just mounted some
mules and asses, and started out under the guardian-
ship of the stately, the princely, the magnificent
Hadji Mohammed Lamarty (may his tribe increase!),
when we came upon a fine Moorish mosque, with tall
tower, rich with checker-work of many-colored porcelain, and every part and portion of the edifice
adorned with the quaint architecture of the Alham-
bra, and Blucher started to ride into the open doorway. A startling "Hi-hi!" from our camp followers, and a loud "Halt!" from an English gentleman in the party, checked the adventurer, and then
we were informed that so dire a profanation is it for
a Christian dog to set foot upon the sacred threshold
of a Moorish mosque, that no amount of purification
can ever make it fit for the faithful to pray in again.
Had Blucher succeeded in entering the place, he
would no doubt have been chased through the town
and stoned; and the time has been, and not many
years ago either, when a Christian would have been

most ruthlessly slaughtered, if captured in a mosque. We caught a glimpse of the handsome tessellated pavements within, and of the devotees performing their ablutions at the fountains; but even that we took that glimpse was a thing not relished by the Moorish bystanders.

Some years ago the clock in the tower of the mosque got out of order. The Moors of Tangier have so degenerated that it has been long since there was an artificer among them capable of curing so delicate a patient as a debilitated clock. The great men of the city met in solemn conclave to consider how the difficulty was to be met. They discussed the matter thoroughly but arrived at no solution. Finally, a patriarch arose and said:

"Oh, children of the Prophet, it is known unto you that a Portuguee dog of a Christian clockmender pollutes the city of Tangier with his presence. Ye know, also, that when mosques are builded, asses bear the stones and the cement, and cross the sacred threshold. Now, therefore, send the Christian dog on all fours, and barefoot, into the holy place to mend the clock, and let him go as an ass!"

And in that way it was done. Therefore, if Blucher ever sees the inside of a mosque, he will have to cast aside his humanity and go in his natural character. We visited the jail, and found Moorish prisoners making mats and baskets. (This thing of utilizing crime savors of civilization.) Murder is punished with death. A short time ago three mur-

derers were taken beyond the city walls and shot.
Moorish guns are not good, and neither are Moorish
marksmen. In this instance, they set up the poor
criminals at long range, like so many targets, and
practiced on them — kept them hopping about and
dodging bullets for half an hour before they managed to drive the center.

When a man steals cattle, they cut off his right
hand and left leg, and nail them up in the market-
place as a warning to everybody. Their surgery is
not artistic. They slice around the bone a little;
then break off the limb. Sometimes the patient gets
well; but, as a general thing, he don't. However,
the Moorish heart is stout. The Moors were always
brave. These criminals undergo the fearful opera-
tion without a wince, without a tremor of any kind,
without a groan! No amount of suffering can bring
down the pride of a Moor, or make him shame his
dignity with a cry.

Here, marriage is contracted by the parents of the
parties to it. There are no valentines, no stolen
interviews, no riding out, no courting in dim parlors,
no lovers' quarrels and reconciliations — no nothing
that is proper to approaching matrimony. The
young man takes the girl his father selects for him,
marries her, and after that she is unveiled, and he
sees her for the first time. If, after due acquaintance,
she suits him, he retains her; but if he suspects her
purity, he bundles her back to her father; if he finds
her diseased, the same; or if, after just and reason-

able time is allowed her, she neglects to bear children, back she goes to the home of her childhood.

Mohammedans here, who can afford it, keep a good many wives on hand. They are called wives, though I believe the Koran only allows four genuine wives — the rest are concubines. The Emperor of Morocco don't know how many wives he has, but thinks he has five hundred. However, that is near enough — a dozen or so, one way or the other, don't matter.

Even the Jews in the interior have a plurality of wives.

I have caught a glimpse of the faces of several Moorish women (for they are only human, and will expose their faces for the admiration of a Christian dog when no male Moor is by), and I am full of veneration for the wisdom that leads them to cover up such atrocious ugliness.

They carry their children at their backs, in a sack, like other savages the world over.

Many of the negroes are held in slavery by the Moors. But the moment a female slave becomes her master's concubine her bonds are broken, and as soon as a male slave can read the first chapter of the Koran (which contains the creed) he can no longer be held in bondage.

They have three Sundays a week in Tangier. The Mohammedan's comes on Friday, the Jew's on Saturday, and that of the Christian Consuls on Sunday. The Jews are the most radical. The Moor goes to his mosque about noon on his Sabbath, as on any other day, removes his shoes at the door, performs his ablutions, makes his salaams, pressing his forehead to the pavement time and again, says his prayers, and goes back to his work.

But the Jew shuts up shop; will not touch copper or bronze money at all; soils his fingers with nothing meaner than silver and gold; attends the synagogue devoutly; will not cook or have anything to do with fire; and religiously refrains from embarking in any enterprise.

The Moor who has made a pilgrimage to Mecca is entitled to high distinction. Men call him Hadji, and he is thenceforward a great personage. Hundreds of Moors come to Tangier every year, and embark for Mecca. They go part of the way in English steamers; and the ten or twelve dollars they pay for passage is about all the trip costs. They take with them a quantity of food, and when the commissary department fails they "skirmish," as Jack terms it in his sinful, slangy way. From the time they leave till they get home again, they never wash, either on land or sea. They are usually gone from five to seven months, and as they do not change their clothes during all that time, they are totally unfit for the drawing-room when they get back.

Many of them have to rake and scrape a long time to gather together the ten dollars their steamer passage costs; and when one of them gets back he
9

is a bankrupt forever after. Few Moors can ever
build up their fortunes again in one short lifetime,
after so reckless an outlay. In order to confine the
dignity of Hadji to gentlemen of patrician blood and
possessions, the Emperor decreed that no man
should make the pilgrimage save bloated aristocrats
who were worth a hundred dollars in specie. But
behold how iniquity can circumvent the law! For a
consideration, the Jewish money-changer lends the
pilgrim one hundred dollars long enough for him to
swear himself through, and then receives it back before the ship sails out of the harbor!

Spain is the only nation the Moors fear. The
reason is, that Spain sends her heaviest ships of war
and her loudest guns to astonish these Moslems;
while America, and other nations, send only a little
contemptible tub of a gunboat occasionally. The
Moors, like other savages, learn by what they see;
not what they hear or read. We have great fleets in
the Mediterranean, but they seldom touch at African
ports. The Moors have a small opinion of England,
France, and America, and put their representatives
to a deal of red-tape circumlocution before they
grant them their common rights, let alone a favor.
But the moment the Spanish minister makes a demand, it is acceded to at once, whether it be just
or not.

Spain chastised the Moors five or six years ago,
about a disputed piece of property opposite Gibraltar, and captured the city of Tetouan. She com-

promised on an augmentation of her territory; twenty million dollars indemnity in money; and peace. And then she gave up the city. But she never gave it up until the Spanish soldiers had eaten up all the cats. They would not compromise as long as the cats held out. Spaniards are very fond of cats. On the contrary, the Moors reverence cats as something sacred. So the Spaniards touched them on a tender point that time. Their unfeline conduct in eating up all the Tetouan cats aroused a hatred toward them in the breasts of the Moors, to which even the driving them out of Spain was tame and passionless. Moors and Spaniards are foes forever now. France had a minister here once who embittered the nation against him in the most innocent way. He killed a couple of battalions of cats (Tangier is full of them) and made a parlor carpet out of their hides. He made his carpet in circles — first a circle of old gray tom-cats, with their tails all pointing toward the center; then a circle of yellow cats; next a circle of black cats and a circle of white ones; then a circle of all sorts of cats; and, finally, a centerpiece of assorted kittens. It was very beautiful; but the Moors curse his memory to this day.

When we went to call on our American Consul-general, to-day, I noticed that all possible games for parlor amusement seemed to be represented on his center-tables. I thought that hinted at lonesomeness. The idea was correct. His is the only American family in Tangier. There are many

foreign Consuls in this place; but much visiting is
not indulged in. Tangier is clear out of the world,
and what is the use of visiting when people have
nothing on earth to talk about? There is none. So
each consul's family stays at home chiefly, and
amuses itself as best it can. Tangier is full of interest for one day, but after that it is a weary prison.
The consul-general has been here five years, and has
got enough of it to do him for a century, and is
going home shortly. His family seize upon their
letters and papers when the mail arrives, read them
over and over again for two days or three, talk them
over and over again for two or three more, till they
wear them out, and after that, for days together,
they eat and drink and sleep, and ride out over the
same old road, and see the same old tiresome things
that even decades of centuries have scarcely changed,
and say never a single word! They have literally
nothing whatever to talk about. The arrival of an
American man-of-war is a godsend to them. " Oh,
solitude, where are the charms which sages have
seen in thy face?" It is the completest exile that I
can conceive of. I would seriously recommend to
the government of the United States that when a
man commits a crime so heinous that the law pro-
vides no adequate punishment for it, they make him
consul-general to Tangier.

I am glad to have seen Tangier — the second
oldest town in the world. But I am ready to bid it
good-bye, I believe.

We shall go hence to Gibraltar this evening or in the morning; and doubtless the *Quaker City* will sail from that port within the next forty-eight hours.

CHAPTER X.

WE passed the Fourth of July on board the *Quaker City*, in mid-ocean. It was in all respects a characteristic Mediterranean day — faultlessly beautiful. A cloudless sky; a refreshing summer wind; a radiant sunshine that glinted cheerily from dancing wavelets instead of crested mountains of water; a sea beneath us that was so wonderfully blue, so richly, brilliantly blue, that it overcame the dullest sensibilities with the spell of its fascination.

They even have fine sunsets on the Mediterranean — a thing that is certainly rare in most quarters of the globe. The evening we sailed away from Gibraltar, that hard-featured rock was swimming in a creamy mist so rich, so soft, so enchantingly vague and dreamy, that even the Oracle, that serene, that inspired, that overpowering humbug, scorned the dinner-gong and tarried to worship!

He said: "Well, that's gorgis, ain't it! They don't have none of them things in our parts, *do* they? I consider that them effects is on account of the superior refragability, as you may say, of the sun's diramic combination with the lymphatic forces of the perihelion of Jubiter. What should you think?"

"Oh, *go* to bed!" Dan said that, and went away.

"Oh, yes, it's all very well to say go to bed when a man makes an argument which another man can't answer. Dan don't never stand any chance in an argument with me. And he knows it, too. What should you say, Jack?"

"Now, doctor, don't you come bothering around me with that dictionary bosh. I don't do you any harm, do I? Then you let *me* alone."

"He's gone, too. Well, them fellows have all tackled the old Oracle, as they say, but the old man's most too many for 'em. Maybe the Poet Lariat ain't satisfied with them deductions?"

The poet replied with a barbarous rhyme, and went below.

"'Pears that *he* can't qualify, neither. Well, I didn't expect nothing out of *him*. I never see one of them poets yet that knowed anything. He'll go down, now, and grind out about four reams of the awfullest slush about that old rock, and give it to a consul or a pilot or a nigger, or anybody he comes across first which he can impose on. Pity but somebody'd take that poor old lunatic and dig all that poetry rubbage out of him. Why can't a man put his intellect onto things that's some value? Gibbons and Hippocratus and Sarcophagus, and all them old ancient philosophers, was down on poets——''

"Doctor," I said, "you are going to invent authorities now, and I'll leave you, too. I always enjoy your conversation, notwithstanding the luxuriance of your syllables, when the philosophy you offer rests on your own responsibility; but when you begin to soar—when you begin to support it with the evidence of authorities who are the creations of your own fancy, I lose confidence."

That was the way to flatter the doctor. He considered it a sort of acknowledgment on my part of a fear to argue with him. He was always persecuting the passengers with abstruse propositions framed in language that no man could understand, and they endured the exquisite torture a minute or two and then abandoned the field. A triumph like this, over half a dozen antagonists, was sufficient for one day; from that time forward he would patrol the decks beaming blandly upon all comers, and so tranquilly, blissfully happy!

But I digress. The thunder of our two brave cannon announced the Fourth of July, at daylight, to all who were awake. But many of us got our information at a later hour, from the almanac. All the flags were sent aloft, except half a dozen that were needed to decorate portions of the ship below, and in a short time the vessel assumed a holiday appearance. During the morning, meetings were held and all manner of committees set to work on the

celebration ceremonies.   In the afternoon the ship's
company assembled aft, on deck, under the awnings;
the flute, the asthmatic melodeon, and the consump-
tive clarinet, crippled the Star Spangled Banner, the
choir chased it to cover, and George came in with a
peculiarly lacerating screech on the final note and
slaughtered it.   Nobody mourned.

We carried out the corpse on three cheers (that
joke was not intentional and I do not indorse it), and
then the President, throned behind a cable-locker
with a national flag spread over it, announced the
"Reader," who rose up and read that same old
Declaration of Independence which we have all
listened to so often without paying any attention to
what it said; and after that the President piped the
Orator of the Day to quarters and he made that
same old speech about our national greatness which
we so religiously believe and so fervently applaud.
Now came the choir into court again, with the com-
plaining instruments, and assaulted Hail Columbia;
and when victory hung wavering in the scale, George
returned with his dreadful wild-goose stop turned on,
and the choir won, of course.   A minister pronounced the benediction, and the patriotic little
gathering disbanded.   The Fourth of July was safe,
as far as the Mediterranean was concerned.

At dinner in the evening, a well-written original
poem was recited with spirit by one of the ship's
captains, and thirteen regular toasts were washed
down with several baskets of champagne.   The

speeches were bad — execrable, almost without exception. In fact, without *any* exception, but one.
Captain Duncan made a good speech; he made the
only good speech of the evening. He said:

"LADIES AND GENTLEMEN: — May we all live to
a green old age, and be prosperous and happy.
Steward, bring up another basket of champagne."

It was regarded as a very able effort.

The festivities, so to speak, closed with another of
those miraculous balls on the promenade deck. We
were not used to dancing on an even keel, though,
and it was only a questionable success. But take it
altogether, it was a bright, cheerful, pleasant Fourth.

Toward nightfall, the next evening, we steamed
into the great artificial harbor of this noble city of
Marseilles, and saw the dying sunlight gild its
clustering spires and ramparts, and flood its leagues
of environing verdure with a mellow radiance that
touched with an added charm the white villas that
flecked the landscape far and near. [Copyright
secured according to law.]

There were no stages out, and we could not get
on the pier from the ship. It was annoying. We
were full of enthusiasm — we wanted to see France!
Just at nightfall our party of three contracted with a
waterman for the privilege of using his boat as a
bridge — its stern was at our companion ladder and
its bow touched the pier. We got in and the fellow
backed out into the harbor. I told him in French
that all we wanted was to walk over his thwarts and

step ashore, and asked him what he went away out there for? He said he could not understand me. I repeated. Still, he could not understand. He appeared to be very ignorant of French. The doctor tried him, but he could not understand the doctor. I asked this boatman to explain his conduct, which he did; and then I couldn't understand *him*. Dan said:

"Oh, go to the pier, you old fool — that's where we want to go!"

We reasoned calmly with Dan that it was useless to speak to this foreigner in English — that he had better let us conduct this business in the French language and not let the stranger see how uncultivated he was.

"Well, go on, go on," he said, "don't mind me. I don't wish to interfere. Only, if you go on telling him in your kind of French he never will find out where we want to go to. That is what I think about it."

We rebuked him severely for this remark, and said we never knew an ignorant person yet but was prejudiced. The Frenchman spoke again, and the doctor said:

"There, now, Dan, he says he is going to *allez* to the *douain*. Means he is going to the hotel. Oh, certainly — *we* don't know the French language."

This was a crusher, as Jack would say. It silenced further criticism from the disaffected member. We coasted past the sharp bows of a navy of great steamships, and stopped at last at a government building on a stone pier. It was easy to remember then that the *douain* was the custom-house, and not the hotel. We did not mention it, however. With winning French politeness, the officers merely opened and closed our satchels, declined to examine our passports, and sent us on our way. We stopped at the first café we came to, and entered. An old woman seated us at a table and waited for orders. The doctor said:

" Avez-vous du vin?"

The dame looked perplexed. The doctor said again, with elaborate distinctness of articulation:

" Avez-vous du — vin!"

The dame looked more perplexed than before. I said:

" Doctor, there is a flaw in your pronunciation somewhere. Let me try her. Madame, avez-vous du vin? It isn't any use, doctor — take the witness."

" Madame, avez-vous du vin — ou fromage — pain — pickled pigs' feet — beurre — des œfs — du beuf — horseradish, sour-crout, hog and hominy — anything, *anything* in the world that can stay a Christian stomach!"

She said:

" Bless you, why didn't you speak English before? — I don't know anything about your plagued French!"

The humiliating taunts of the disaffected member

spoiled the supper, and we dispatched it in angry silence and got away as soon as we could. Here we were in beautiful France — in a vast stone house of quaint architecture — surrounded by all manner of curiously worded French signs — stared at by strangely-habited, bearded French people — everything gradually and surely forcing upon us the coveted consciousness that at last, and beyond all question, we *were* in beautiful France and absorbing its nature to the forgetfulness of everything else, and coming to feel the happy romance of the thing in all its enchanting delightfulness — and to think of this skinny veteran intruding with her vile English, at such a moment, to blow the fair vision to the winds! It was exasperating.

We set out to find the center of the city, inquiring the direction every now and then. We never did succeed in making anybody understand just exactly what we wanted, and neither did we ever succeed in comprehending just exactly what they said in reply — but then they always pointed — they always did that, and we bowed politely and said " Merci, Monsieur," and so it was a blighting triumph over the disaffected member, anyway. He was restive under these victories and often asked:

" What did that pirate say?"

" Why, he told us which way to go, to find the Grand Casino."

" Yes, but what did he *say?*"

" Oh, it don't matter what he said — *we* understood him. These are educated people — not like that absurd boatman.''

" Well, I wish they were educated enough to tell a man a direction that goes *some*where — for we've been going around in a circle for an hour — I've passed this same old drug store seven times.''

We said it was a low, disreputable falsehood (but we knew it was not). It was plain that it would not do to pass that drug store again, though — we might go on asking directions, but we must cease from following finger pointings if we hoped to check the suspicions of the disaffected member.

A long walk through smooth, asphaltum-paved streets, bordered by blocks of vast new mercantile houses of cream-colored stone,— every house and every block precisely like all the other houses and all the other blocks for a mile, and all brilliantly lighted,— brought us at last to the principal thoroughfare. On every hand were bright colors, flashing constellations of gas-burners, gaily-dressed men and women thronging the sidewalks — hurry, life, activity, cheerfulness, conversation, and laughter everywhere! We found the Grand Hotel du Louvre et de la Paix, and wrote down who we were, where we were born, what our occupations were, the place we came from last, whether we were married or single, how we liked it, how old we were, where we were bound for and when we expected to get there, and a great deal of information of similar importance —all for the benefit of the landlord and the secret

THE DAME LOOKED PERPLEXED

police. We hired a guide and began the business of sight-seeing immediately. That first night on French soil was a stirring one. I cannot think of half the places we went to, or what we particularly saw; we had no disposition to examine carefully into any-thing at all — we only wanted to glance and go — to move, keep moving! The spirit of the country was upon us. We sat down, finally, at a late hour, in the great Casino, and called for unstinted cham-pagne. It is so easy to be bloated aristocrats where it costs nothing of consequence! There were about five hundred people in that dazzling place, I sup-pose, though the walls being papered entirely with mirrors, so to speak, one could not really tell but that there were a hundred thousand. Young, daintily-dressed exquisites and young, stylishly-dressed women, and also old gentlemen and old ladies, sat in couples and groups about innumerable marble-topped tables, and ate fancy suppers, drank wine, and kept up a chattering din of conversation that was dazing to the senses. There was a stage at the far end, and a large orchestra; and every now and then actors and actresses in preposterous comic dresses came out and sang the most extravagantly funny songs, to judge by their absurd actions; but that audience merely suspended its chatter, stared cynically, and never once smiled, never once ap-plauded! I had always thought that Frenchmen were ready to laugh at anything.

CHAPTER XI.

WE are getting foreignized rapidly, and with facility. We are getting reconciled to halls and bed-chambers with unhomelike stone floors, and no carpets — floors that ring to the tread of one's heels with a sharpness that is death to sentimental musing. We are getting used to tidy, noiseless waiters, who glide hither and thither, and hover about your back and your elbows like butterflies, quick to comprehend orders, quick to fill them; thankful for a gratuity without regard to the amount; and always polite — never otherwise than polite. That is the strangest curiosity yet — a really polite hotel waiter who isn't an idiot. We are getting used to driving right into the central court of the hotel, in the midst of a fragrant circle of vines and flowers, and in the midst, also, of parties of gentlemen sitting quietly reading the paper and smoking. We are getting used to ice frozen by artificial process in ordinary bottles — the only kind of ice they have here. We are getting used to all these things; but we are *not* getting used to carrying our own soap. We are sufficiently civilized to carry our own combs

(140)

and tooth-brushes; but this thing of having to ring for soap every time we wash is new to us, and not pleasant at all. We think of it just after we get our heads and faces thoroughly wet, or just when we think we have been in the bath-tub long enough, and then, of course, an annoying delay follows. These Marseillaise make Marseillaise hymns, and Marseilles vests, and Marseilles soap for all the world; but they never sing their hymns, or wear their vests, or wash with their soap themselves.

We have learned to go through the lingering routine of the table d'hôte with patience, with serenity, with satisfaction. We take soup; then wait a few minutes for the fish; a few minutes more and the plates are changed, and the roast beef comes; another change and we take peas; change again and take lentils; change and take snail patties (I prefer grasshoppers); change and take roast chicken and salad; then strawberry pie and ice cream; then green figs, pears, oranges, green almonds, etc., finally coffee. Wine with every course, of course, being in France. With such a cargo on board, digestion is a slow process, and we must sit long in the cool chambers and smoke — and read French newspapers, which have a strange fashion of telling a perfectly straight story till you get to the "nub" of it, and then a word drops in that no man can translate, and that story is ruined. An embankment fell on some Frenchmen yesterday, and the papers are full of it to-day — but whether those sufferers were killed, or crippled, or bruised, or only scared, is more than I can possibly make out, and yet I would just give anything to know.

We were troubled a little at dinner to-day, by the conduct of an American, who talked very loudly and coarsely, and laughed boisterously where all others were so quiet and well-behaved. He ordered wine with a royal flourish, and said: "I never dine without wine, sir" (which was a pitiful falsehood), and looked around upon the company to bask in the admiration he expected to find in their faces. All these airs in a land where they would as soon expect to leave the soup out of the bill of fare as the wine! — in a land where wine is nearly as common among all ranks as water! This fellow said: "I am a free-born sovereign, sir, an American, sir, and I want everybody to know it!" He did not mention that he was a lineal descendant of Balaam's ass; but everybody knew that without his telling it.

We have driven in the Prado — that superb avenue bordered with patrician mansions and noble shade trees — and have visited the Chateau Borély and its curious museum. They showed us a miniature cemetery there — a copy of the first graveyard that was ever in Marseilles, no doubt. The delicate little skeletons were lying in broken vaults, and had their household gods and kitchen utensils with them. The original of this cemetery was dug up in the principal street of the city a few years ago. It had remained there, only twelve feet under ground, for a matter of twenty-five hundred years, or there-abouts. Romulus was here before he built Rome, and thought something of founding a city on this spot, but gave up the idea. He may have been personally acquainted with some of these Phœnicians whose skeletons we have been examining.

In the great Zoölogical Gardens we found speci-mens of all the animals the world produces, I think, including a dromedary, a monkey ornamented with tufts of brilliant blue and carmine hair — a very gorgeous monkey he was — a hippopotamus from the Nile, and a sort of tall, long-legged bird with a beak like a powder-horn, and close-fitting wings like the tails of a dress-coat. This fellow stood up with his eyes shut and his shoulders stooped forward a little, and looked as if he had his hands under his coat-tails. Such tranquil stupidity, such supernatural gravity, such self-righteousness, and such ineffable self-complacency as were in the countenance and attitude of that gray-bodied, dark-winged, bald-headed, and preposterously uncomely bird! He was so ungainly, so pimply about the head, so scaly about the legs; yet so serene, so unspeakably satis-fied! He was the most comical-looking creature that can be imagined. It was good to hear Dan and the doctor laugh — such natural and such enjoyable laughter had not been heard among our excursionists since our ship sailed away from America. This bird was a godsend to us, and I should be an ingrate if I forgot to make honorable mention of him in these

pages. Ours was a pleasure excursion; therefore
we stayed with that bird an hour, and made the
most of him. We stirred him up occasionally, but
he only unclosed an eye and slowly closed it again,
abating no jot of his stately piety of demeanor or
his tremendous seriousness. He only seemed to
say, "Defile not Heaven's anointed with unsanctified
hands." We did not know his name, and so we
called him "The Pilgrim." Dan said:

"All he wants now is a Plymouth Collection."

The boon companion of the colossal elephant was
a common cat! This cat had a fashion of climbing
up the elephant's hind legs, and roosting on his
back. She would sit up there, with her paws curved
under her breast, and sleep in the sun half the afternoon. It used to annoy the elephant at first, and
he would reach up and take her down, but she
would go aft and climb up again. She persisted
until she finally conquered the elephant's prejudices,
and now they are inseparable friends. The cat
plays about her comrade's forefeet or his trunk
often, until dogs approach, and then she goes aloft
out of danger. The elephant has annihilated several
dogs lately, that pressed his companion too closely.

We hired a sailboat and a guide and made an
excursion to one of the small islands in the harbor
to visit the Castle d'If. This ancient fortress has a
melancholy history. It has been used as a prison
for political offenders for two or three hundred
years, and its dungeon walls are scarred with the

rudely-carved names of many and many a captive
who fretted his life away here, and left no record of
himself but these sad epitaphs wrought with his own
hands. How thick the names were! And their
long-departed owners seemed to throng the gloomy
cells and corridors with their phantom shapes. We
loitered through dungeon after dungeon, away down
into the living rock below the level of the sea, it
seemed. Names everywhere! — some plebeian, some
noble, some even princely. Plebeian, prince, and
noble, had one solicitude in common — they would
not be forgotten! They could suffer solitude, inac-
tivity, and the horrors of a silence that no sound
ever disturbed; but they could not bear the thought
of being utterly forgotten by the world. Hence
the carved names. In one cell, where a little light
penetrated, a man had lived twenty-seven years
without seeing the face of a human being — lived in
filth and wretchedness, with no companionship but
his own thoughts, and they were sorrowful enough,
and hopeless enough, no doubt. Whatever his
jailers considered that he needed was conveyed to
his cell by night, through a wicket. This man
carved the walls of his prison-house from floor to
roof with all manner of figures of men and animals,
grouped in intricate designs. He had toiled there
year after year, at his self-appointed task, while in-
fants grew to boyhood — to vigorous youth — idled
through school and college — acquired a profession
— claimed man's mature estate — married and

10*

looked back to infancy as to a thing of some vague, ancient time, almost. But who shall tell how many ages it seemed to this prisoner? With the one, time flew sometimes; with the other, never — it crawled always. To the one, nights spent in dancing had seemed made of minutes instead of hours; to the other, those self-same nights had been like all other nights of dungeon life, and seemed made of slow, dragging weeks, instead of hours and minutes.

One prisoner of fifteen years had scratched verses upon his walls, and brief prose sentences — brief, but full of pathos. These spoke not of himself and his hard estate; but only of the shrine where his spirit fled the prison to worship — of home and the idols that were templed there. He never lived to see them.

The walls of these dungeons are as thick as some bed-chambers at home are wide — fifteen feet. We saw the damp, dismal cells in which two of Dumas' heroes passed their confinement — heroes of "Monte Cristo." It was here that the brave Abbé wrote a book with his own blood; with a pen made of a piece of iron hoop, and by the light of a lamp made out of shreds of cloth soaked in grease obtained from his food; and then dug through the thick wall with some trifling instrument which he wrought himself out of a stray piece of iron or table cutlery, and freed Dantés from his chains. It was a pity that so many weeks of dreary labor should have come to naught at last.

They showed us the noisome cell where the celebrated "Iron Mask"—that ill-starred brother of a
hard-hearted king of France—was confined for a
season, before he was sent to hide the strange mystery of his life from the curious in the dungeons of
St. Marguerite. The place had a far greater interest
for us than it could have had if we had known beyond all question who the Iron Mask was, and what
his history had been, and why this most unusual
punishment had been meted out to him. Mystery!
That was the charm. That speechless tongue, those
prisoned features, that heart so freighted with unspoken troubles, and that breast so oppressed with
its piteous secret, had been here. These dank
walls had known the man whose dolorous story is a
sealed book forever! There was fascination in the
spot.

CHAPTER XII.

WE have come five hundred miles by rail through the heart of France. What a bewitching land it is! What a garden! Surely the leagues of bright green lawns are swept and brushed and watered every day and their grasses trimmed by the barber. Surely the hedges are shaped and measured and their symmetry preserved by the most architectural of gardeners. Surely the long, straight rows of stately poplars that divide the beautiful landscape like the squares of a checker-board are set with line and plummet, and their uniform height determined with a spirit level. Surely the straight, smooth, pure white turnpikes are jack-planed and sand-papered every day. How else are these marvels of symmetry, cleanliness, and order attained? It is wonderful. There are no unsightly stone walls, and never a fence of any kind. There is no dirt, no decay, no rubbish anywhere — nothing that even hints at untidiness — nothing that ever suggests neglect. All is orderly and beautiful — everything is charming to the eye.

We had such glimpses of the Rhone gliding along

between its grassy banks; of cosy cottages buried
in flowers and shrubbery; of quaint old red-tiled
villages with mossy mediæval cathedrals looming
out of their midst; of wooded hills with ivy-grown
towers and turrets of feudal castles projecting above
the foliage; such glimpses of Paradise, it seemed to
us, such visions of fabled fairy-land!

We knew, then, what the poet meant, when he
sang of —

> " — thy cornfields green, and sunny vines,
>   O pleasant land of France!"

And it *is* a pleasant land. No word described it
so felicitously as that one. They say there is no
word for "home" in the French language. Well,
considering that they have the article itself in such
an attractive aspect, they ought to manage to get
along without the word. Let us not waste too much
pity on "homeless" France. I have observed that
Frenchmen abroad seldom wholly give up the idea
of going back to France some time or other. I am
not surprised at it now.

We are not infatuated with these French railway
cars, though. We took first-class passage, not because we wished to attract attention by doing a thing
which is uncommon in Europe, but because we
could make our journey quicker by so doing. It is
hard to make railroading pleasant, in any country.
It is too tedious. Stage-coaching is infinitely more
delightful. Once I crossed the plains and deserts
and mountains of the West, in a stage-coach, from

the Missouri line to California, and since then all
my pleasure-trips must be measured to that rare
holiday frolic. Two thousand miles of ceaseless
rush and rattle and clatter, by night and by day, and
never a weary moment, never a lapse of interest!
The first seven hundred miles a level continent, its
grassy carpet greener and softer and smoother than
any sea, and figured with designs fitted to its magnitude — the shadows of the clouds. Here were no
scenes but summer scenes, and no disposition inspired by them but to lie at full length on the mail
sacks, in the grateful breeze, and dreamily smoke the
pipe of peace — what other, where all was repose
and contentment? In cool mornings, before the
sun was fairly up, it was worth a lifetime of city
toiling and moiling, to perch in the foretop with the
driver and see the six mustangs scamper under the
sharp snapping of a whip that never touched them;
to scan the blue distances of a world that knew no
lords but us; to cleave the wind with uncovered head
and feel the sluggish pulses rousing to the spirit of a
speed that pretended to the resistless rush of a
typhoon! Then thirteen hundred miles of desert
solitudes; of limitless panoramas of bewildering
perspective; of mimic cities, of pinnacled cathedrals, of massive fortresses, counterfeited in the
eternal rocks and splendid with the crimson and
gold of the setting sun; of dizzy altitudes among
fog-wreathed peaks and never-melting snows, where
thunders and lightnings and tempests warred mag-

nificently at our feet and the storm-clouds above
swung their shredded banners in our very faces!

But I forgot. I am in elegant France, now, and
not skurrying through the great South Pass and the
Wind River Mountains, among antelopes and buffa-
loes, and painted Indians on the warpath. It is
not meet that I should make too disparaging com-
parisons between humdrum travel on a railway and
that royal summer flight across a continent in a
stage-coach. I meant, in the beginning, to say that
railway journeying is tedious and tiresome, and so it
is — though, at the time, I was thinking particularly
of a dismal fifty-hour pilgrimage between New York
and St. Louis. Of course our trip through France
was not really tedious, because all its scenes and
experiences were new and strange; but as Dan says,
it had its "discrepancies."

The cars are built in compartments that hold eight
persons each. Each compartment is partially sub-
divided, and so there are two tolerably distinct
parties of four in it. Four face the other four.
The seats and backs are thickly padded and cushioned, and are very comfortable; you can smoke, if
you wish; there are no bothersome peddlers; you
are saved the infliction of a multitude of disagreeable fellow-passengers. So far, so well. But then
the conductor locks you in when the train starts;
there is no water to drink in the car; there is no
heating apparatus for night travel; if a drunken
rowdy should get in, you could not remove a matter

of twenty seats from him, or enter another car; but, above all, if you are worn out and must sleep, you must sit up and do it in naps, with cramped legs and in a torturing misery that leaves you withered and lifeless the next day — for behold, they have not that culmination of all charity and human kindness, a sleeping car, in all France. I prefer the American system. It has not so many grievous "discrepancies."

In France, all is clockwork, all is order. They make no mistakes. Every third man wears a uniform, and whether he be a marshal of the empire or a brakeman, he is ready and perfectly willing to answer all your questions with tireless politeness, ready to tell you which car to take, yea, and ready to go and put you into it to make sure that you shall not go astray. You cannot pass into the waiting-room of the depot till you have secured your ticket, and you cannot pass from its only exit till the train is at its threshold to receive you. Once on board, the train will not start till your ticket has been examined — till every passenger's ticket has been inspected. This is chiefly for your own good. If by any possibility you have managed to take the wrong train, you will be handed over to a polite official who will take you whither you belong, and bestow you with many an affable bow. Your ticket will be inspected every now and then along the route, and when it is time to change cars you will know it. You are in the hands of officials who zealously study your welfare and your interest, instead of turning their talents to the invention of new methods of discommoding and snubbing you, as is very often the main employment of that exceedingly self-satisfied monarch, the railroad conductor of America.

But the happiest regulation in French railway government, is — thirty minutes to dinner! No five-minute boltings of flabby rolls, muddy coffee, questionable eggs, gutta-percha beef, and pies whose conception and execution are a dark and bloody mystery to all save the cook who created them! No; we sat calmly down — it was in old Dijon, which is so easy to spell and so impossible to pronounce, except when you civilize it and call it Demijohn — and poured out rich Burgundian wines and munched calmly through a long table d'hôte bill of fare, snail patties, delicious fruits and all, then paid the trifle it cost and stepped happily aboard the train again, without once cursing the railroad company. A rare experience, and one to be treasured forever.

They say they do not have accidents on these French roads, and I think it must be true. If I remember rightly, we passed high above wagon roads, or through tunnels under them, but never crossed them on their own level. About every quarter of a mile, it seemed to me, a man came out and held up a club till the train went by, to signify that everything was safe ahead. Switches were changed a mile in advance, by pulling a wire rope that passed along the ground by the rail, from station to station. Signals for the day and signals for the night gave constant and timely notice of the position of switches.

No, they have no railroad accidents to speak of in France. But why? Because when one occurs, *somebody* has to hang for it!* Not hang, maybe, but be punished at least with such vigor of emphasis as to make negligence a thing to be shuddered at by railroad officials for many a day thereafter. "No blame attached to the officers"— that lying and disaster-breeding verdict so common to our soft-hearted juries, is seldom rendered in France. If the trouble occurred in the conductor's department, that officer must suffer if his subordinate cannot be proven guilty; if in the engineer's department, and the case be similar, the engineer must answer.

The Old Travelers — those delightful parrots who have "been here before," and know more about the country than Louis Napoleon knows now or ever will know,— tell us these things, and we believe them because they are pleasant things to believe, and because they are plausible and savor of the rigid subjection to law and order which we behold about us everywhere.

But we love the Old Travelers. We love to hear them prate and drivel and lie. We can tell them

* They go on the principle that it is better that one innocent man should suffer than five hundred.

the moment we see them. They always throw out
a few feelers: they never cast themselves adrift till
they have sounded every individual and know that
he has not traveled. Then they open their throttle-
valves, and how they do brag, and sneer, and swell,
and soar, and blaspheme the sacred name of Truth!
Their central idea, their grand aim, is to subjugate
you, keep you down, make you feel insignificant
and humble in the blaze of their cosmopolitan glory!
They will not let you know anything. They sneer
at your most inoffensive suggestions; they laugh
unfeelingly at your treasured dreams of foreign
lands; they brand the statements of your traveled
aunts and uncles as the stupidest absurdities; they
deride your most trusted authors and demolish the
fair images they have set up for your willing worship
with the pitiless ferocity of the fanatic iconoclast!
But still I love the Old Travelers. I love them for
their witless platitudes; for their supernatural ability
to bore; for their delightful asinine vanity; for their
luxuriant fertility of imagination; for their startling,
their brilliant, their overwhelming mendacity!

By Lyons and the Saône (where we saw the Lady
of Lyons and thought little of her comeliness); by
Villa Franca, Tonnerre, venerable Sens, Melun, Fon-
tainebleau, and scores of other beautiful cities, we
swept, always noting the absence of hog-wallows,
broken fences, cowlots, unpainted houses, and mud,
and always noting, as well, the presence of cleanliness,
grace, taste in adorning and beautifying, even to the

disposition of a tree or the turning of a hedge, the marvel of roads in perfect repair, void of ruts and guiltless of even an inequality of surface — we bowled along, hour after hour, that brilliant summer day, and as nightfall approached we entered a wilderness of odorous flowers and shrubbery, sped through it, and then, excited, delighted, and half persuaded that we were only the sport of a beautiful dream, lo, we stood in magnificent Paris!

What excellent order they kept about that vast depot! There was no frantic crowding and jostling, no shouting and swearing, and no swaggering intrusion of services by rowdy hackmen. These latter gentry stood outside — stood quietly by their long line of vehicles and said never a word. A kind of hackman-general seemed to have the whole matter of transportation in his hands. He politely received the passengers and ushered them to the kind of conveyance they wanted, and told the driver where to deliver them. There was no "talking back," no dissatisfaction about overcharging, no grumbling about anything. In a little while we were speeding through the streets of Paris, and delightfully recognizing certain names and places with which books had long ago made us familiar. It was like meeting an old friend when we read " *Rue de Rivoli* " on the street corner; we knew the genuine vast palace of the Louvre as well as we knew its picture; when we passed by the Column of July we needed no one to tell us what it was, or to remind us that on its site

once stood the grim Bastile, that grave of human
hopes and happiness, that dismal prison-house
within whose dungeons so many young faces put on
the wrinkles of age, so many proud spirits grew
humble, so many brave hearts broke.

We secured rooms at the hotel, or rather, we had
three beds put into one room, so that we might be
together, and then we went out to a restaurant, just
after lamp-lighting, and ate a comfortable, satisfactory, lingering dinner. It was a pleasure to eat
where everything was so tidy, the food so well
cooked, the waiters so polite, and the coming and
departing company so moustached, so frisky, so
affable, so fearfully and wonderfully Frenchy! All
the surroundings were gay and enlivening. Two
hundred people sat at little tables on the sidewalk,
sipping wine and coffee; the streets were thronged
with light vehicles and with joyous pleasure-seekers;
there was music in the air, life and action all about
us, and a conflagration of gaslight everywhere!

After dinner we felt like seeing such Parisian
specialties as we might see without distressing exer-
tion, and so we sauntered through the brilliant streets
and looked at the dainty trifles in variety stores and
jewelry shops. Occasionally, merely for the pleasure
of being cruel, we put unoffending Frenchmen on
the rack with questions framed in the incomprehen-
sible jargon of their native language, and while they
writhed, we impaled them, we peppered them, we
scarified them, with their own vile verbs and participles.

11

We noticed that in the jewelry stores they had some of the articles marked "gold," and some labeled "imitation." We wondered at this extravagance of honesty, and inquired into the matter. We were informed that inasmuch as most people are not able to tell false gold from the genuine article, the government compels jewelers to have their gold work assayed and stamped officially according to its fineness, and their imitation work duly labeled with the sign of its falsity. They told us the jewelers would not dare to violate this law, and that whatever a stranger bought in one of their stores might be depended upon as being strictly what it was represented to be. Verily, a wonderful land is France!

Then we hunted for a barber-shop. From earliest infancy it had been a cherished ambition of mine to be shaved some day in a palatial barber-shop of Paris. I wished to recline at full length in a cushioned invalid-chair, with pictures about me, and sumptuous furniture; with frescoed walls and gilded arches above me, and vistas of Corinthian columns stretching far before me; with perfumes of Araby to intoxicate my senses, and the slumbrous drone of distant noises to soothe me to sleep. At the end of an hour I would wake up regretfully and find my face as smooth and as soft as an infant's. Departing, I would lift my hands above that barber's head and say, "Heaven bless you, my son!"

So we searched high and low, for a matter of two hours, but never a barber-shop could we see. We

saw only wig-making establishments, with shocks of
dead and repulsive hair bound upon the heads of
painted waxen brigands who stared out from glass
boxes upon the passer-by, with their stony eyes,
and scared him with the ghostly white of their countenances. We shunned these signs for a time, but
finally we concluded that the wig-makers must of
necessity be the barbers as well, since we could
find no single legitimate representative of the frater-
nity. We entered and asked, and found that it
was even so.

I said I wanted to be shaved. The barber inquired where my room was. I said, never mind
where my room was, I wanted to be shaved — there,
on the spot. The doctor said he would be shaved
also. Then there was an excitement among those
two barbers! There was a wild consultation, and
afterward a hurrying to and fro and a feverish gathering up of razors from obscure places and a ransack-
ing for soap. Next they took us into a little mean,
shabby back room; they got two ordinary sitting-
room chairs and placed us in them, with our coats
on. My old, old dream of bliss vanished into thin
air!

I sat bolt upright, silent, sad, and solemn. One
of the wig-making villains lathered my face for ten
terrible minutes and finished by plastering a mass of
suds into my mouth. I expelled the nasty stuff with
a strong English expletive and said, "Foreigner,
beware!" Then this outlaw strapped his razor on

his boot, hovered over me ominously for six fearful
seconds, and then swooped down upon me like the
genius of destruction.   The first rake of his razor
loosened the very hide from my face and lifted me
out of the chair.   I stormed and raved, and the
other boys enjoyed it.   Their beards are not strong
and thick.   Let us draw the curtain over this harrow-
ing scene.   Suffice it that I submitted, and went
through with the cruel infliction of a shave by a
French barber; tears of exquisite agony coursed down
my cheeks, now and then, but I survived.   Then the
incipient assassin held a basin of water under my
chin and slopped its contents over my face, and into
my bosom, and down the back of my neck, with a
mean pretense of washing away the soap and blood.
He dried my features with a towel, and was going
to comb my hair; but I asked to be excused.   I
said, with withering irony, that it was sufficient to
be skinned — I declined to be scalped.

I went away from there with my handkerchief
about my face, and never, never, never desired to
dream of palatial Parisian barber-shops any more.
The truth is, as I believe I have since found out,
that they have no barber-shops worthy of the name
in Paris — and no barbers, either, for that matter.
The impostor who does duty as a barber brings his
pans and napkins and implements of torture to your
residence and deliberately skins you in your private
apartments.   Ah, I have suffered, suffered, suffered,
here in Paris, but never mind — the time is coming

when I shall have a dark and bloody revenge. Some day a Parisian barber will come to my room to skin me, and from that day forth that barber will never be heard of more.

At eleven o'clock we alighted upon a sign which manifestly referred to billiards. Joy! We had played billiards in the Azores with balls that were not round, and on an ancient table that was very little smoother than a brick pavement — one of those wretched old things with dead cushions, and with patches in the faded cloth and invisible obstructions that made the balls describe the most astonishing and unsuspected angles, and perform feats in the way of unlooked-for and almost impossible "scratches," that were perfectly bewildering. We had played at Gibraltar with balls the size of a walnut, on a table like a public square — and in both instances we achieved far more aggravation than amusement. We expected to fare better here, but we were mistaken. The cushions were a good deal higher than the balls, and as the balls had a fashion of always stopping under the cushions, we accomplished very little in the way of caroms. The cushions were hard and unelastic, and the cues were so crooked that in making a shot you had to allow for the curve or you would infallibly put the "English" on the wrong side of the ball. Dan was to mark while the doctor and I played. At the end of an hour neither of us had made a count, and so Dan was tired of keeping tally with nothing to tally, and

11.

we were heated and angry and disgusted. We paid the heavy bill — about six cents — and said we would call around some time when we had a week to spend, and finish the game.

We adjourned to one of those pretty cafés and took supper and tested the wines of the country, as we had been instructed to do, and found them harmless and unexciting. They might have been exciting, however, if we had chosen to drink a sufficiency of them.

To close our first day in Paris cheerfully and pleasantly, we now sought our grand room in the Grand Hotel du Louvre and climbed into our sumptuous bed, to read and smoke — but alas!

> It was pitiful,
> In a whole city-full,
> Gas we had none.

No gas to read by — nothing but dismal candles. It was a shame. We tried to map out excursions for the morrow; we puzzled over French "Guides to Paris"; we talked disjointedly, in a vain endeavor to make head or tail of the wild chaos of the day's sights and experiences; we subsided to indolent smoking; we gaped and yawned, and stretched — then feebly wondered if we were really and truly in renowned Paris, and drifted drowsily away into that vast mysterious void which men call sleep.

CHAPTER XIII.

THE next morning we were up and dressed at ten o'clock. We went to the *commissionaire* of the hotel — I don't know what a *commissionaire* is, but that is the man we went to — and told him we wanted a guide. He said the great International Exposition had drawn such multitudes of Englishmen and Americans to Paris that it would be next to impossible to find a good guide unemployed. He said he usually kept a dozen or two on hand, but he only had three now. He called them. One looked so like a very pirate that we let him go at once. The next one spoke with a simpering precision of pronunciation that was irritating, and said:

"If ze zhentlemans will to me make ze grande honneur to me rattain in hees serveece, I shall show to him everysing zat is magnifique to look upon in ze beautiful Parree. I speaky ze Angleesh pairfaitemaw."

He would have done well to have stopped there, because he had that much by heart and said it right off without making a mistake. But his self-complacency seduced him into attempting a flight into

K*

regions of unexplored English, and the reckless experiment was his ruin. Within ten seconds he was so tangled up in a maze of mutilated verbs and torn and bleeding forms of speech that no human ingenuity could ever have gotten him out of it with credit. It was plain enough that he could not "speaky" the English quite as "pairfaitemaw" as he had pretended he could.

The third man captured us. He was plainly dressed, but he had a noticeable air of neatness about him. He wore a high silk hat which was a little old, but had been carefully brushed. He wore second-hand kid gloves, in good repair, and carried a small rattan cane with a curved handle — a female leg, of ivory. He stepped as gently and as daintily as a cat crossing a muddy street; and oh, he was urbanity; he was quiet, unobtrusive self-possession; he was deference itself! He spoke softly and guardedly; and when he was about to make a statement on his sole responsibility, or offer a suggestion, he weighed it by drachms and scruples first, with the crook of his little stick placed meditatively to his teeth. His opening speech was perfect. It was perfect in construction, in phraseology, in grammar, in emphasis, in pronunciation — everything. He spoke little and guardedly, after that. We were charmed. We were more than charmed — we were overjoyed. We hired him at once. We never even asked him his price. This man — our lackey, our servant, our unquestioning slave though he was, was still a gentleman — we could see that — while of the other two one was coarse and awkward, and the other was a born pirate. We asked our man Friday's name. He drew from his pocket-book a snowy little card, and passed it to us with a profound bow:

A. BILLFINGER,
Guide to Paris, France, Germany,
Spain, &c., &c.,
Grande Hotel du Louvre.

"Billfinger! Oh, carry me home to die!"

That was an "aside" from Dan. The atrocious name grated harshly on my ear, too. The most of us can learn to forgive, and even to like, a counte-nance that strikes us unpleasantly at first, but few of us, I fancy, become reconciled to a jarring name so easily. I was almost sorry we had hired this man, his name was so unbearable. However, no matter. We were impatient to start. Billfinger stepped to the door to call a carriage, and then the doctor said:

"Well, the guide goes with the barber-shop, with the billiard table, with the gasless room, and maybe with many another pretty romance of Paris. I ex-pected to have a guide named Henri de Mont-morency, or Armand de la Chartreuse, or something that would sound grand in letters to the villagers at home; but to think of a Frenchman by the name of Billfinger! Oh! this is absurd, you know. This will never do. We can't say Billfinger; it is nause-

ating.   Name him over again; what had we better
call him?   Alexis du Caulaincourt?"

"Alphonse Henri Gustave de Hauteville," I suggested.

"Call him Ferguson," said Dan.

That was practical, unromantic good sense.
Without debate, we expunged Billfinger *as* Billfinger, and called him Ferguson.

The carriage — an open barouche — was ready.
Ferguson mounted beside the driver, and we whirled
away to breakfast.   As was proper, Mr. Ferguson
stood by to transmit our orders and answer questions.   By and by, he mentioned casually — the
artful adventurer — that he would go and get his
breakfast as soon as we had finished ours.   He
knew he could not get along without him, and that
we would not want to loiter about and wait for him.
We asked him to sit down and eat with us.   He
begged, with many a bow, to be excused.   It
was not proper, he said; he would sit at another
table.   We ordered him peremptorily to sit down
with us.

Here endeth the first lesson.   It was a mistake.

As long as we had the fellow after that, he was
always hungry; he was always thirsty.   He came
early; he stayed late; he could not pass a restaurant;
he looked with a lecherous eye upon every wine-shop.
Suggestions to stop, excuses to eat and to drink
were forever on his lips.   We tried all we could to
fill him so full that he would have no room to spare

for a fortnight; but it was a failure. He did not hold enough to smother the cravings of his super-human appetite.

He had another "discrepancy" about him. He was always wanting us to buy things. On the shallowest pretenses, he would inveigle us into shirt-stores, boot-stores, tailor-shops, glove-shops — anywhere under the broad sweep of the heavens that there seemed a chance of our buying anything. Any one could have guessed that the shopkeepers paid him a percentage on the sales; but in our blessed innocence we didn't, until this feature of his conduct grew unbearably prominent. One day, Dan happened to mention that he thought of buying three or four silk dress-patterns for presents. Ferguson's hungry eye was upon him in an instant. In the course of twenty minutes, the carriage stopped.

"What's this?"

"Zis is ze finest silk magazin in Paris — ze most celebrate."

"What did you come here for? We told you to take us to the palace of the Louvre."

"I suppose ze gentleman say he wish to buy some silk."

"You are not required to 'suppose' things for the party, Ferguson. We do not wish to tax your energies too much. We will bear some of the burden and heat of the day ourselves. We will endeavor to do such 'supposing' as is really necessary to be done. Drive on." So spake the doctor

Within fifteen minutes the carriage halted again, and before another silk-store. The doctor said:

"Ah, the palace of the Louvre; beautiful, beautiful edifice! Does the Emperor Napoleon live here now, Ferguson?"

"Ah, doctor! you do jest; zis is not ze palace; we come there directly. But since we pass right by zis store, where is such beautiful silk——"

"Ah! I see, I see. I meant to have told you that we did not wish to purchase any silks to-day; but in my absentmindedness I forgot it. I also meant to tell you we wished to go directly to the Louvre; but I forgot that also. However, we will go there now. Pardon my seeming carelessness, Ferguson. Drive on."

Within the half-hour, we stopped again—in front of another silk-store. We were angry; but the doctor was always serene, always smooth-voiced. He said.

"At last! How imposing the Louvre is, and yet how small! how exquisitely fashioned! how charmingly situated! Venerable, venerable pile——"

"Pairdon, doctor, zis is not ze Louvre—it is——"

"*What* is it?"

"I have ze idea—it come to me in a moment—zat ze silk in zis magazin——"

"Ferguson, how heedless I am! I fully intended to tell you that we did not wish to buy any silks to-day, and I also intended to tell you that we yearned

to go immediately to the palace of the Louvre, but
enjoying the happiness of seeing you devour four
breakfasts this morning has so filled me with pleasur-
able emotions that I neglect the commonest interests
of the time. However, we will proceed now to the
Louvre, Ferguson.''

"But, doctor" (excitedly), "it will take not a
minute — not but one small minute! Ze gentleman
need not to buy if he not wish to — but only *look* at
ze silk — *look* at ze beautiful fabric." [Then plead-
ingly.] " *Sair* — just only one *leetle* moment!''

Dan said, "Confound the idiot! I don't want to
see any silks to-day, and I *won't* look at them.
Drive on.''

And the doctor: "We need no silks now, Ferguson. Our hearts yearn for the Louvre. Let us
journey on — let us journey on.''

"But, *doctor!* it is only one moment — one leetle
moment. And ze time will be save — entirely save!
Because zere is nothing to see, now — it is too late.
It want ten minute to four and ze Louvre close at
four — *only* one leetle moment, doctor!''

The treacherous miscreant! After four breakfasts
and a gallon of champagne, to serve us such a scurvy
trick. We got no sight of the countless treasures of
art in the Louvre galleries that day, and our only
poor little satisfaction was in the reflection that
Ferguson sold not a solitary silk dress-pattern.

I am writing this chapter partly for the satisfaction of abusing that accomplished knave, Billfinger,

and partly to show whosoever shall read this how Americans fare at the hands of the Paris guides, and what sort of people Paris guides are. It need not be supposed that we were a stupider or an easier prey than our countrymen generally are, for we were not. The guides deceive and defraud every American who goes to Paris for the first time and sees its sights alone or in company with others as little experienced as himself. I shall visit Paris again some day, and then let the guides beware! I shall go in my war-paint — I shall carry my tomahawk along.

I think we have lost but little time in Paris. We have gone to bed every night tired out. Of course, we visited the renowned International Exposition. All the world did that. We went there on our third day in Paris — and we stayed there *nearly two hours*. That was our first and last visit. To tell the truth, we saw at a glance that one would have to spend weeks — yea, even months — in that monstrous establishment, to get an intelligible idea of it. It was a wonderful show, but the moving masses of people of all nations we saw there were a still more wonderful show. I discovered that if I were to stay there a month, I should still find myself looking at the people instead of the inanimate objects on exhibition. I got a little interested in some curious old tapestries of the thirteenth century, but a party of Arabs came by, and their dusky faces and quaint costumes called my attention away at once. I

watched a silver swan, which had a living grace
about his movements, and a living intelligence in his
eyes — watched him swimming about as comfortably
and as unconcernedly as if he had been born in a
morass instead of a jeweler's shop — watched him
seize a silver fish from under the water and hold up
his head and go through all the customary and
elaborate motions of swallowing it — but the moment
it disappeared down his throat some tattooed South
Sea Islanders approached and I yielded to their
attractions. Presently I found a revolving pistol
several hundred years old which looked strangely
like a modern Colt, but just then I heard that the
Empress of the French was in another part of the
building, and hastened away to see what she might
look like. We heard martial music — we saw an
unusual number of soldiers walking hurriedly about
— there was a general movement among the people.
We inquired what it was all about, and learned that
the Emperor of the French and the Sultan of Turkey
were about to review twenty-five thousand troops at
the *Arc de l'Étoile.* We immediately departed. I
had a greater anxiety to see these men than I could
have had to see twenty expositions.

We drove away and took up a position in an open
space opposite the American minister's house. A
speculator bridged a couple of barrels with a board
and we hired standing places on it. Presently there
was a sound of distant music; in another minute a
pillar of dust came moving slowly toward us; a mo-

ment more, and then, with colors flying and a grand
crash of military music, a gallant array of cavalry-
men emerged from the dust and came down the
street on a gentle trot. After them came a long
line of artillery; then more cavalry, in splendid
uniforms; and then their Imperial Majesties, Napoleon III and Abdul Aziz. The vast concourse of
people swung their hats and shouted — the windows
and housetops in the wide vicinity burst into a
snow-storm of waving handkerchiefs, and the wavers
of the same mingled their cheers with those of the
masses below. It was a stirring spectacle.

But the two central figures claimed all my attention. Was ever such a contrast set up before a
multitude till then? Napoleon, in military uniform
— a long-bodied, short-legged man, fiercely mus-
tached, old, wrinkled, with eyes half closed, and
such a deep, crafty, scheming expression about
them! Napoleon, bowing ever so gently to the
loud plaudits, and watching everything and everybody with his cat-eyes from under his depressed hat-
brim, as if to discover any sign that those cheers
were not heartfelt and cordial.

Abdul Aziz, absolute lord of the Ottoman Empire,— clad in dark green European clothes, almost
without ornament or insignia of rank; a red Turkish
fez on his head — a short, stout, dark man, black-
bearded, black-eyed, stupid, unprepossessing — a
man whose whole appearance somehow suggested
that if he only had a cleaver in his hand and a white

apron on, one would not be at all surprised to hear him say: "A mutton roast to-day, or will you have a nice porterhouse steak?"

Napoleon III, the representative of the highest modern civilization, progress, and refinement; Abdul Aziz, the representative of a people by nature and training filthy, brutish, ignorant, unprogressive, superstitious — and a government whose Three Graces are Tyranny, Rapacity, Blood. Here in brilliant Paris, under this majestic Arch of Triumph, the First Century greets the Nineteenth!

Napoleon III, Emperor of France! Surrounded by shouting thousands, by military pomp, by the splendors of his capital city, and companioned by kings and princes — this is the man who was sneered at, and reviled, and called Bastard — yet who was dreaming of a crown and an empire all the while; who was driven into exile — but carried his dreams with him; who associated with the common herd in America, and ran foot-races for a wager — but still sat upon a throne, in fancy; who braved every danger to go to his dying mother — and grieved that she could not be spared to see him cast aside his plebeian vestments for the purple of royalty; who kept his faithful watch and walked his weary beat a common policeman of London — but dreamed the while of a coming night when he should tread the long-drawn corridors of the Tuileries; who made the miserable *fiasco* of Strasbourg; saw his poor, shabby eagle, forgetful of its lesson, refuse to perch upon his shoulder; delivered his carefully prepared, sententious burst of eloquence upon unsympathetic ears; found himself a prisoner, the butt of small wits, a mark for the pitiless ridicule of all the world — yet went on dreaming of coronations and splendid pageants as before; who lay a forgotten captive in the dungeons of Ham — and still schemed and planned and pondered over future glory and future power; President of France at last! a *coup d'état* and surrounded by applauding armies, welcomed by the thunders of cannon, he mounts a throne and waves before an astounded world the scepter of a mighty empire! Who talks of the marvels of fiction? Who speaks of the wonders of romance? Who prates of the tame achievements of Aladdin and the Magi of Arabia?

ABDUL AZIZ, Sultan of Turkey, Lord of the Ottoman Empire! Born to a throne; weak, stupid, ignorant, almost, as his meanest slave; chief of a vast royalty, yet the puppet of his premier and the obedient child of a tyrannical mother; a man who sits upon a throne — the beck of whose finger moves navies and armies — who holds in his hands the power of life and death over millions — yet who sleeps, sleeps, eats, eats, idles with his eight hundred concubines, and when he is surfeited with eating and sleeping and idling, and would rouse up and take the reins of government and threaten to *be* a Sultan, is charmed from his purpose by wary Fuad Pacha with a pretty plan for a new palace or a new ship —

charmed away with a new toy, like any other restless child; a man who sees his people robbed and oppressed by soulless tax-gatherers, but speaks no word to save them; who believes in gnomes and genii and the wild fables of the Arabian Nights, but has small regard for the mighty magicians of to-day, and is nervous in the presence of their mysterious railroads and steamboats and telegraphs; who would see undone in Egypt all that great Mehemet Ali achieved, and would prefer rather to forget than emulate him; a man who found his great empire a blot upon the earth — a degraded, poverty-stricken, miserable, infamous agglomeration of ignorance, crime, and brutality, and will idle away the allotted days of his trivial life, and then pass to the dust and the worms and leave it so!

Napoleon has augmented the commercial prosperity of France, in ten years, to such a degree that figures can hardly compute it. He has rebuilt Paris, and has partly rebuilt every city in the state. He condemns a whole street at a time, assesses the damages, pays them, and rebuilds superbly. Then speculators buy up the ground and sell, but the original owner is given the first choice by the government at a stated price before the speculator is permitted to purchase. But above all things, he has taken the sole control of the empire of France into his hands, and made it a tolerably free land — for people who will not attempt to go too far in meddling with government affairs. No country offers greater security to life and property than France, and one has all the freedom he wants, but no license — no license to interfere with anybody, or make any one uncomfortable.

As for the Sultan, one could set a trap anywhere and catch a dozen abler men in a night.

The bands struck up, and the brilliant adventurer, Napoleon III, the genius of Energy, Persistence, Enterprise; and the feeble Abdul Aziz, the genius of Ignorance, Bigotry, and Indolence, prepared for the Forward — March!

We saw the splendid review, we saw the white-moustached old Crimean soldier, Canrobert, Marshal of France, we saw — well, we saw everything, and then we went home satisfied.

CHAPTER XIV.

WE went to see the Cathedral of Notre Dame. We had heard of it before. It surprises me, sometimes, to think how much we *do* know, and how intelligent we are. We recognized the brown old Gothic pile in a moment; it was like the pictures. We stood at a little distance and changed from one point of observation to another, and gazed long at its lofty square towers and its rich front, clustered thick with stony, mutilated saints who had been looking calmly down from their perches for ages. The Patriarch of Jerusalem stood under them in the old days of chivalry and romance, and preached the third Crusade, more than six hundred years ago; and since that day they have stood there and looked quietly down upon the most thrilling scenes, the grandest pageants, the most extraordinary spectacles that have grieved or delighted Paris. These battered and broken-nosed old fellows saw many and many a cavalcade of mail-clad knights come marching home from Holy Land; they heard the bells above them toll the signal for the St. Bartholomew's Massacre, and they saw the slaughter that followed;

later, they saw the Reign of Terror, the carnage of
the Revolution, the overthrow of a king, the coronation of two Napoleons, the christening of the young
prince that lords it over a regiment of servants in
the Tuileries to-day — and they may possibly continue to stand there until they see the Napoleon
dynasty swept away and the banners of a great Republic floating above its ruins. I wish these old
parties could speak. They could tell a tale worth
the listening to.

They say that a pagan temple stood where Notre
Dame now stands, in the old Roman days, eighteen
or twenty centuries ago — remains of it are still preserved in Paris; and that a Christian church took
its place about A. D. 300; another took the place
of that in A. D. 500; and that the foundations of
the present cathedral were laid about A. D. 1100.
The ground ought to be measurably sacred by this
time, one would think. One portion of this noble
old edifice is suggestive of the quaint fashions of
ancient times. It was built by Jean Sans-Peur,
Duke of Burgundy, to set his conscience at rest —
he had assassinated the Duke of Orleans. Alas!
those good old times are gone, when a murderer
could wipe the stain from his name and soothe his
troubles to sleep simply by getting out his bricks
and mortar and building an addition to a church.

The portals of the great western front are bisected
by square pillars. They took the central one away,
in 1852, on the occasion of thanksgivings for the

reinstitution of the Presidential power — but precious
soon they had occasion to reconsider that motion
and put it back again! And they did.

We loitered through the grand aisles for an hour
or two, staring up at the rich stained-glass windows
embellished with blue and yellow and crimson saints
and martyrs, and trying to admire the numberless
great pictures in the chapels, and then we were ad-
mitted to the sacristy and shown the magnificent
robes which the Pope wore when he crowned Napoleon I; a wagon-load of solid gold and silver utensils used in the great public processions and ceremonies of the church; some nails of the true cross,
a fragment of the cross itself, a part of the crown
of thorns. We had already seen a large piece of the
true cross in a church in the Azores, but no nails.
They showed us likewise the bloody robe which that
Archbishop of Paris wore who exposed his sacred
person and braved the wrath of the insurgents of
1848, to mount the barricades and hold aloft the
olive branch of peace in the hope of stopping the
slaughter. His noble effort cost him his life. He
was shot dead. They showed us a cast of his face,
taken after death, the bullet that killed him, and the
two vertebræ in which it lodged. These people
have a somewhat singular taste in the matter of
relics. Ferguson told us that the silver cross which
the good archbishop wore at his girdle was seized
and thrown into the Seine, where it lay embedded
in the mud for fifteen years, and then an angel ap-

L*

peared to a priest and told him where to dive for it;
he *did* dive for it and got it, and now it is there on
exhibition at Notre Dame, to be inspected by anybody who feels an interest in inanimate objects of
miraculous intervention.

Next we went to visit the Morgue, that horrible
receptacle for the dead who die mysteriously and
leave the manner of their taking off a dismal secret.
We stood before a grating and looked through into
a room which was hung all about with the clothing
of dead men; coarse blouses, water-soaked; the
delicate garments of women and children; patrician
vestments, flecked and stabbed and stained with red;
a hat that was crushed and bloody. On a slanting
stone lay a drowned man, naked, swollen, purple;
clasping the fragment of a broken bush with a grip
which death had so petrified that human strength
could not unloose it — mute witness of the last despairing effort to save the life that was doomed
beyond all help. A stream of water trickled ceaselessly over the hideous face. We knew that the
body and the clothing were there for identification
by friends, but still we wondered if anybody could
love that repulsive object or grieve for its loss. We
grew meditative and wondered if, some forty years
ago, when the mother of that ghastly thing was
dandling it upon her knee, and kissing it and petting
it and displaying it with satisfied pride to the passers-
by, a prophetic vision of this dread ending ever
flitted through her brain. I half feared that the

mother, or the wife or a brother of the dead man might come while we stood there, but nothing of the kind occurred. Men and women came, and some looked eagerly in, and pressed their faces against the bars; others glanced carelessly at the body, and turned away with a disappointed look — people, I thought, who live upon strong excitements, and who attend the exhibitions of the Morgue regularly, just as other people go to see theatrical spectacles every night. When one of these looked in and passed on, I could not help thinking —

"Now this don't afford you any satisfaction — a party with his head shot off is what *you* need."

One night we went to the celebrated *Jardin Mabille*, but only stayed a little while. We wanted to see some of this kind of Paris life, however, and therefore the next night we went to a similar place of entertainment in a great garden in the suburb of Asniéres. We went to the railroad depot, toward evening, and Ferguson got tickets for a second-class carriage. Such a perfect jam of people I have not often seen — but there was no noise, no disorder, no rowdyism. Some of the women and young girls that entered the train we knew to be of the *demi-monde*, but others we were not at all sure about.

The girls and women in our carriage behaved themselves modestly and becomingly all the way out, except that they smoked. When we arrived at the garden in Asniéres, we paid a franc or two admission, and entered a place which had flower-beds in it, and grass-plats, and long, curving rows of ornamental shrubbery, with here and there a secluded bower convenient for eating ice-cream in. We moved along the sinuous gravel walks, with the great concourse of girls and young men, and suddenly a domed and filigreed white temple, starred over and over and over again with brilliant gas jets, burst upon us like a fallen sun. Near by was a large, handsome house with its ample front illuminated in the same way, and above its roof floated the Star Spangled Banner of America.

"Well!" I said. "How is this?" It nearly took my breath away.

Ferguson said an American — a New Yorker — kept the place, and was carrying on quite a stirring opposition to the *Jardin Mabille*.

Crowds, composed of both sexes and nearly all ages, were frisking about the garden or sitting in the open air in front of the flagstaff and the temple, drinking wine and coffee, or smoking. The dancing had not begun yet. Ferguson said there was to be an exhibition. The famous Blondin was going to perform on a tight rope in another part of the garden. We went thither. Here the light was dim, and the masses of people were pretty closely packed together. And now I made a mistake which any donkey might make, but a sensible man never. I committed an error which I find myself repeating every day of my life. Standing right before a young lady, I said:

"Dan, just look at this girl, how beautiful she is!"

'I thank you more for the evident sincerity of the compliment, sir, than for the extraordinary publicity you have given to it!" This in good, pure English.

We took a walk, but my spirits were very, very sadly dampened. I did not feel right comfortable for some time afterward. Why *will* people be so stupid as to suppose themselves the only foreigners among a crowd of ten thousand persons?

But Blondin came out shortly. He appeared on a stretched cable, far away above the sea of tossing hats and handkerchiefs, and in the glare of the hundreds of rockets that whizzed heavenward by him he looked like a wee insect. He balanced his pole and walked the length of his rope — two or three hundred feet; he came back and got a man and carried him across; he returned to the center and danced a jig; next he performed some gymnastic and balancing feats too perilous to afford a pleasant spectacle; and he finished by fastening to his person a thousand Roman candles, Catherine wheels, serpents and rockets of all manner of brilliant colors, setting them on fire all at once and walking and waltzing across his rope again in a blinding blaze of glory that lit up the garden and the people's faces like a great conflagration at midnight.

The dance had begun, and we adjourned to the temple. Within it was a drinking-saloon; and all around it was a broad circular platform for the dancers. I backed up against the wall of the temple, and waited. Twenty sets formed, the music struck up, and then — I placed my hands before my face for very shame. But I looked through my fingers. They were dancing the renowned *"Can-can."* A handsome girl in the set before me tripped forward lightly to meet the opposite gentleman — tripped back again, grasped her dresses vigorously on both sides with her hands, raised them pretty high, danced an extraordinary jig that had more activity and exposure about it than any jig I ever saw before, and then, drawing her clothes still higher, she advanced gaily to the center and launched a vicious kick full at her *vis-a-vis* that must infallibly have removed his nose if he had been seven feet high. It was a mercy he was only six.

That is the *can-can.* The idea of it is to dance as wildly, as noisily, as furiously as you can; expose yourself as much as possible if you are a woman; and kick as high as you can, no matter which sex you belong to. There is no word of exaggeration in this. Any of the staid, respectable, aged people who were there that night can testify to the truth of that statement. There were a good many such people present. I suppose French morality is not of that strait-laced description which is shocked at trifles.

I moved aside and took a general view of the *can-can.* Shouts, laughter, furious music, a bewildering chaos of darting and intermingling forms, stormy jerking and snatching of gay dresses, bobbing heads, flying arms, lightning flashes of white-stockinged calves and dainty slippers in the air, and then a grand final rush, riot, a terrific hubbub, and a wild stampede! Heavens! Nothing like it has been seen on earth since trembling Tam O'Shanter saw the devil and the witches at their orgies that stormy night in "Alloway's auld haunted kirk."

We visited the Louvre, at a time when we had no silk purchases in view, and looked at its miles of paintings by the old masters. Some of them were beautiful, but at the same time they carried such evidences about them of the cringing spirit of those great men that we found small pleasure in examining them. Their nauseous adulation of princely patrons was more prominent to me and chained my attention more surely than the charms of color and expression which are claimed to be in the pictures. Gratitude for kindnesses is well, but it seems to me that some of those artists carried it so far that it ceased to be gratitude, and became worship. If there is a plausible excuse for the worship of men, then by all means let us forgive Rubens and his brethren.

But I will drop the subject, lest I say something about the old masters that might as well be left unsaid.

Of course we drove in the *Bois de Boulogne*, that limitless park, with its forests, its lakes, its cascades, and its broad avenues. There were thousands upon thousands of vehicles abroad, and the scene was full of life and gayety. There were very common hacks, with father and mother and all the children in them; conspicuous little open carriages with celebrated ladies of questionable reputation in them; there were Dukes and Duchesses abroad, with gorgeous footmen perched behind, and equally gorgeous outriders perched on each of the six horses; there were blue and silver, and green and gold, and pink and black, and all sorts and descriptions of stunning and startling liveries out, and I almost yearned to be a flunkey myself, for the sake of the fine clothes.

But presently the Emperor came along and he outshone them all. He was preceded by a bodyguard of gentlemen on horseback in showy uniforms, his carriage horses (there appeared to be somewhere in the remote neighborhood of a thousand of them) were bestridden by gallant looking fellows, also in stylish uniforms, and after the carriage followed another detachment of body-guards. Everybody got out of the way; everybody bowed to the Emperor and his friend the Sultan, and they went by on a swinging trot and disappeared.

I will not describe the *Bois de Boulogne*. I cannot do it. It is simply a beautiful, cultivated, endless, wonderful wilderness. It is an enchanting place. It is in Paris, now, one may say, but a crumbling old cross in one portion of it reminds one that it was not always so. The cross marks the spot where a celebrated troubadour was waylaid and mur-

dered in the fourteenth century. It was in this park
that that fellow with an unpronounceable name made
the attempt upon the Russian Czar's life last spring
with a pistol. The bullet struck a tree. Ferguson
showed us the place. Now in America that interesting tree would be chopped down or forgotten
within the next five years, but it will be treasured
here. The guides will point it out to visitors for
the next eight hundred years, and when it decays
and falls down they will put up another there and go
on with the same old story just the same.

CHAPTER XV.

ONE of our pleasantest visits was to Père la Chaise, the national burying-ground of France, the honored resting-place of some of her greatest and best children, the last home of scores of illustrious men and women who were born to no titles, but achieved fame by their own energy and their own genius. It is a solemn city of winding streets, and of miniature marble temples and mansions of the dead gleaming white from out a wilderness of foliage and fresh flowers. Not every city is so well peopled as this, or has so ample an area within its walls. Few palaces exist in any city that are so exquisite in design, so rich in art, so costly in material, so graceful, so beautiful.

We had stood in the ancient church of St. Denis, where the marble effigies of thirty generations of kings and queens lay stretched at length upon the tombs, and the sensations invoked were startling and novel; the curious armor, the obsolete costumes, the placid faces, the hands placed palm to palm in eloquent supplication — it was a vision of gray antiquity. It seemed curious enough to be standing

face to face, as it were, with old Dagobert I, and
Clovis and Charlemagne, those vague, colossal
heroes, those shadows, those myths of a thousand
years ago! I touched their dust-covered faces with
my finger, but Dagobert was deader than the sixteen
centuries that have passed over him, Clovis slept
well after his labor for Christ, and old Charlemagne
went on dreaming of his paladins, of bloody Ronces-
valles, and gave no heed to me.

The great names of Père la Chaise impress one,
too, but differently. There the suggestion brought
constantly to his mind is, that this place is sacred
to a nobler royalty — the royalty of heart and brain.
Every faculty of mind, every noble trait of human
nature, every high occupation which men engage in,
seems represented by a famous name. The effect is
a curious medley. Davoust and Massena, who
wrought in many a battle-tragedy, are here, and so
also is Rachel, of equal renown in mimic tragedy on
the stage. The Abbé Sicard sleeps here — the first
great teacher of the deaf and dumb — a man whose
heart went out to every unfortunate, and whose life
was given to kindly offices in their service; and not
far off, in repose and peace at last, lies Marshal
Ney, whose stormy spirit knew no music like the
bugle call to arms. The man who originated public
gas lighting, and that other benefactor who introduced the cultivation of the potato and thus blessed
millions of his starving countrymen, lie with the
Prince of Masserano, and with exiled queens and

13

princes of Further India. Gay-Lussac, the chemist; Laplace, the astronomer; Larrey, the surgeon; de Sèze, the advocate, are here, and with them are Talma, Bellini, Rubini; de Balzac, Beaumarchais, Béranger; Molière and Lafontaine, and scores of other men whose names and whose worthy labors are as familiar in the remote byplaces of civilization as are the historic deeds of the kings and princes that sleep in the marble vaults of St. Denis.

But among the thousands and thousands of tombs in Père la Chaise, there is one that no man, no woman, no youth of either sex, ever passes by without stopping to examine. Every visitor has a sort of indistinct idea of the history of its dead, and comprehends that homage is due there, but not one in twenty thousand clearly remembers the story of that tomb and its romantic occupants. This is the grave of Abelard and Heloise — a grave which has been more revered, more widely known, more written and sung about and wept over, for seven hundred years, than any other in Christendom, save only that of the Saviour. All visitors linger pensively about it; all young people capture and carry away keepsakes and mementoes of it; all Parisian youths and maidens who are disappointed in love come there to bail out when they are full of tears; yea, many stricken lovers make pilgrimages to this shrine from distant provinces to weep and wail and " grit" their teeth over their heavy sorrows, and to purchase the sympathies of the chastened spirits of

that tomb with offerings of immortelles and budding
flowers.

Go when you will, you find somebody snuffling
over that tomb. Go when you will, you find it
furnished with those bouquets and immortelles. Go
when you will, you find a gravel train from Marseilles
arriving to supply the deficiencies caused by
memento-cabbaging vandals whose affections have
miscarried.

Yet who really knows the story of Abelard and
Heloise? Precious few people. The names are
perfectly familiar to everybody, and that is about
all. With infinite pains I have acquired a knowledge
of that history, and I propose to narrate it here,
partly for the honest information of the public and
partly to show that public that they have been wast-
ing a good deal of marketable sentiment very un-
necessarily.

STORY OF ABELARD AND HELOISE.

Heloise was born seven hundred and sixty-six
years ago. She may have had parents. There is
no telling. She lived with her uncle Fulbert, a
canon of the cathedral of Paris. I do not know
what a canon of a cathedral is, but that is what he
was. He was nothing more than a sort of a mountain howitzer, likely, because they had no heavy
artillery in those days. Suffice it, then, that Heloise
lived with her uncle the howitzer, and was happy.
She spent the most of her childhood in the convent of

Argenteuil — never heard of Argenteuil before, but suppose there was really such a place. She then returned to her uncle, the old gun, or son of a gun, as the case may be, and he taught her to write and speak Latin, which was the language of literature and polite society at that period.

Just at this time, Pierre Abelard, who had already made himself widely famous as a rhetorician, came to found a school of rhetoric in Paris. The originality of his principles, his eloquence, and his great physical strength and beauty created a profound sensation. He saw Heloise, and was captivated by her blooming youth, her beauty, and her charming disposition. He wrote to her; she answered. He wrote again, she answered again. He was now in love. He longed to know her — to speak to her face to face.

His school was near Fulbert's house. He asked Fulbert to allow him to call. The good old swivel saw here a rare opportunity; his niece, whom he so much loved, would absorb knowledge from this man, and it would not cost him a cent. Such was Fulbert — penurious.

Fulbert's first name is not mentioned by any author, which is unfortunate. However, George W. Fulbert will answer for him as well as any other. We will let him go at that. He asked Abelard to teach her.

Abelard was glad enough of the opportunity. He came often and stayed long. A letter of his shows

In its very first sentence that he came under that
friendly roof, like a cold-hearted villain as he was,
with the deliberate intention of debauching a confiding, innocent girl.   This is the letter:

"I cannot cease to be astonished at the simplicity of Fulbert; I was
as much surprised as if he had placed a lamb in the power of a hungry
wolf.   Heloise and I, under pretext of study, gave ourselves up wholly
to love, and the solitude that love seeks our studies procured for us.
Books were open before us, but we spoke oftener of love than philosophy,
and kisses came more readily from our lips than words."

And so, exulting over an honorable confidence
which to his degraded instinct was a ludicrous
"simplicity," this unmanly Abelard seduced the
niece of the man whose guest he was.   Paris found
it out.   Fulbert was told of it — told often — but
refused to believe it.   He could not comprehend
how a man could be so depraved as to use the sacred
protection and security of hospitality as a means for
the commission of such a crime as that.   But when
he heard the rowdies in the streets singing the love-
songs of Abelard to Heloise, the case was too plain
— love-songs come not properly within the teachings
of rhetoric and philosophy.

He drove Abelard from his house.   Abelard returned secretly and carried Heloise away to Palais,
in Brittany, his native country.   Here, shortly afterward, she bore a son, who, from his rare beauty,
was surnamed Astrolabe — William G.   The girl's
flight enraged Fulbert, and he longed for vengeance,
but feared to strike lest retaliation visit Heloise —

13.

for he still loved her tenderly. At length Abelard offered to marry Heloise — but on a shameful condition: that the marriage should be kept secret from the world, to the end that (while her good name remained a wreck, as before) his priestly reputation might be kept untarnished. It was like that miscreant. Fulbert saw his opportunity and consented. He would see the parties married, and then violate the confidence of the man who had taught him that trick; he would divulge the secret and so remove somewhat of the obloquy that attached to his niece's fame. But the niece suspected his scheme. She refused the marriage at first; she said Fulbert would betray the secret to save her, and besides, she did not wish to drag down a lover who was so gifted, so honored by the world, and who had such a splendid career before him. It was noble, self-sacrificing love, and characteristic of the pure-souled Heloise, but it was not good sense.

But she was overruled, and the private marriage took place. Now for Fulbert! The heart so wounded should be healed at last; the proud spirit so tortured should find rest again; the humbled head should be lifted up once more. He proclaimed the marriage in the high places of the city, and rejoiced that dishonor had departed from his house. But lo! Abelard denied the marriage! Heloise denied it! The people, knowing the former circumstances, might have believed Fulbert, had only Abelard denied it, but when the person chiefly inter ested — the girl herself — denied it, they laughed despairing Fulbert to scorn.

The poor canon of the cathedral of Paris was spiked again. The last hope of repairing the wrong that had been done his house was gone. What next? Human nature suggested revenge. He compassed it. The historian says:

"Ruffians, hired by Fulbert, fell upon Abelard by night, and inflicted upon him a terrible and nameless mutilation."

I am seeking the last resting-place of those "ruffians." When I find it I shall shed some tears on it, and stack up some bouquets and immortelles, and cart away from it some gravel whereby to remember that howsoever blotted by crime their lives may have been, these ruffians did one just deed, at any rate, albeit it was not warranted by the strict letter of the law.

Heloise entered a convent and gave good-bye to the world and its pleasures for all time. For twelve years she never heard of Abelard — never even heard his name mentioned. She had become prioress of Argenteuil, and led a life of complete seclusion. She happened one day to see a letter written by him, in which he narrated his own history. She cried over it, and wrote him. He answered, addressing her as his "sister in Christ." They continued to correspond, she in the unweighed language of unwavering affection, he in the chilly phraseology of the polished rhetorician. She poured out her heart

M.*

in passionate, disjointed sentences; he replied with
finished essays, divided deliberately into heads and
sub-heads, premises and argument. She showered
upon him the tenderest epithets that love could
devise, he addressed her from the North Pole of his
frozen heart as the " Spouse of Christ!" The
abandoned villain!

On account of her too easy government of her
nuns, some disreputable irregularities were discovered among them, and the Abbot of St. Denis broke
up her establishment. Abelard was the official head
of the monastery of St. Gildas de Ruys, at that
time, and when he heard of her homeless condition
a sentiment of pity was aroused in his breast (it is a
wonder the unfamiliar emotion did not blow his
head off), and he placed her and her troop in the
little oratory of the Paraclete, a religious establishment which he had founded. She had many priva-
tions and sufferings to undergo at first, but her worth
and her gentle disposition won influential friends for
her, and she built up a wealthy and flourishing
nunnery. She became a great favorite with the
heads of the church, and also the people, though
she seldom appeared in public. She rapidly advanced in esteem, in good report and in usefulness,
and Abelard as rapidly lost ground. The Pope so
honored her that he made her the head of her order.
Abelard, a man of splendid talents, and ranking as
the first debater of his time, became timid, irreso-
lute, and distrustful of his powers. He only needed

a great misfortune to topple him from the high position he held in the world of intellectual excellence, and it came. Urged by kings and princes to meet the subtle St. Bernard in debate and crush him, he stood up in the presence of a royal and illustrious assemblage, and when his antagonist had finished he looked about him, and stammered a commencement; but his courage failed him, the cunning of his tongue was gone; with his speech unspoken, he trembled and sat down, a disgraced and vanquished champion.

He died a nobody, and was buried at Cluny, A.D. 1144. They removed his body to the Paraclete afterward, and when Heloise died, twenty years later, they buried her with him, in accordance with her last wish. He died at the ripe age of 64, and she at 63. After the bodies had remained entombed three hundred years, they were removed once more. They were removed again in 1800, and finally, seventeen years afterward, they were taken up and transferred to Père la Chaise, where they will remain in peace and quiet until it comes time for them to get up and move again.

History is silent concerning the last acts of the mountain howitzer. Let the world say what it will about him, *I*, at least, shall always respect the memory and sorrow for the abused trust, and the broken heart, and the troubled spirit of the old smooth-bore. Rest and repose be his!

Such is the story of Abelard and Heloise. Such is the history that Lamartine has shed such cataracts of tears over. But that man never could come within the influence of a subject in the least pathetic without overflowing his banks. He ought to be dammed — or leveed, I should more properly say. Such is the history — not as it is usually told, but as it is when stripped of the nauseous sentimentality that would enshrine for our loving worship a dastardly seducer like Pierre Abelard. I have not a word to say against the misused, faithful girl, and would not withhold from her grave a single one of those simple tributes which blighted youths and maidens offer to her memory, but I am sorry enough that I have not time and opportunity to write four or five volumes of my opinion of her friend the founder of the Parachute, or the Paraclete, or whatever it was.

The tons of sentiment I have wasted on that unprincipled humbug, in my ignorance! I shall throttle down my emotions hereafter, about this sort of people, until I have read them up and know whether they are entitled to any tearful attentions or not. I wish I had my immortelles back, now, and that bunch of radishes.

In Paris we often saw in shop windows the sign, "*English Spoken Here,*" just as one sees in the windows at home the sign, "*Ici on parle française.*" We always invaded these places at once — and invariably received the information, framed in faultless French, that the clerk who did the English for the establishment had just gone to dinner and would be

back in an hour — would Monsieur buy something?
We wondered why those parties happened to take
their dinners at such erratic and extraordinary
hours, for we never called at a time when an exem-
plary Christian would be in the least likely to be
abroad on such an errand. The truth was, it was a
base fraud — a snare to trap the unwary — chaff to
catch fledglings with. They had no English-
murdering clerk. They trusted to the sign to inveigle foreigners into their lairs, and trusted to their
own blandishments to keep them there till they
bought something.

We ferreted out another French imposition — a
frequent sign to this effect: "ALL MANNER OF
AMERICAN DRINKS ARTISTICALLY PREPARED
HERE." We procured the services of a gentleman
experienced in the nomenclature of the American
bar, and moved upon the works of one of these im-
postors. A bowing, aproned Frenchman skipped
forward and said:

"Que voulez les messieurs?" I do not know
what "Que voulez les messieurs" means, but such
was his remark.

Our General said, "We will take a whisky-
straight."

[A stare from the Frenchman.]

"Well, if you don't know what that is, give us a
champagne cock-tail."

[A stare and a shrug.]

"Well, then, give us a sherry cobbler."

The Frenchman was checkmated. This was all Greek to him.

" Give us a brandy smash!"

The Frenchman began to back away, suspicious of the ominous vigor of the last order — began to back away, shrugging his shoulders and spreading his hands apologetically.

The General followed him up and gained a complete victory. The uneducated foreigner could not even furnish a Santa Cruz Punch, an Eye-Opener, a Stone-Fence, or an Earthquake. It was plain that he was a wicked impostor.

An acquaintance of mine said, the other day, that he was doubtless the only American visitor to the Exposition who had had the high honor of being escorted by the Emperor's body-guard. I said with unobtrusive frankness that I was astonished that such a long-legged, lantern-jawed, unprepossessing looking specter as he should be singled out for a distinction like that, and asked how it came about. He said he had attended a great military review in the *Champ de Mars*, some time ago, and while the multitude about him was growing thicker and thicker every moment, he observed an open space inside the railing. He left his carriage and went into it. He was the only person there, and so he had plenty of room, and the situation being central, he could see all the preparations going on about the field. By and by there was a sound of music, and soon the Emperor of the French and the Emperor of

Austria, escorted by the famous *Cent Gardes*, entered the inclosure. They seemed not to observe him, but directly, in response to a sign from the commander of the Guard, a young lieutenant came toward him with a file of his men following, halted, raised his hand and gave the military salute, and then said in a low voice that he was sorry to have to disturb a stranger and a gentleman, but the place was sacred to royalty. Then this New Jersey phantom rose up and bowed and begged pardon, then with the officer beside him, the file of men marching behind him, and with every mark of respect, he was escorted to his carriage by the imperial *Cent Gardes!* The officer saluted again and fell back, the New Jersey sprite bowed in return and had presence of mind enough to pretend that he had simply called on a matter of private business with those emperors, and so waved them an adieu, and drove from the field!

Imagine a poor Frenchman ignorantly intruding upon a public rostrum sacred to some sixpenny dignitary in America. The police would scare him to death, first, with a storm of their elegant blasphemy, and then pull him to pieces getting him away from there. We are measurably superior to the French in some things, but they are immeasurably our betters in others.

Enough of Paris for the present. We have done our whole duty by it. We have seen the Tuileries, the Napoleon Column, the Madeleine, that wonder of wonders the tomb of Napoleon, all the great churches and museums, libraries, imperial palaces, and sculpture and picture galleries, the Pantheon, *Jardin des Plantes*, the opera, the circus, the legislative body, the billiard-rooms, the barbers, the *grisettes* —

Ah, the *grisettes* ! I had almost forgotten. They are another romantic fraud. They were (if you let the books of travel tell it) always so beautiful — so neat and trim, so graceful — so naïve and trusting — so gentle, so winning — so faithful to their shop duties, so irresistible to buyers in their prattling importunity — so devoted to their poverty-stricken students of the Latin Quarter — so light hearted and happy on their Sunday picnics in the suburbs — and oh, so charmingly, so delightfully immoral!

Stuff! For three or four days I was constantly saying:

"Quick, Ferguson! is that a *grisette ?*"

And he always said "No."

He comprehended, at last, that I wanted to see a grisette. Then he showed me dozens of them. They were like nearly all the Frenchwomen I ever saw — homely. They had large hands, large feet, large mouths; they had pug noses as a general thing, and moustaches that not even good breeding could overlook; they combed their hair straight back without parting; they were ill-shaped, they were not winning, they were not graceful; I knew by their looks that they ate garlic and onions; and lastly and finally, to my thinking it would be base flattery to call them immoral.

Aroint thee, wench! I sorrow for the vagabond student of the Latin Quarter now, even more than formerly I envied him. Thus topples to earth another idol of my infancy.

We have seen everything, and to-morrow we go to Versailles. We shall see Paris only for a little while as we come back to take up our line of march for the ship, and so I may as well bid the beautiful city a regretful farewell. We shall travel many thousands of miles after we leave here, and visit many great cities, but we shall find none so enchanting as this.

Some of our party have gone to England, intending to take a roundabout course and rejoin the vessel at Leghorn or Naples, several weeks hence. We came near going to Geneva, but have concluded to return to Marseilles and go up through Italy from Genoa.

I will conclude this chapter with a remark that I am sincerely proud to be able to make — and glad, as well, that my comrades cordially indorse it, to wit: by far the handsomest women we have seen in France were born and reared in America.

I feel, now, like a man who has redeemed a failing reputation and shed luster upon a dimmed escutcheon, by a single just deed done at the eleventh hour.

Let the curtain fall, to slow music.

CHAPTER XVI.

VERSAILLES! It is wonderfully beautiful! You gaze, and stare, and try to understand that it is real, that it is on the earth, that it is not the Garden of Eden — but your brain grows giddy, stupefied by the world of beauty around you, and you half believe you are the dupe of an exquisite dream. The scene thrills one like military music! A noble palace, stretching its ornamented front block upon block away, till it seemed that it would never end; a grand promenade before it, whereon the armies of an empire might parade; all about it rainbows of flowers, and colossal statues that were almost numberless, and yet seemed only scattered over the ample space; broad flights of stone steps leading down from the promenade to lower grounds of the park — stairways that whole regiments might stand to arms upon and have room to spare; vast fountains whose great bronze effigies discharged rivers of sparkling water into the air and mingled a hundred curving jets together in forms of matchless beauty; wide grass-carpeted avenues that branched hither and thither in every direction and wandered

(204)

to seemingly interminable distances, walled all the way on either side with compact ranks of leafy trees whose branches met above and formed arches as faultless and as symmetrical as ever were carved in stone; and here and there were glimpses of sylvan lakes with miniature ships glassed in their surfaces. And everywhere — on the palace steps, and the great promenade, around the fountains, among the trees, and far under the arches of the endless avenues, hundreds and hundreds of people in gay costumes walked or ran or danced, and gave to the fairy picture the life and animation which was all of perfection it could have lacked.

It was worth a pilgrimage to see. Everything is on so gigantic a scale. Nothing is small — nothing is cheap. The statues are all large; the palace is grand; the park covers a fair-sized county; the avenues are interminable. All the distances and all the dimensions about Versailles are vast. I used to think the pictures exaggerated these distances and these dimensions beyond all reason, and that they made Versailles more beautiful than it was possible for any place in the world to be. I know now that the pictures never came up to the subject in any respect, and that no painter could represent Versailles on canvas as beautiful as it is in reality. I used to abuse Louis XIV for spending two hundred millions of dollars in creating this marvelous park, when bread was so scarce with some of his subjects; but I have forgiven him now. He took a tract of land

14

sixty miles in circumference and set to work to
make this park and build this palace and a road to
it from Paris. He kept 36,000 men employed daily
on it, and the labor was so unhealthy that they used
to die and be hauled off by cart-loads every night.
The wife of a nobleman of the time speaks of this as
an "*inconvenience*," but naïvely remarks that "it
does not seem worthy of attention in the happy
state of tranquillity we now enjoy."

I always thought ill of people at home, who
trimmed their shrubbery into pyramids and squares
and spires and all manner of unnatural shapes, and
when I saw the same thing being practiced in this
great park I began to feel dissatisfied. But I soon
saw the idea of the thing and the wisdom of it.
They seek the *general* effect. We distort a dozen
sickly trees into unaccustomed shapes in a little
yard no bigger than a dining-room, and then surely
they look absurd enough. But here they take two
hundred thousand tall forest trees and set them in a
double row; allow no sign of leaf or branch to grow
on the trunk lower down than six feet above the
ground; from that point the boughs begin to project, and very gradually they extend outward further
and further till they meet overhead, and a faultless
tunnel of foliage is formed. The arch is mathematically precise. The effect is then very fine.
They make trees take fifty different shapes, and so
these quaint effects are infinitely varied and picturesque. The trees in no two avenues are shaped

alike, and consequently the eye is not fatigued with anything in the nature of monotonous uniformity. I will drop this subject now, leaving it to others to determine how these people manage to make endless ranks of lofty forest trees grow to just a certain thickness of trunk (say a foot and two-thirds); how they make them spring to precisely the same height for miles; how they make them grow so close together; how they compel one huge limb to spring from the same identical spot on each tree and form the main sweep of the arch; and how all these things are kept exactly in the same condition, and in the same exquisite shapeliness and symmetry month after month and year after year — for I have tried to reason out the problem, and have failed.

We walked through the great hall of sculpture and the one hundred and fifty galleries of paintings in the palace of Versailles, and felt that to be in such a place was useless unless one had a whole year at his disposal. These pictures are all battle-scenes, and only one solitary little canvas among them all treats of anything but great French victories. We wandered, also, through the Grand Trianon and the Petit Trianon, those monuments of royal prodigality, and with histories so mournful — filled, as it is, with souvenirs of Napoleon the First, and three dead kings and as many queens. In one sumptuous bed they had all slept in succession, but no one occupies it now. In a large dining-room stood the table at which Louis XIV and his mistress, Madame Main-

tenon, and after them Louis XV, and Pompadour,
had sat at their meals naked and unattended — for
the table stood upon a trap-door, which descended
with it to regions below when it was necessary to
replenish its dishes.   In a room of the Petit Trianon
stood the furniture, just as poor Marie Antoinette
left it when the mob came and dragged her and the
King to Paris, never to return.   Near at hand, in
the stables, were prodigious carriages that showed
no color but gold — carriages used by former kings
of France on state occasions, and never used now
save when a kingly head is to be crowned, or an
imperial infant christened.   And with them were
some curious sleighs, whose bodies were shaped
like lions, swans, tigers, etc.— vehicles that had once
been handsome with pictured designs and fine workmanship, but were dusty and decaying now.   They
had their history.   When Louis XIV had finished
the Grand Trianon, he told Maintenon he had
created a Paradise for her, and asked if she could
think of anything now to wish for.   He said he
wished the Trianon to be perfection — nothing less.
She said she could think of but one thing — it was
summer, and it was balmy France — yet she would like
well to sleigh-ride in the leafy avenues of Versailles!
The next morning found miles and miles of grassy
avenues spread thick with snowy salt and sugar, and
a procession of those quaint sleighs waiting to receive the chief concubine of the gayest and most
unprincipled court that France has ever seen!

From sumptuous Versailles, with its palaces, its statues, its gardens and its fountains, we journeyed back to Paris and sought its antipodes — the Faubourg St. Antoine. Little, narrow streets; dirty children blockading them; greasy, slovenly women capturing and spanking them; filthy dens on first floors, with rag stores in them (the heaviest business in the Faubourg is the chiffonier's); other filthy dens where whole suits of second and third-hand clothing are sold at prices that would ruin any proprietor who did not steal his stock; still other filthy dens where they sold groceries — sold them by the half-pennyworth — five dollars would buy the man out, good-will and all. Up these little crooked streets they will murder a man for seven dollars and dump the body in the Seine. And up some other of these streets — most of them, I should say — live lorettes.

All through this Faubourg St. Antoine, misery, poverty, vice, and crime go hand in hand, and the evidences of it stare one in the face from every side. Here the people live who begin the revolutions. Whenever there is anything of that kind to be done, they are always ready. They take as much genuine pleasure in building a barricade as they do in cutting a throat or shoving a friend into the Seine. It is these savage-looking ruffians who storm the splendid halls of the Tuileries, occasionally, and swarm into Versailles when a king is to be called to account.

14.

But they will build no more barricades, they will break no more soldiers' heads with paving-stones. Louis Napoleon has taken care of all that. He is annihilating the crooked streets, and building in their stead noble boulevards as straight as an arrow — avenues which a cannon-ball could traverse from end to end without meeting an obstruction more irresistible than the flesh and bones of men — boulevards whose stately edifices will never afford refuges and plotting-places for starving, discontented revolution-breeders. Five of these great thoroughfares radiate from one ample center —a center which is exceedingly well adapted to the accommodation of heavy artillery. The mobs used to riot there, but they must seek another rallying-place in future. And this ingenious Napoleon paves the streets of his great cities with a smooth, compact composition of asphaltum and sand. No more barricades of flag-stones — no more assaulting his Majesty's troops with cobbles. I cannot feel friendly toward my quondam fellow-American, Napoleon III, especially at this time,* when in fancy I see his credulous victim, Maximilian, lying stark and stiff in Mexico, and his maniac widow watching eagerly from her French asylum for the form that will never come — but I do admire his nerve, his calm self-reliance, his shrewd good sense.

* July, 1867.

CHAPTER XVII.

WE had a pleasant journey of it seaward again. We found that for the three past nights our ship had been in a state of war. The first night the sailors of a British ship, being happy with grog, came down on the pier and challenged our sailors to a free fight. They accepted with alacrity, repaired to the pier and gained — their share of a drawn battle. Several bruised and bloody members of both parties were carried off by the police, and imprisoned until the following morning. The next night the British boys came again to renew the fight, but our men had had strict orders to remain on board and out of sight. They did so, and the besieging party grew noisy, and more and more abusive as the fact became apparent (to them) that our men were afraid to come out. They went away, finally, with a closing burst of ridicule and offensive epithets. The third night they came again, and were more obstreperous than ever. They swaggered up and down the almost deserted pier, and hurled curses, obscenity, and stinging sarcasms at our crew. It was more than human nature could bear. The

N*   (211)

executive officer ordered our men ashore — with instructions not to fight. They charged the British and gained a brilliant victory. I probably would not have mentioned this war had it ended differently. But I travel to learn, and I still remember that they picture no French defeats in the battle-galleries of Versailles.

It was like home to us to step on board the comfortable ship again, and smoke and lounge about her breezy decks. And yet it was not altogether like home, either, because so many members of the family were away. We missed some pleasant faces which we would rather have found at dinner, and at night there were gaps in the euchre-parties which could not be satisfactorily filled. "Moult." was in England, Jack in Switzerland, Charley in Spain. Blucher was gone, none could tell where. But we were at sea again, and we had the stars and the ocean to look at, and plenty of room to meditate in.

In due time the shores of Italy were sighted, and as we stood gazing from the decks early in the bright summer morning, the stately city of Genoa rose up out of the sea and flung back the sunlight from her hundred palaces.

Here we rest, for the present — or rather, here we have been trying to rest, for some little time, but we run about too much to accomplish a great deal in that line.

I would like to remain here. I had rather not go any further. There may be prettier women in

Europe, but I doubt it. The population of Genoa
is 120,000; two-thirds of these are women, I think,
and at least two-thirds of the women are beautiful.
They are as dressy and as tasteful and as graceful
as they could possibly be without being angels.
However, angels are not very dressy, I believe. At
least the angels in pictures are not — they wear
nothing but wings. But these Genoese women do
look so charming. Most of the young demoiselles
are robed in a cloud of white from head to foot,
though many trick themselves out more elaborately.
Nine-tenths of them wear nothing on their heads but
a filmy sort of veil, which falls down their backs like
a white mist. They are very fair, and many of
them have blue eyes, but black and dreamy dark
brown ones are met with oftenest.

The ladies and gentlemen of Genoa have a
pleasant fashion of promenading in a large park on
the top of a hill in the center of the city, from six
till nine in the evening, and then eating ices in a
neighboring garden an hour or two longer. We
went to the park on Sunday evening. Two thousand persons were present, chiefly young ladies and
gentlemen. The gentlemen were dressed in the very
latest Paris fashions, and the robes of the ladies
glinted among the trees like so many snow-flakes.
The multitude moved round and round the park in
a great procession. The bands played, and so did
the fountains; the moon and the gas-lamps lit up
the scene, and altogether it was a brilliant and an

animated picture. I scanned every female face that passed, and it seemed to me that all were handsome. I never saw such a freshet of loveliness before. I do not see how a man of only ordinary decision of character could marry here, because, before he could get his mind made up he would fall in love with somebody else.

Never smoke any Italian tobacco. Never do it on any account. It makes me shudder to think what it must be made of. You cannot throw an old cigar "stub" down anywhere, but some vagabond will pounce upon it on the instant. I like to smoke a good deal, but it wounds my sensibilities to see one of these stub-hunters watching me out of the corners of his hungry eyes and calculating how long my cigar will be likely to last. It reminded me too painfully of that San Francisco undertaker who used to go to sick beds with his watch in his hand and time the corpse. One of these stub-hunters followed us all over the park last night, and we never had a smoke that was worth anything. We were always moved to appease him with the stub before the cigar was half gone, because he looked so viciously anxious. He regarded us as his own legitimate prey, by right of discovery, I think, because he drove off several other professionals who wanted to take stock in us.

Now, they surely must chew up those old stubs, and dry and sell them for smoking tobacco. Therefore, give your custom to other than Italian brands of the article.

"The Superb" and the "City of Palaces" are names which Genoa has held for centuries. She is full of palaces, certainly, and the palaces are sumptuous inside, but they are very rusty without, and make no pretensions to architectural magnificence. "Genoa, the Superb," would be a felicitous title if it referred to the women.

We have visited several of the palaces — immense thick-walled piles, with great stone staircases, tessellated marble pavements on the floors (sometimes they make a mosaic work, of intricate designs, wrought in pebbles, or little fragments of marble laid in cement), and grand *salons* hung with pictures by Rubens, Guido, Titian, Paul Veronese, and so on, and portraits of heads of the family, in plumed helmets and gallant coats of mail, and patrician ladies, in stunning costumes of centuries ago. But, of course, the folks were all out in the country for the summer, and might not have known enough to ask us to dinner if they had been at home, and so all the grand empty *salons*, with their resounding pavements, their grim pictures of dead ancestors, and tattered banners with the dust of bygone centuries upon them, seemed to brood solemnly of death and the grave, and our spirits ebbed away, and our cheerfulness passed from us. We never went up to the eleventh story. We always began to suspect ghosts. There was always an undertaker-looking servant along, too, who handed us a programme, pointed to the picture that began the list of the *salon* he was in, and then stood stiff and stark and unsmiling in his petrified livery till we were ready to move on to the next chamber, whereupon he marched sadly ahead and took up another malignantly respectful position as before. I wasted so much time praying that the roof would fall in on these dispiriting flunkeys that I had but little left to bestow upon palace and pictures.

And besides, as in Paris, we had a guide. Perdition catch all the guides. This one said he was the most gifted linguist in Genoa, as far as English was concerned, and that only two persons in the city beside himself could talk the language at all. He showed us the birthplace of Christopher Columbus, and after we had reflected in silent awe before it for fifteen minutes, he said it was not the birthplace of Columbus, but of Columbus's grandmother! When we demanded an explanation of his conduct he only shrugged his shoulders and answered in barbarous Italian. I shall speak further of this guide in a future chapter. All the information we got out of him we shall be able to carry along with us, I think.

I have not been to church so often in a long time as I have in the last few weeks. The people in these old lands seem to make churches their specialty. Especially does this seem to be the case with the citizens of Genoa. I think there is a church every three or four hundred yards all over town. The streets are sprinkled from end to end with shovel-hatted, long-robed, well-fed priests, and the church

bells by dozens are pealing all the day long, nearly.
Every now and then one comes across a friar of
orders gray, with shaven head, long, coarse robe,
rope girdle and beads, and with feet cased in sandals
or entirely bare. These worthies suffer in the flesh,
and do penance all their lives, I suppose, but they
look like consummate famine-breeders. They are
all fat and serene.

The old Cathedral of San Lorenzo is about as
notable a building as we have found in Genoa. It
is vast, and has colonnades of noble pillars, and a
great organ, and the customary pomp of gilded
moldings, pictures, frescoed ceilings, and so forth.
I cannot describe it, of course — it would require a
good many pages to do that. But it is a curious
place. They said that half of it — from the front
door half way down to the altar — was a Jewish
Synagogue before the Saviour was born, and that no
alteration had been made in it since that time. We
doubted the statement, but did it reluctantly. We
would much rather have believed it. The place
looked in too perfect repair to be so ancient.

The main point of interest about the cathedral is
the little Chapel of St. John the Baptist. They only
allow women to enter it on one day in the year, on
account of the animosity they still cherish against
the sex because of the murder of the Saint to gratify
a caprice of Herodias. In this chapel is a marble
chest, in which, they told us, were the ashes of St.
John; and around it was wound a chain, which,

they said, had confined him when he was in prison.
We did not desire to disbelieve these statements, and
yet we could not feel certain that they were correct
— partly because we could have broken that chain,
and so could St. John, and partly because we had
seen St. John's ashes before, in another church.
We could not bring ourselves to think St. John had
two sets of ashes.

They also showed us a portrait of the Madonna
which was painted by St. Luke, and it did not look
half as old and smoky as some of the pictures by
Rubens. We could not help admiring the Apostle's
modesty in never once mentioning in his writings
that he could paint.

But isn't this relic matter a little overdone? We
find a piece of the true cross in every old church we
go into, and some of the nails that held it together.
I would not like to be positive, but I think we have
seen as much as a keg of these nails. Then there
is the crown of thorns; they have part of one in
Sainte Chapelle, in Paris, and part of one, also, in
Notre Dame. And as for bones of St. Denis, I feel
certain we have seen enough of them to duplicate
him, if necessary.

I only meant to write about the churches, but I
keep wandering from the subject. I could say that
the Church of the Annunciation is a wilderness of
beautiful columns, of statues, gilded moldings, and
pictures almost countless, but that would give no
one an entirely perfect idea of the thing, and so

where is the use? One family built the whole
edifice, and have got money left. There is where
the mystery lies. We had an idea at first that only
a mint could have survived the expense.

These people here live in the heaviest, highest,
broadest, darkest, solidest houses one can imagine.
Each one might "laugh a siege to scorn." A
hundred feet front and a hundred high is about the
style, and you go up three flights of stairs before
you begin to come upon signs of occupancy.
Everything is stone, and stone of the heaviest —
floors, stairways, mantels, benches — everything.
The walls are four to five feet thick. The streets
generally are four or five to eight feet wide and as
crooked as a corkscrew. You go along one of these
gloomy cracks, and look up and behold the sky like
a mere ribbon of light, far above your head, where
the tops of the tall houses on either side of the
street bend almost together. You feel as if you
were at the bottom of some tremendous abyss, with
all the world far above you. You wind in and out
and here and there, in the most mysterious way,
and have no more idea of the points of the compass
than if you were a blind man. You can never persuade yourself that these are actually streets, and
the frowning, dingy, monstrous houses dwellings,
till you see one of these beautiful, prettily-dressed
women emerge from them — see her emerge from a
dark, dreary-looking den that looks dungeon all
over, from the ground away half-way up to heaven.

And then you wonder that such a charming moth could come from such a forbidding shell as that. The streets are wisely made narrow and the houses heavy and thick and stony, in order that the people may be cool in this roasting climate. And they are cool, and stay so. And while I think of it — the men wear hats and have very dark complexions, but the women wear no headgear but a flimsy veil like a gossamer's web, and yet are exceedingly fair as a general thing. Singular, isn't it?

The huge palaces of Genoa are each supposed to be occupied by one family, but they could accommodate a hundred, I should think. They are relics of the grandeur of Genoa's palmy days — the days when she was a great commercial and maritime power several centuries ago. These houses, solid marble palaces though they be, are, in many cases, of a dull pinkish color, outside, and from pavement to eaves are pictured with Genoese battle-scenes, with monstrous Jupiters and Cupids and with familiar illustrations from Grecian mythology. Where the paint has yielded to age and exposure and is peeling off in flakes and patches, the effect is not happy. A noseless Cupid, or a Jupiter with an eye out, or a Venus with a fly-blister on her breast, are not attractive features in a picture. Some of these painted walls reminded me somewhat of the tall van, plastered with fanciful bills and posters, that follows the band wagon of a circus about a country village. I have not read or heard that the outsides of the houses of any other European city are frescoed in this way.

I cannot conceive of such a thing as Genoa in ruins. Such massive arches, such ponderous substructions as support these towering broad-winged edifices, we have seldom seen before; and surely the great blocks of stone of which these edifices are built can never decay; walls that are as thick as an ordinary American doorway is high, cannot crumble.

The Republics of Genoa and Pisa were very powerful in the Middle Ages. Their ships filled the Mediterranean, and they carried on an extensive commerce with Constantinople and Syria. Their warehouses were the great distributing depots from whence the costly merchandise of the East was sent abroad over Europe. They were warlike little nations, and defied, in those days, governments that overshadow them now as mountains overshadow molehills. The Saracens captured and pillaged Genoa nine hundred years ago, but during the following century Genoa and Pisa entered into an offensive and defensive alliance and besieged the Saracen colonies in Sardinia and the Balearic Isles with an obstinacy that maintained its pristine vigor and held to its purpose for forty long years. They were victorious at last, and divided their conquests equably among their great patrician families. Descendants of some of those proud families still inhabit the palaces of Genoa, and trace in their own features a resemblance to the grim knights whose

15

portraits hang in their stately halls, and to pictured beauties with pouting lips and merry eyes whose originals have been dust and ashes for many a dead and forgotten century.

The hotel we live in belonged to one of those great orders of Knights of the Cross in the times of the Crusades, and its mailed sentinels once kept watch and ward in its massive turrets and woke the echoes of these halls and corridors with their iron heels.

But Genoa's greatness has degenerated into an unostentatious commerce in velvets and silver filigree work. They say that each European town has its specialty. These filigree things are Genoa's specialty. Her smiths take silver ingots and work them up into all manner of graceful and beautiful forms. They make bunches of flowers, from flakes and wires of silver, that counterfeit the delicate creations the frost weaves upon a window pane; and we were shown a miniature silver temple whose fluted columns, whose Corinthian capitals and rich entablatures, whose spire, statues, bells, and ornate lavishness of sculpture were wrought in polished silver, and with such matchless art that every detail was a fascinating study, and the finished edifice a wonder of beauty.

We are ready to move again, though we are not really tired, yet, of the narrow passages of this old marble cave. Cave is a good word — when speaking of Genoa under the stars. When we have been prowling at midnight through the gloomy crevices they call streets, where no footfalls but ours were echoing, where only ourselves were abroad, and lights appeared only at long intervals and at a distance, and mysteriously disappeared again, and the houses at our elbows seemed to stretch upward farther than ever toward the heavens, the memory of a cave I used to know at home was always in my mind, with its lofty passages, its silence and solitude, its shrouding gloom, its sepulchral echoes, its flitting lights, and more than all, its sudden revelations of branching crevices and corridors where we least expected them.

We are not tired of the endless processions of cheerful, chattering gossipers that throng these courts and streets all day long, either; nor of the coarse-robed monks; nor of the "Asti" wines, which that old doctor (whom we call the Oracle) with customary felicity in the matter of getting everything wrong, misterms "nasty." But we must go, nevertheless.

Our last sight was the cemetery (a burial place intended to accommodate 60,000 bodies), and we shall continue to remember it after we shall have forgotten the palaces. It is a vast marble colonnaded corridor extending around a great unoccupied square of ground; its broad floor is marble, and on every slab is an inscription — for every slab covers a corpse. On either side, as one walks down the middle of the passage, are monuments, tombs, and sculptured figures that are exquisitely wrought and are full of grace and beauty. They are new and snowy; every outline is perfect, every feature guiltless of mutilation, flaw, or blemish; and, therefore, to us these far-reaching ranks of bewitching forms are a hundredfold more lovely than the damaged and dingy statuary they have saved from the wreck of ancient art and set up in the galleries of Paris for the worship of the world.

Well provided with cigars and other necessaries of life, we are now ready to take the cars for Milan.

CHAPTER XVIII.

ALL day long we sped through a mountainous country whose peaks were bright with sunshine, whose hillsides were dotted with pretty villas sitting in the midst of gardens and shrubbery, and whose deep ravines were cool and shady, and looked ever so inviting from where we and the birds were winging our flight through the sultry upper air.

We had plenty of chilly tunnels wherein to check our perspiration, though. We timed one of them. We were twenty minutes passing through it, going at the rate of thirty to thirty-five miles an hour.

Beyond Alessandria we passed the battlefield of Marengo.

Toward dusk we drew near Milan, and caught glimpses of the city and the blue mountain-peaks beyond. But we were not caring for these things — they did not interest us in the least. We were in a fever of impatience; we were dying to see the renowned cathedral! We watched — in this direction and that — all around — everywhere. We needed no one to point it out — we did not wish any one to

15* (225)

point it out — we would recognize it, even in the desert of the great Sahara.

At last, a forest of graceful needles, shimmering in the amber sunlight, rose slowly above the pigmy housetops, as one sometimes sees, in the far horizon, a gilded and pinnacled mass of cloud lift itself above the waste of waves, at sea,— the cathedral! We knew it in a moment.

Half of that night, and all of the next day, this architectural autocrat was our sole object of interest. What a wonder it is! So grand, so solemn, so vast! And yet so delicate, so airy, so graceful! A very world of solid weight, and yet it seems in the soft moonlight only a fairy delusion of frostwork that might vanish with a breath! How sharply its pinnacled angles and its wilderness of spires were cut against the sky, and how richly their shadows fell upon its snowy roof! It was a vision! — a miracle! — an anthem sung in stone, a poem wrought in marble!

Howsoever you look at the great cathedral, it is noble, it is beautiful! Wherever you stand in Milan, or within seven miles of Milan, it is visible — and when it is visible, no other object can chain your whole attention. Leave your eyes unfettered by your will but a single instant and they will surely turn to seek it. It is the first thing you look for when you rise in the morning, and the last your lingering gaze rests upon at night. Surely, it must be the princeliest creation that ever brain of man conceived.

At nine o'clock in the morning we went and stood
before this marble colossus. The central one of its
five great doors is bordered with a bas-relief of birds
and fruits and beasts and insects, which have been
so ingeniously carved out of the marble that they
seem like living creatures — and the figures are so
numerous and the design so complex, that one
might study it a week without exhausting its
interest. On the great steeple — surmounting the
myriad of spires — inside of the spires — over the
doors, the windows — in nooks and corners — everywhere that a niche or a perch can be found about the
enormous building, from summit to base, there is a
marble statue, and every statue is a study in itself!
Raphael, Angelo, Canova — giants like these gave
birth to the designs, and their own pupils carved
them. Every face is eloquent with expression, and
every attitude is full of grace. Away above, on
the lofty roof, rank on rank of carved and fretted
spires spring high in the air, and through their rich
tracery one sees the sky beyond. In their midst the
central steeple towers proudly up like the mainmast
of some great Indiaman among a fleet of coasters.

We wished to go aloft. The sacristan showed us
a marble stairway (of course it was marble, and of
the purest and whitest — there is no other stone, no
brick, no wood, among its building materials), and
told us to go up one hundred and eighty-two steps
and stop till he came. It was not necessary to say
stop — we should have done that anyhow. We

O*

were tired by the time we got there. This was the
roof. Here, springing from its broad marble flag-
stones, were the long files of spires, looking very
tall close at hand, but diminishing in the distance
like the pipes of an organ. We could see, now, that
the statue on the top of each was the size of a large
man, though they all looked like dolls from the
street. We could see, also, that from the inside of
each and every one of these hollow spires, from
sixteen to thirty-one beautiful marble statues looked
out upon the world below.

From the eaves to the comb of the roof stretched
in endless succession great curved marble beams,
like the fore-and-aft braces of a steamboat, and
along each beam from end to end stood up a row of
richly carved flowers and fruits — each separate and
distinct in kind, and over 15,000 species represented. At a little distance these rows seem to
close together like the ties of a railroad track, and
then the mingling together of the buds and blossoms
of this marble garden forms a picture that is very
charming to the eye.

We descended and entered. Within the church,
long rows of fluted columns, like huge monuments,
divided the building into broad aisles, and on the
figured pavement fell many a soft blush from the
painted windows above. I knew the church was
very large, but I could not fully appreciate its great
size until I noticed that the men standing far down
by the altar looked like boys, and seemed to glide,

rather than walk.   We loitered about gazing aloft at
the monster windows all aglow with brilliantly
colored scenes in the lives of the Saviour and his
followers.   Some of these pictures are mosaics, and
so artistically are their thousand particles of tinted
glass or stone put together that the work has all the
smoothness and finish of a painting.   We counted
sixty panes of glass in one window, and each pane
was adorned with one of these master achievements
of genius and patience.

The guide showed us a coffee-colored piece of
sculpture which he said was considered to have come
from the hand of Phidias, since it was not possible
that any other artist, of any epoch, could have
copied nature with such faultless accuracy.   The
figure was that of a man without a skin; with every
vein, artery, muscle, every fibre and tendon and
tissue of the human frame, represented in minute
detail.   It looked natural, because somehow it looked
as if it were in pain.   A skinned man would be likely
to look that way, unless his attention were occupied
with some other matter.   It was a hideous thing,
and yet there was a fascination about it somewhere.
I am very sorry I saw it, because I shall always see
it, now.   I shall dream of it, sometimes.   I shall
dream that it is resting its corded arms on the bed's
head and looking down on me with its dead eyes; I
shall dream that it is stretched between the sheets
with me and touching me with its exposed muscles
and its stringy cold legs.

It is hard to forget repulsive things. I remember yet how I ran off from school once, when I was a boy, and then, pretty late at night, concluded to climb into the window of my father's office and sleep on a lounge, because I had a delicacy about going home and getting thrashed. As I lay on the lounge and my eyes grew accustomed to the darkness, I fancied I could see a long, dusky, shapeless thing stretched upon the floor. A cold shiver went through me. I turned my face to the wall. That did not answer. I was afraid that that thing would creep over and seize me in the dark. I turned back and stared at it for minutes and minutes — they seemed hours. It appeared to me that the lagging moonlight never, never would get to it. I turned to the wall and counted twenty, to pass the feverish time away. I looked — the pale square was nearer. I turned again and counted fifty — it was almost touching it. With desperate will I turned again and counted one hundred, and faced about, all in a tremble. A white human hand lay in the moonlight! Such an awful sinking at the heart — such a sudden gasp for breath! I felt — I cannot tell *what* I felt. When I recovered strength enough, I faced the wall again. But no boy could have remained so, with that mysterious hand behind him. I counted again, and looked — the most of a naked arm was exposed. I put my hands over my eyes and counted till I could stand it no longer, and then — the pallid face of a man was there, with the corners of the mouth drawn down, and the eyes fixed and glassy in death! I raised to a sitting posture and glowered on that corpse till the light crept down the bare breast,— line by line — inch by inch — past the nipple, — and then it disclosed a ghastly stab!

I went away from there. I do not say that I went away in any sort of a hurry, but I simply went — that is sufficient. I went out at the window, and I carried the sash along with me. I did not need the sash, but it was handier to take it than it was to leave it, and so I took it. I was not scared, but I was considerably agitated.

When I reached home, they whipped me, but I enjoyed it. It seemed perfectly delightful. That man had been stabbed near the office that afternoon, and they carried him in there to doctor him, but he only lived an hour. I have slept in the same room with him often, since then — in my dreams.

Now we will descend into the crypt, under the grand altar of Milan cathedral, and receive an impressive sermon from lips that have been silent and hands that have been gestureless for three hundred years.

The priest stopped in a small dungeon and held up his candle. This was the last resting-place of a good man, a warm-hearted, unselfish man; a man whose whole life was given to succoring the poor, encouraging the faint-hearted, visiting the sick; in relieving distress, whenever and wherever he found it.   His heart, his hand, and his purse were always open.   With his story in one's mind he can almost see his benignant countenance moving calmly among the haggard faces of Milan in the days when the plague swept the city, brave where all others were cowards, full of compassion where pity had been crushed out of all other breasts by the instinct of self-preservation gone mad with terror, cheering all, praying with all, helping all, with hand and brain and purse, at a time when parents forsook their children, the friend deserted the friend, and the brother turned away from the sister while her pleadings were still wailing in his ears.

This was good St. Charles Borromeo, Bishop of Milan.   The people idolized him; princes lavished uncounted treasures upon him.   We stood in his tomb.   Near by was the sarcophagus, lighted by the dripping candles.   The walls were faced with bas-reliefs representing scenes in his life done in massive silver.   The priest put on a short white lace garment over his black robe, crossed himself, bowed reverently, and began to turn a windlass slowly.   The sarcophagus separated in two parts, lengthwise, and the lower part sank down and disclosed a coffin of rock crystal as clear as the atmosphere.   Within lay the body, robed in costly habiliments covered with gold embroidery and starred with scintillating gems.   The decaying head was black with age, the dry skin was drawn tight to the bones, the eyes were gone, there was a hole in the temple and another in the cheek, and the skinny lips were parted as in a ghastly smile! Over this dreadful face, its dust and decay, and its mocking grin, hung a crown sown thick with flashing brilliants; and upon the breast lay crosses and croziers of solid gold that were splendid with emeralds and diamonds.

How poor, and cheap, and trivial these gewgaws seemed in presence of the solemnity, the grandeur, the awful majesty of Death! Think of Milton, Shakespeare, Washington, standing before a reverent world tricked out in the glass beads, the brass earrings, and tin trumpery of the savages of the plains!

Dead Borromeo preached his pregnant sermon, and its burden was: You that worship the vanities of earth — you that long for worldly honor, worldly wealth, worldly fame — behold their worth!

To us it seemed that so good a man, so kind a heart, so simple a nature, deserved rest and peace in a grave sacred from the intrusion of prying eyes, and believed that he himself would have preferred to have it so, but peradventure our wisdom was at fault in this regard.

As we came out upon the floor of the church again, another priest volunteered to show us the treasures of the church. What, more? The furniture of the narrow chamber of death we had just visited, weighed six millions of francs in ounces and carats alone, without a penny thrown into the account for the costly workmanship bestowed upon them! But we followed into a large room filled

with tall wooden presses like wardrobes. He threw
them open, and behold, the cargoes of "crude
bullion" of the assay offices of Nevada faded out of
my memory. There were Virgins and bishops there,
above their natural size, made of solid silver, each
worth, by weight, from eight hundred thousand to
two millions of francs, and bearing gemmed books
in their hands worth eighty thousand; there were
bas-reliefs that weighed six hundred pounds, carved
in solid silver; croziers and crosses, and candlesticks
six and eight feet high, all of virgin gold, and
brilliant with precious stones; and beside these were
all manner of cups and vases, and such things, rich
in proportion. It was an Aladdin's palace. The
treasures here, by simple weight, without counting
workmanship, were valued at fifty millions of francs!
If I could get the custody of them for a while, I fear
me the market price of silver bishops would advance
shortly, on acccunt of their exceeding scarcity in
the Cathedral of Milan.

The priests showed us two of St. Paul's fingers,
and one of St. Peter's; a bone of Judas Iscariot (it
was black), and also bones of all the other disciples;
a handkerchief in which the Saviour had left the
impression of his face. Among the most precious
of the relics were, a stone from the Holy Sepulchre,
part of the crown of thorns (they have a whole one
at Notre Dame), a fragment of the purple robe
worn by the Saviour, a nail from the Cross, and a
picture of the Virgin and Child painted by the

veritable hand of St. Luke. This is the second of St. Luke's Virgins we have seen. Once a year all these holy relics are carried in procession through the streets of Milan.

I like to revel in the dryest details of the great cathedral. The building is five hundred feet long by one hundred and eighty wide, and the principal steeple is in the neighborhood of four hundred feet high. It has 7,148 marble statues, and will have upward of three thousand more when it is finished. In addition, it has one thousand five hundred bas-reliefs. It has one hundred and thirty-six spires — twenty-one more are to be added. Each spire is surmounted by a statue six and a half feet high. Everything about the church is marble, and all from the same quarry; it was bequeathed to the Archbishopric for this purpose centuries ago. So nothing but the mere workmanship costs; still that is expensive — the bill foots up six hundred and eighty-four millions of francs, thus far (considerably over a hundred millions of dollars), and it is estimated that it will take a hundred and twenty years yet to finish the cathedral. It looks complete, but is far from being so. We saw a new statue put in its niche yesterday, alongside of one which had been standing these four hundred years, they said. There are four staircases leading up to the main steeple, each of which cost a hundred thousand dollars, with the four hundred and eight statues which adorn them. Marcoda Campione was the architect who de-

signed the wonderful structure more than five hundred years ago, and it took him forty-six years to
work out the plan and get it ready to hand over to
the builders. He is dead now. The building was
begun a little less than five hundred years ago, and
the third generation hence will not see it completed.

The building looks best by moonlight, because
the older portions of it being stained with age, contrast unpleasantly with the newer and whiter portions. It seems somewhat too broad for its height,
but may be familiarity with it might dissipate this
impression.

They say that the Cathedral of Milan is second
only to St. Peter's at Rome. I cannot understand
how it can be second to anything made by human
hands.

We bid it good-bye now — possibly for all time.
How surely, in some future day, when the memory
of it shall have lost its vividness, shall we half
believe we have seen it in a wonderful dream, but
never with waking eyes!

CHAPTER XIX.

" DO you wis zo haut can be?"

That was what the guide asked, when we were looking up at the bronze horses on the Arch of Peace. It meant, Do you wish to go up there? I give it as a specimen of guide-English. These are the people that make life a burthen to the tourist. Their tongues are never still. They talk forever and forever, and that is the kind of billingsgate they use. Inspiration itself could hardly comprehend them. If they would only show you a masterpiece of art, or a venerable tomb, or a prison-house, or a battlefield, hallowed by touching memories, or historical reminiscences, or grand traditions, and then step aside and hold still for ten minutes and let you think, it would not be so bad. But they interrupt every dream, every pleasant train of thought, with their tiresome cackling. Sometimes when I have been standing before some cherished old idol of mine that I remembered years and years ago in pictures in the geography at school, I have thought I would give a whole world if the human parrot at my side would

16

suddenly perish where he stood and leave me to
gaze, and ponder, and worship.

No, we did not "wis zo haut can be." We
wished to go to La Scala, the largest theater in the
world, I think they call it. We did so. It was a
large place. Seven separate and distinct masses of
humanity — six great circles and a monster par-
quette.

We wished to go to the Ambrosian Library, and
we did that also. We saw a manuscript of Virgil,
with annotations in the handwriting of Petrarch, the
gentleman who loved another man's Laura, and
lavished upon her all through life a love which was a
clear waste of the raw material. It was sound sentiment, but bad judgment. It brought both parties
fame, and created a fountain of commiseration for
them in sentimental breasts that is running yet. But
who says a word in behalf of poor Mr. Laura? (I
do not know his other name.) Who glorifies him?
Who bedews him with tears? Who writes poetry
about him? Nobody. How do you suppose *he*
liked the state of things that has given the world so
much pleasure? How did he enjoy having another
man following his wife everywhere and making her
name a familiar word in every garlic-exterminating
mouth in Italy with his sonnets to her pre-empted
eyebrows? *They* got fame and sympathy — he got
neither. This is a peculiarly felicitous instance of
what is called poetical justice. It is all very fine;
but it does not chime with my notions of right. It

is too one-sided — too ungenerous. Let the world
go on fretting about Laura and Petrarch if it will;
but as for me, my tears and my lamentations shall
be lavished upon the unsung defendant.

We saw also an autograph letter of Lucrezia
Borgia, a lady for whom I have always entertained
the highest respect, on account of her rare histrionic
capabilities, her opulence in solid gold goblets made
of gilded wood, her high distinction as an operatic
screamer, and the facility with which she could order
a sextuple funeral and get the corpses ready for it.
We saw one single coarse yellow hair from Lucrezia's head, likewise. It awoke emotions, but we
still live. In this same library we saw some drawings
by Michael Angelo (these Italians call him Mickel
Angelo), and Leonardo da Vinci. (They spell it
Vinci and pronounce it Vinchy; foreigners always
spell better than they pronounce.) We reserve our
opinion of these sketches.

In another building they showed us a fresco
representing some lions and other beasts drawing
chariots; and they seemed to project so far from
the wall that we took them to be sculptures. The
artist had shrewdly heightened the delusion by painting dust on the creatures' backs, as if it had fallen
there naturally and properly. Smart fellow — if it
be smart to deceive strangers.

Elsewhere we saw a huge Roman amphitheater,
with its stone seats still in good preservation.
Modernized, it is now the scene of more peaceful

recreations than the exhibition of a party of wild beasts with Christians for dinner. Part of the time, the Milanese use it for a race track, and at other seasons they flood it with water and have spirited yachting regattas there. The guide told us these things, and he would hardly try so hazardous an experiment as the telling of a falsehood, when it is all he can do to speak the truth in English without getting the lockjaw.

In another place we were shown a sort of summer arbor, with a fence before it. We said that was nothing. We looked again, and saw, through the arbor, an endless stretch of garden, and shrubbery, and grassy lawn. We were perfectly willing to go in there and rest, but it could not be done. It was only another delusion — a painting by some ingenious artist with little charity in his heart for tired folk. The deception was perfect. No one could have imagined the park was not real. We even thought we smelled the flowers at first.

We got a carriage at twilight and drove in the shaded avenues with the other nobility, and after dinner we took wine and ices in a fine garden with the great public. The music was excellent, the flowers and shrubbery were pleasant to the eye, the scene was vivacious, everybody was genteel and well-behaved, and the ladies were slightly moustached, and handsomely dressed, but very homely.

We adjourned to a café and played billiards an hour, and I made six or seven points by the

doctor pocketing his ball, and he made as many by
my pocketing my ball. We came near making a
carom sometimes, but not the one we were trying to
make. The table was of the usual European style —
cushions dead and twice as high as the balls; the
cues in bad repair. The natives play only a sort of
pool on them. We have never seen anybody play
ing the French three-ball game yet, and I doubt if
there is any such game known in France, or that
there lives any man mad enough to try to play it on
one of these European tables. We had to stop
playing, finally, because Dan got to sleeping fifteen
minutes between the counts and paying no attention
to his marking.

Afterward we walked up and down one of the
most popular streets for some time, enjoying other
people's comfort and wishing we could export some
of it to our restless, driving, vitality-consuming
marts at home. Just in this one matter lies the
main charm of life in Europe — comfort. In
America, we hurry — which is well; but when the
day's work is done, we go on thinking of losses and
gains, we plan for the morrow, we even carry our
business cares to bed with us, and toss and worry
over them when we ought to be restoring our racked
bodies and brains with sleep. We burn up our
energies with these excitements, and either die early
or drop into a lean and mean old age at a time of
life which they call a man's prime in Europe.
When an acre of ground has produced long and

well, we let it lie fallow and rest for a season; we take no man clear across the continent in the same coach he started in — the coach is stabled somewhere on the plains and its heated machinery allowed to cool for a few days; when a razor has seen long service and refuses to hold an edge, the barber lays it away for a few weeks, and the edge comes back of its own accord. We bestow thoughtful care upon inanimate objects, but none upon ourselves. What a robust people, what a nation of thinkers we might be, if we would only lay ourselves on the shelf occasionally and renew our edges!

I do envy these Europeans the comfort they take. When the work of the day is done, they forget it. Some of them go, with wife and children, to a beer hall, and sit quietly and genteelly drinking a mug or two of ale and listening to music; others walk the streets, others drive in the avenues; others assemble in the great ornamental squares in the early evening to enjoy the sight and the fragrance of flowers and to hear the military bands play — no European city being without its fine military music at eventide; and yet others of the populace sit in the open air in front of the refreshment houses and eat ices and drink mild beverages that could not harm a child. They go to bed moderately early, and sleep well. They are always quiet, always orderly, always cheerful, comfortable, and appreciative of life and its manifold blessings. One never sees a drunken man among them. The change that has come over our little party is surprising. Day by day we lose some of our restlessness and absorb some of the spirit of quietude and ease that is in the tranquil atmosphere about us and in the demeanor of the people. We grow wise apace. We begin to comprehend what life is for.

We have had a bath in Milan, in a public bathhouse. They were going to put all three of us in one bathtub, but we objected. Each of us had an Italian farm on his back. We could have felt affluent if we had been officially surveyed and fenced in. We chose to have three bathtubs, and large ones — tubs suited to the dignity of aristocrats who had real estate, and brought it with them. After we were stripped and had taken the first chilly dash, we discovered that haunting atrocity that has embittered our lives in so many cities and villages of Italy and France — there was no soap. I called. A woman answered, and I barely had time to throw myself against the door — she would have been in, in another second. I said:

"Beware, woman! Go away from here — go away, now, or it will be the worse for you. I am an unprotected male, but I will preserve my honor at the peril of my life!"

These words must have frightened her, for she skurried away very fast.

Dan's voice rose on the air:

"Oh, bring some soap, why don't you!"

The reply was Italian. Dan resumed:

R *

"Soap, you know — soap. That is what I want — soap. S-o-a-p, soap; s-o-p-e, soap; s-o-u-p, soap. Hurry up! I don't know how you Irish spell it, but I want it. Spell it to suit yourself, but fetch it. I'm freezing."

I heard the doctor say, impressively:

"Dan, how often have we told you that these foreigners cannot understand English? Why will you not depend upon us? Why will you not tell *us* what you want, and let us ask for it in the language of the country? It would save us a great deal of the humiliation your reprehensible ignorance causes us. I will address this person in his mother tongue: 'Here, cospetto! corpo di Bacco! Sacramento! Solferino! — Soap, you son of a gun!' Dan, if you would let *us* talk for you, you would never expose your ignorant vulgarity."

Even this fluent discharge of Italian did not bring the soap at once, but there was a good reason for it. There was not such an article about the establishment. It is my belief that there never had been. They had to send far up town, and to several different places before they finally got it, so they said. We had to wait twenty or thirty minutes. The same thing had occurred the evening before, at the hotel. I think I have divined the reason for this state of things at last. The English know how to travel comfortably, and they carry soap with them; other foreigners do not use the article.

At every hotel we stop at we always have to send

out for soap, at the last moment, when we are grooming ourselves for dinner, and they put it in the bill along with the candles and other nonsense. In Marseilles they make half the fancy toilet soap we consume in America, but the Marseillaise only have a vague theoretical idea of its use, which they have obtained from books of travel, just as they have acquired an uncertain notion of clean shirts, and the peculiarities of the gorilla, and other curious matters. This reminds me of poor Blucher's note to the landlord in Paris:

> "PARIS, le 7 Juillet.
>
> "*Monsieur le Landlord* — Sir: *Pourquoi* don't you *mettez* some *savon* in your bedchambers? *Est-ce que vous pensez* I will steal it? *La nuit passée* you charged me *pour deux chandelles* when I only had one; *hier vous avez* charged me *avec glace* when I had none at all; *tout les jours* you are coming some fresh game or other on me, *mais vous ne pouvez pas* play this *savon* dodge on me twice. *Savon* is a necessary *de la vie* to anybody but a Frenchman, *et je l'aurai hors de cet hôtel* or make trouble. You hear *me. Allons.* BLUCHER."

I remonstrated against the sending of this note, because it was so mixed up that the landlord would never be able to make head or tail of it; but Blucher said he guessed the old man could read the French of it and average the rest.

Blucher's French is bad enough, but it is not much worse than the English one finds in advertisements all over Italy every day. For instance, observe the printed card of the hotel we shall probably stop at on the shores of Lake Como:

"NOTISH."

"This hotel which the best it is in Italy and most superb, is handsome locate on the best situation of the lake, with the most splendid view near the Villas Melzy, to the King of Belgian, and Serbelloni. This hotel have recently enlarge, do offer all commodities on moderate price, at the strangers gentlemen who whish spend the seasons on the Lake Come."

How is that for a specimen? In the hotel is a handsome little chapel where an English clergyman is employed to preach to such of the guests of the house as hail from England and America, and this fact is also set forth in barbarous English in the same advertisement. Wouldn't you have supposed that the adventurous linguist who framed the card would have known enough to submit it to that clergyman before he sent it to the printer?

Here, in Milan, in an ancient tumble-down ruin of a church, is the mournful wreck of the most celebrated painting in the world — "The Last Supper," by Leonardo da Vinci. We are not infallible judges of pictures, but, of course, we went there to see this wonderful painting, once so beautiful, always so worshiped by masters in art, and forever to be famous in song and story. And the first thing that occurred was the infliction on us of a placard fairly reeking with wretched English. Take a morsel of it:

"Bartholomew (that is the first figure on the left hand side at the spectator), uncertain and doubtful about what he thinks to have heard, and upon which he wants to be assured by himself at Christ and by no others."

Good, isn't it? And then Peter is described as "argumenting in a threatening and angrily condition at Judas Iscariot."

This paragraph recalls the picture. "The Last Supper" is painted on the dilapidated wall of what was a little chapel attached to the main church in ancient times, I suppose. It is battered and scarred in every direction, and stained and discolored by time, and Napoleon's horses kicked the legs off most the disciples when they (the horses, not the disciples) were stabled there more than half a century ago.

I recognized the old picture in a moment — the Saviour with bowed head seated at the center of a long, rough table with scattering fruits and dishes upon it, and six disciples on either side in their long robes, talking to each other — the picture from which all engravings and all copies have been made for three centuries. Perhaps no living man has ever known an attempt to paint the Lord's Supper differently. The world seems to have become settled in the belief, long ago, that it is not possible for human genius to outdo this creation of Da Vinci's. I suppose painters will go on copying it as long as any of the original is left visible to the eye. There were a dozen easels in the room, and as many artists transferring the great picture to their canvases. Fifty proofs of steel engravings and lithographs were scattered around, too. And as usual, I could not help noticing how superior the copies were to the original, that is, to my inexperienced eye. Where-

ever you find a Raphael, a Rubens, a Michael
Angelo, a Caracci, or a Da Vinci (and we see them
every day) you find artists copying them, and the
copies are always the handsomest. Maybe the
originals were handsome when they were new, but
they are not now.

This picture is about thirty feet long, and ten or
twelve high, I should think, and the figures are at
least life size. It is one of the largest paintings in
Europe.

The colors are dimmed with age; the countenances
are scaled and marred, and nearly all expression is
gone from them; the hair is a dead blur upon the
wall, and there is no life in the eyes. Only the
attitudes are certain.

People come here from all parts of the world, and
glorify this masterpiece. They stand entranced before it with bated breath and parted lips, and when
they speak, it is only in the catchy ejaculations of
rapture:

" Oh, wonderful !"
" Such expression !"
" Such grace of attitude !"
" Such dignity !"
" Such faultless drawing !"
" Such matchless coloring !"
" Such feeling !"
" What delicacy of touch !"
" What sublimity of conception !"
" A vision ! a vision !"

I only envy these people; I envy them their honest admiration, if it be honest — their delight, if they feel delight. I harbor no animosity toward any of them. But at the same time the thought *will* intrude itself upon me, How can they see what is not visible? What would you think of a man who looked at some decayed, blind, toothless, pock-marked Cleopatra, and said: "What matchless beauty! What soul! What expression!" What would you think of a man who gazed upon a dingy, foggy sunset, and said: "What sublimity! what feeling! what richness of coloring!" What would you think of a man who stared in ecstasy upon a desert of stumps and said: "Oh, my soul, my beating heart, what a noble forest is here!"

You would think that those men had an astonishing talent for seeing things that had already passed away. It was what I thought when I stood before the Last Supper and heard men apostrophizing wonders and beauties and perfections which had faded out of the picture and gone, a hundred years before they were born. We can imagine the beauty that was once in an aged face; we can imagine the forest if we see the stumps; but we cannot absolutely *see* these things when they are not there. I am willing to believe that the eye of the practiced artist can rest upon the Last Supper and renew a lustre where only a hint of it is left, supply a tint that has faded away, restore an expression that is gone; patch, and color, and add to the dull canvas

until at last its figures shall stand before him aglow
with the life, the feeling, the freshness, yea, with all
the noble beauty that was theirs when first they
came from the hand of the master. But *I* cannot
work this miracle. Can those other uninspired
visitors do it, or do they only happily imagine they
do?

After reading so much about it, I am satisfied that
the Last Supper was a very miracle of art once. But
it was three hundred years ago.

It vexes me to hear people talk so glibly of "feeling," "expression," "tone," and those other
easily-acquired and inexpensive technicalities of art
that make such a fine show in conversations concerning pictures. There is not one man in seventy-five
hundred that can tell *what* a pictured face is intended
to express. There is not one man in five hundred
that can go into a court-room and be sure that he
will not mistake some harmless innocent of a jury-
man for the black-hearted assassin on trial. Yet
such people talk of "character" and presume to
interpret "expression" in pictures. There is an
old story that Matthews, the actor, was once lauding
the ability of the human face to express the passions
and emotions hidden in the breast. He said the
countenance could disclose what was passing in the
heart plainer than the tongue could.

"Now," he said, "observe my face — what does
it express?"

"Despair!"

"Bah, it expresses peaceful resignation! What does *this* express?"

"Rage!"

"Stuff! it means terror! *This!*"

"Imbecility!"

"Fool! It is smothered ferocity! Now *this!*"

"Joy!"

"Oh, perdition! *Any* ass can see it means insanity!"

Expression! People coolly pretend to read it who would think themselves presumptuous if they pretended to interpret the hieroglyphics on the obelisk of Luxor — yet they are fully as competent to do the one thing as the other. I have heard two very intelligent critics speak of Murillo's Immaculate Conception (now in the museum at Seville) within the past few days. One said:

"Oh, the Virgin's face is full of the ecstasy of a joy that is complete — that leaves nothing more to be desired on earth!"

The other said:

"Ah, that wonderful face is so humble, so pleading — it says as plainly as words could say it: 'I fear; I tremble; I am unworthy. But Thy will be done; sustain Thou Thy servant!'"

The reader can see the picture in any drawing-room; it can be easily recognized; the Virgin (the only young and really beautiful Virgin that was ever painted by one of the old masters, some of us think) stands in the crescent of the new moon, with a multitude of cherubs hovering about her, and more coming; her hands are crossed upon her breast, and upon her uplifted countenance falls a glory out of the heavens. The reader may amuse himself, if he chooses, in trying to determine which of these gentlemen read the Virgin's " expression " aright, or if either of them did it.

Any one who is acquainted with the old masters will comprehend how much the Last Supper is damaged when I say that the spectator cannot really tell, now, whether the disciples are Hebrews or Italians. These ancient painters never succeeded in denationalizing themselves. The Italian artists painted Italian Virgins, the Dutch painted Dutch Virgins, the Virgins of the French painters were Frenchwomen — none of them ever put into the face of the Madonna that indescribable something which proclaims the Jewess, whether you find her in New York, in Constantinople, in Paris, Jerusalem, or in the Empire of Morocco. I saw in the Sandwich Islands, once, a picture, copied by a talented German artist from an engraving in one of the American illustrated papers. It was an allegory, representing Mr. Davis in the act of signing a secession act or some such document. Over him hovered the ghost of Washington in warning attitude, and in the background a troop of shadowy soldiers in Continental uniform were limping with shoeless, bandaged feet through a driving snowstorm. Valley Forge was suggested, of course. The copy seemed accurate, and yet there was a discrepancy somewhere. After a long examination I discovered what it was — the shadowy soldiers were all Germans! Jeff. Davis was a German! even the hovering ghost was a German ghost! The artist had unconsciously worked his nationality into the picture. To tell the truth, I am getting a little perplexed about John the Baptist and his portraits. In France I finally grew reconciled to him as a Frenchman; here he is unquestionably an Italian. What next? Can it be possible that the painters make John the Baptist a Spaniard in Madrid and an Irishman in Dublin?

We took an open barouche and drove two miles out of Milan to "see ze echo," as the guide expressed it. The road was smooth, it was bordered by trees, fields, and grassy meadows, and the soft air was filled with the odor of flowers. Troops of picturesque peasant girls, coming from work, hooted at us, shouted at us, made all manner of game of us, and entirely delighted me. My long-cherished judgment was confirmed. I always did think those frowsy, romantic, unwashed peasant girls I had read so much about in poetry were a glaring fraud.

We enjoyed our jaunt. It was an exhilarating relief from tiresome sightseeing.

We distressed ourselves very little about the astonishing echo the guide talked so much about. We were growing accustomed to encomiums on wonders that too often proved no wonders at all. And so we were most happily disappointed to find

17

in the sequel that the guide had even failed to rise to the magnitude of his subject.

We arrived at a tumble-down old rookery called the Palazzo Simonetti — a massive hewn-stone affair occupied by a family of ragged Italians. A good-looking young girl conducted us to a window on the second floor which looked out on a court walled on three sides by tall buildings. She put her head out at the window and shouted. The echo answered more times than we could count. She took a speaking-trumpet and through it she shouted, sharp and quick, a single

"Ha!" The echo answered:

"Ha————ha!!———ha!——ha!—ha!–ha! ha! h-a-a-a-a-a!" and finally went off into a rollicking convulsion of the jolliest laughter that could be imagined. It was so joyful, so long-continued, so perfectly cordial and hearty, that everybody was forced to join in. There was no resisting it.

Then the girl took a gun and fired it. We stood ready to count the astonishing clatter of reverberations. We could not say one, two, three, fast enough, but we could dot our note-books with our pencil-points almost rapidly enough to take down a sort of shorthand report of the result. My page revealed the following account. I could not keep up, but I did as well as I could.

I set down fifty-two distinct repetitions, and then the echo got the advantage of me. The doctor set down sixty-four, and thenceforth the echo moved

too fast for him, also. After the separate concus‑
sions could no longer be noted, the reverberations
dwindled to a wild, long-sustained clatter of sounds
such as a watchman's rattle produces. It is likely
that this is the most remarkable echo in the world.

The doctor, in jest, offered to kiss the young girl,
and was taken a little aback when she said he might
for a franc! The commonest gallantry compelled
him to stand by his offer, and so he paid the franc
and took the kiss. She was a philosopher. She
said a franc was a good thing to have, and she did
not care anything for one paltry kiss, because she
had a million left. Then our comrade, always a
shrewd business man, offered to take the whole cargo
at thirty days, but that little financial scheme was a
failure.

CHAPTER XX.

WE left Milan by rail. The cathedral six or seven miles behind us — vast, dreamy, bluish, snow-clad mountains twenty miles in front of us,— these were the accented points in the scenery. The more immediate scenery consisted of fields and farmhouses outside the car and a monster-headed dwarf and a moustached woman inside it. These latter were not show-people. Alas, deformity and female beards are too common in Italy to attract attention.

We passed through a range of wild, picturesque hills, steep, wooded, cone-shaped, with rugged crags projecting here and there, and with dwellings and ruinous castles perched away up toward the drifting clouds. We lunched at the curious old town of Como, at the foot of the lake, and then took the small steamer and had an afternoon's pleasure excursion to this place,— Bellagio.

When we walked ashore, a party of policemen (people whose cocked hats and showy uniforms would shame the finest uniform in the military service of the United States) put us into a little stone cell and locked us in. We had the whole passenger list for company, but their room would have been preferable, for there was no light, there were no windows, no ventilation. It was close and hot. We were much crowded. It was the Black Hole of Calcutta on a small scale. Presently a smoke rose about our feet — a smoke that smelt of all the dead things of earth, of all the putrefaction and corruption imaginable.

We were there five minutes, and when we got out it was hard to tell which of us carried the vilest fragrance.

These miserable outcasts called that "fumigating" us, and the term was a tame one, indeed. They fumigated us to guard themselves against the cholera, though we hailed from no infected port. We had left the cholera far behind us all the time. However, they must keep epidemics away somehow or other, and fumigation is cheaper than soap. They must either wash themselves or fumigate other people. Some of the lower classes had rather die than wash, but the fumigation of strangers causes them no pangs. They need no fumigation themselves. Their habits make it unnecessary. They carry their preventive with them; they sweat and fumigate all the day long. I trust I am a humble and a consistent Christian. I try to do what is right. I know it is my duty to "pray for them that despitefully use me"; and therefore, hard as it is, I shall still try to pray for these fumigating, macaroni-stuffing organ-grinders.

Our hotel sits at the water's edge — at least its
front garden does — and we walk among the shrubbery and smoke at twilight; we look afar off at
Switzerland and the Alps, and feel an indolent
willingness to look no closer; we go down the steps
and swim in the lake; we take a shapely little boat
and sail abroad among the reflections of the stars;
lie on the thwarts and listen to the distant laughter,
the singing, the soft melody of flutes and guitars
that comes floating across the water from pleasuring
gondolas; we close the evening with exasperating
billiards on one of those same old execrable tables.
A midnight luncheon in our ample bed-chamber; a
final smoke in its contracted veranda facing the
water, the gardens, and the mountains; a summing
up of the day's events. Then to bed, with drowsy
brains harassed with a mad panorama that mixes up
pictures of France, of Italy, of the ship, of the
ocean, of home, in grotesque and bewildering disorder. Then a melting away of familiar faces, of
cities and of tossing waves, into a great calm of
forgetfulness and peace.

After which, the nightmare.

Breakfast in the morning, and then the lake.

I did not like it yesterday. I thought Lake Tahoe
was *much* finer. I have to confess now, however,
that my judgment erred somewhat, though not extravagantly. I always had an idea that Como was a
vast basin of water, like Tahoe, shut in by great
mountains. Well, the border of huge mountains is

here, but the lake itself is not a basin. It is as crooked as any brook, and only from one-quarter to two-thirds as wide as the Mississippi. There is not a yard of low ground on either side of it — nothing but endless chains of mountains that spring abruptly from the water's edge, and tower to altitudes varying from a thousand to two thousand feet. Their craggy sides are clothed with vegetation, and white specks of houses peep out from the luxuriant foliage everywhere; they are even perched upon jutting and picturesque pinnacles a thousand feet above your head.

Again, for miles along the shores, handsome country seats, surrounded by gardens and groves, sit fairly in the water, sometimes in nooks carved by Nature out of the vine-hung precipices, and with no ingress or egress save by boats. Some have great broad stone staircases leading down to the water, with heavy stone balustrades ornamented with statuary and fancifully adorned with creeping vines and bright-colored flowers — for all the world like a drop-curtain in a theater, and lacking nothing but long-waisted, high-heeled women and plumed gallants in silken tights coming down to go serenading in the splendid gondola in waiting.

A great feature of Como's attractiveness is the multitude of pretty houses and gardens that cluster upon its shores and on its mountain sides. They look so snug and so homelike, and at eventide when everything seems to slumber, and the music of the vesper bells comes stealing over the water, one almost believes that nowhere else than on the Lake of Como can there be found such a paradise of tranquil repose.

From my window here in Bellagio, I have a view of the other side of the lake now, which is as beautiful as a picture. A scarred and wrinkled precipice rises to a height of eighteen hundred feet; on a tiny bench half way up its vast wall, sits a little snow-flake of a church, no bigger than a martin-box, apparently; skirting the base of the cliff are a hundred orange groves and gardens, flecked with glimpses of the white dwellings that are buried in them; in front, three or four gondolas lie idle upon the water — and in the burnished mirror of the lake, mountain, chapel, houses, groves, and boats are counterfeited so brightly and so clearly that one scarce knows where the reality leaves off and the reflection begins !

The surroundings of this picture are fine. A mile away, a grove-plumed promontory juts far into the lake and glasses its palace in the blue depths; in midstream a boat is cutting the shining surface and leaving a long track behind, like a ray of light; the mountains beyond are veiled in a dreamy purple haze; far in the opposite direction a tumbled mass of domes and verdant slopes and valleys bars the lake, and here, indeed, does distance lend enchantment to the view — for on this broad canvas, sun and clouds and the richest of atmospheres have blended a thousand tints together, and over its surface the filmy lights and shadows drift, hour after hour, and glorify it with a beauty that seems reflected out of Heaven itself. Beyond all question, this is the most voluptuous scene we have yet looked upon.

Last night the scenery was striking and picturesque. On the other side crags and trees and snowy houses were reflected in the lake with a wonderful distinctness, and streams of light from many a distant window shot far abroad over the still waters. On this side, near at hand, great mansions, white with moonlight, glared out from the midst of masses of foliage that lay black and shapeless in the shadows that fell from the cliff above — and down in the margin of the lake every feature of the weird vision was faithfully repeated.

To-day we have idled through a wonder of a garden attached to a ducal estate — but enough of description is enough, I judge. I suspect that this was the same place the gardener's son deceived the Lady of Lyons with, but I do not know. You may have heard of the passage somewhere:

> "A deep vale,
> Shut out by Alpine hills from the rude world,
> Near a clear lake margined by fruits of gold
> And whispering myrtles:
> Glassing softest skies, cloudless,
> Save with rare and roseate shadows;
> A palace, lifting to eternal heaven its marbled walls,
> From out a glossy bower of coolest foliage musical
> with birds."

That is all very well, except the " clear " part of

the lake. It certainly is clearer than a great many lakes, but how dull its waters are compared with the wonderful transparence of Lake Tahoe! I speak of the north shore of Tahoe, where one can count the scales on a trout at a depth of a hundred and eighty feet. I have tried to get this statement off at par here, but with no success; so I have been obliged to negotiate it at fifty per cent. discount. At this rate I find some takers; perhaps the reader will receive it on the same terms — ninety feet instead of one hundred and eighty. But let it be remembered that those are forced terms — sheriff's-sale prices. As far as I am privately concerned, I abate not a jot of the original assertion that in those strangely-magnifying waters one may count the scales on a trout (a trout of the large kind) at a depth of a hundred and eighty feet — may see every pebble on the bottom — might even count a paper of dray-pins. People talk of the transparent waters of the Mexican Bay of Acapulco, but in my own experience I know they cannot compare with those I am speaking of. I have fished for trout in Tahoe, and at a measured depth of eighty-four feet I have seen them put their noses to the bait and I could see their gills open and shut. I could hardly have seen the trout themselves at that distance in the open air.

As I go back in spirit and recall that noble sea, reposing among the snow-peaks six thousand feet above the ocean, the conviction comes strong upon me again that Como would only seem a bedizened little courtier in that august presence.

Sorrow and misfortune overtake the legislature that still from year to year permits Tahoe to retain its unmusical cognomen! Tahoe! It suggests no crystal waters, no picturesque shores, no sublimity. Tahoe for a sea in the clouds; a sea that has character, and asserts it in solemn calms, at times, at times in savage storms; a sea, whose royal seclusion is guarded by a cordon of sentinel peaks that lift their frosty fronts nine thousand feet above the level world; a sea whose every aspect is impressive, whose belongings are all beautiful, whose lonely majesty types the Deity!

Tahoe means grasshoppers. It means grasshopper soup. It is Indian, and suggestive of Indians. They say it is Pi-ute — possibly it is Digger. I am satisfied it was named by the Diggers — those degraded savages who roast their dead relatives, then mix the human grease and ashes of bones with tar, and "gaum" it thick all over their heads and foreheads and ears, and go caterwauling about the hills and call it *mourning*. *These* are the gentry that named the lake.

People say that Tahoe means "Silver Lake"—"Limpid Water"—"Falling Leaf." Bosh! It means grasshopper soup, the favorite dish of the Digger tribe — and of the Pi-utes as well. It isn't worth while, in these practical times, for people to talk about Indian poetry — there never was any in

them — except in the Fenimore Cooper Indians.
But *they* are an extinct tribe that never existed. I
know the Noble Red Man. I have camped with the
Indians; I have been on the warpath with them,
taken part in the chase with them — for grasshoppers; helped them steal cattle; I have roamed
with them, scalped them, had them for breakfast.
I would gladly eat the whole race if I had a chance.

But I am growing unreliable. I will return to my
comparison of the lakes. Como is a little deeper
than Tahoe, if people here tell the truth. They say
it is eighteen hundred feet deep at this point, but it
does not look a dead enough blue for that. Tahoe
is one thousand five hundred and twenty-five feet
deep in the center, by the State Geologist's measure-
ment. They say the great peak opposite this town
is five thousand feet high; but I feel sure that three
thousand feet of that statement is a good, honest lie.
The lake is a mile wide here, and maintains about
that width from this point to its northern extremity
— which is distant sixteen miles; from here to its
southern extremity — say fifteen miles — it is not
over half a mile wide in any place, I should think.
Its snow-clad mountains one hears so much about
are only seen occasionally, and then in the distance,
the Alps. Tahoe is from ten to eighteen miles
wide, and its mountains shut it in like a wall. Their
summits are never free from snow the year round.
One thing about it is very strange: it never has even
a skim of ice upon its surface. although lakes in the

same range of mountains, lying in a lower and warmer temperature, freeze over in winter.

It is cheerful to meet a shipmate in these out-of-the-way places and compare notes with him. We have found one of ours here — an old soldier of the war, who is seeking bloodless adventures and rest from his campaigns, in these sunny lands.*

* Col. J. Heron Foster, editor of a Pittsburgh journal, and a most estimable gentleman.   As these sheets are being prepared for the press, I am pained to learn of his decease shortly after his return home. — M. T.

CHAPTER XXI.

WE voyaged by steamer down the Lago di Lecco, through wild mountain scenery, and by hamlets and villas, and disembarked at the town of Lecco. They said it was two hours, by carriage, to the ancient city of Bergamo, and that we would arrive there in good season for the railway train. We got an open barouche and a wild, boisterous driver, and set out. It was delightful. We had a fast team and a perfectly smooth road. There were towering cliffs on our left, and the pretty Lago di Lecco on our right, and every now and then it rained on us. Just before starting, the driver picked up, in the street, a stump of a cigar an inch long, and put it in his mouth. When he had carried it thus about an hour, I thought it would be only Christian charity to give him a light. I handed him my cigar, which I had just lit, and he put it in his mouth and returned his stump to his pocket! I never saw a more sociable man. At least I never saw a man who was more sociable on a short acquaintance.

We saw interior Italy now. The houses were of

solid stone, and not often in good repair. The
peasants and their children were idle, as a general
thing, and the donkeys and chickens made themselves at home in drawing-room and bed-chamber
and were not molested. The drivers of each and
every one of the slow-moving market-carts we met
were stretched in the sun upon their merchandise,
sound asleep. Every three or four hundred yards,
it seemed to me, we came upon the shrine of some
saint or other — a rude picture of him built into a
huge cross or a stone pillar by the roadside. Some
of the pictures of the Saviour were curiosities in
their way. They represented him stretched upon
the cross, his countenance distorted with agony.
From the wounds of the crown of thorns; from the
pierced side; from the mutilated hands and feet;
from the scourged body — from every hand-breadth
of his person, streams of blood were flowing! Such
a gory, ghastly spectacle would frighten the children
out of their senses, I should think. There were
some unique auxiliaries to the painting which added
to its spirited effect. These were genuine wooden
and iron implements, and were prominently disposed
round about the figure: a bundle of nails; the
hammer to drive them; the sponge; the reed that
supported it; the cup of vinegar; the ladder for the
ascent of the cross; the spear that pierced the
Saviour's side. The crown of thorns was made of
real thorns, and was nailed to the sacred head. In
some Italian church paintings, even by the old

masters, the Saviour and the Virgin wear silver or gilded crowns that are fastened to the pictured head with nails. The effect is as grotesque as it is incongruous.

Here and there, on the fronts of roadside inns, we found huge, coarse frescoes of suffering martyrs like those in the shrines. It could not have diminished their sufferings any to be so uncouthly represented. We were in the heart and home of priestcraft — of a happy, cheerful, contented ignorance, superstition, degradation, poverty, indolence, and everlasting unaspiring worthlessness. And we said fervently, It suits these people precisely; let them enjoy it, along with the other animals, and Heaven forbid that they be molested. *We* feel no malice toward these fumigators.

We passed through the strangest, funniest, undreamt-of old towns, wedded to the customs and steeped in the dreams of the elder ages, and perfectly unaware that the world turns round! And perfectly indifferent, too, as to whether it turns around or stands still. *They* have nothing to do but eat and sleep and sleep and eat, and toil a little when they can get a friend to stand by and keep them awake. *They* are not paid for thinking — *they* are not paid to fret about the world's concerns. They were not respectable people — they were not worthy people — they were not learned and wise and brilliant people — but in their breasts, all their stupid lives long, resteth a peace that passeth under-

standing! How can men, calling themselves men,
consent to be so degraded and happy.

We whisked by many a gray old medieval castle,
clad thick with ivy that swung its green banners
down from towers and turrets where once some old
Crusader's flag had floated. The driver pointed to
one of these ancient fortresses, and said (I translate):

"Do you see that great iron hook that projects
from the wall just under the highest window in the
ruined tower?"

We said we could not see it at such a distance,
but had no doubt it was there.

"Well," he said, "there is a legend connected
with that iron hook. Nearly seven hundred years
ago, that castle was the property of the noble Count
Luigi Gennaro Guido Alphonso di Genova——"

"What was his other name?" said Dan.

"He had no other name. The name I have
spoken was all the name he had. He was the son
of——"

"Poor but honest parents — that is all right —
never mind the particulars — go on with the legend."

THE LEGEND.

Well, then, all the world, at that time, was in a
wild excitement about the Holy Sepulchre. All the
great feudal lords in Europe were pledging their
lands and pawning their plate to fit out men-at-arms
so that they might join the grand armies of Christen-

18

dom and win renown in the Holy Wars. The Count Luigi raised money, like the rest, and one mild September morning, armed with battle-axe, portcullis and thundering culverin, he rode through the greaves and bucklers of his donjon-keep with as gallant a troop of Christian bandits as ever stepped in Italy. He had his sword, Excalibur, with him. His beautiful countess and her young daughter waved him a tearful adieu from the battering-rams and buttresses of the fortress, and he galloped away with a happy heart.

He made a raid on a neighboring baron and completed his outfit with the booty secured. He then razed the castle to the ground, massacred the family, and moved on. They were hardy fellows in the grand old days of chivalry. Alas! those days will never come again.

Count Luigi grew high in fame in Holy Land. He plunged into the carnage of a hundred battles, but his good Excalibur always brought him out alive, albeit often sorely wounded. His face became browned by exposure to the Syrian sun in long marches; he suffered hunger and thirst; he pined in prisons, he languished in loathsome plague-hospitals. And many and many a time he thought of his loved ones at home, and wondered if all was well with them. But his heart said, Peace, is not thy brother watching over thy household?

* * * * * *

Forty-two years waxed and waned; the good fight

was won; Godfrey reigned in Jerusalem — the Christian hosts reared the banner of the cross above the Holy Sepulchre!

Twilight was approaching. Fifty harlequins, in flowing robes, approached this castle wearily, for they were on foot, and the dust upon their garments betokened that they had traveled far. They overtook a peasant, and asked him if it were likely they could get food and a hospitable bed there, for love of Christian charity, and if, perchance, a moral parlor entertainment might meet with generous countenance — "for," said they, "this exhibition hath no feature that could offend the most fastidious taste."

"Marry," quoth the peasant, "an' it please your worships, ye had better journey many a good rood hence with your juggling circus than trust your bones in yonder castle."

"How now, sirrah!" exclaimed the chief monk, "explain thy ribald speech, or by'r Lady it shall go hard with thee."

"Peace, good mountebank, I did but utter the truth that was in my heart. San Paolo be my witness that did ye but find the stout Count Leonardo in his cups, sheer from the castle's topmost battlements would he hurl ye all! Alack-a-day! the good Lord Luigi reigns not here in these sad times."

"The good Lord Luigi?"

"Aye, none other, please your worship. In his

day, the poor rejoiced in plenty and the rich he did oppress; taxes were not known, the fathers of the church waxed fat upon his bounty; travelers went and came, with none to interfere; and whosoever would, might tarry in his halls in cordial welcome, and eat his bread and drink his wine, withal. But woe is me! some two and forty years agone the good count rode hence to fight for Holy Cross, and many a year hath flown since word or token have we had of him. Men say his bones lie bleaching in the fields of Palestine."

" And now?"

" *Now!* God 'a mercy, the cruel Leonardo lords it in the castle. He wrings taxes from the poor; he robs all travelers that journey by his gates; he spends his days in feuds and murders, and his nights in revel and debauch; he roasts the fathers of the church upon his kitchen spits, and enjoyeth the same, calling it pastime. These thirty years Luigi's countess hath not been seen by any he in all this land, and many whisper that she pines in the dungeons of the castle for that she will not wed with Leonardo, saying her dear lord still liveth and that she will die ere she prove false to him. They whisper likewise that her daughter is a prisoner as well. Nay, good jugglers, seek ye refreshment otherwheres. 'Twere better that ye perished in a Christian way than that ye plunged from off yon dizzy tower. Give ye good-day."

" God keep ye, gentle knave — farewell."

But heedless of the peasant's warning, the players moved straightway toward the castle.

Word was brought to Count Leonardo that a company of mountebanks besought his hospitality.

"'Tis well. Dispose of them in the customary manner. Yet stay! I have need of them. Let them come hither. Later, cast them from the battlements — or — how many priests have ye on hand?"

"The day's results are meager, good my lord. An abbot and a dozen beggarly friars is all we have."

"Hell and furies! Is the estate going to seed? Send hither the mountebanks. Afterward, broil them with the priests."

The robed and close-cowled harlequins entered. The grim Leonardo sate in state at the head of his council board. Ranged up and down the hall on either hand stood near a hundred men-at-arms.

"Ha, villains!" quoth the count, "What can ye do to earn the hospitality ye crave?"

"Dread lord and mighty, crowded audiences have greeted our humble efforts with rapturous applause. Among our body count we the versatile and talented Ugolino; the justly celebrated Rodolpho; the gifted and accomplished Roderigo; the management have spared neither pains nor expense ——"

"S'death! what can ye *do?* Curb thy prating tongue."

"Good my lord, in acrobatic feats, in practice with the dumb-bells, in balancing and ground and

18.

lofty tumbling are we versed — and sith your highness asketh me, I venture here to publish that in the truly marvelous and entertaining Zampillaerostation———''

"Gag him! throttle him! Body of Bacchus! am I a dog that I am to be assailed with polysyllabled blasphemy like to this? But hold! Lucretia, Isabel, stand forth! Sirrah, behold this dame, this weeping wench. The first I marry, within the hour; the other shall dry her tears or feed the vultures. Thou and thy vagabonds shall crown the wedding with thy merry-makings. Fetch hither the priest!"

The dame sprang toward the chief player.

"Oh, save me!" she cried; "save me from a fate far worse than death! Behold these sad eyes, these sunken cheeks, this withered frame! See thou the wreck this fiend hath made, and let thy heart be moved with pity! Look upon this damosel; note her wasted form, her halting step, her bloomless cheeks where youth should blush and happiness exult in smiles! Hear us, and have compassion. This monster was my husband's brother. He who should have been our shield against all harm, hath kept us shut within the noisome caverns of his donjon-keep for, lo, these thirty years. And for what crime? None other than that I would not belie my troth, root out my strong love for him who marches with the legions of the cross in Holy Land (for oh, he is not dead), and wed with him! Save us, oh, save thy persecuted suppliants!"

She flung herself at his feet and clasped his knees.

"Ha!-ha!-ha!" shouted the brutal Leonardo. "Priest, to thy work!" and he dragged the weeping dame from her refuge. "Say, once for all, *will* you be mine?—for by my halidome, that breath that uttereth thy refusal shall be thy last on earth!"

"NE-VER!"

"Then die!" and the sword leaped from its scabbard.

Quicker than thought, quicker than the lightning's flash, fifty monkish habits disappeared, and fifty knights in splendid armor stood revealed! fifty falchions gleamed in air above the men-at-arms, and brighter, fiercer than them all, flamed Excalibur aloft, and cleaving downward struck the brutal Leonardo's weapon from his grasp!

"A Luigi to the rescue! Whoop!"

"A Leonardo! tare an ouns!"

"Oh, God, oh, God, my husband!"

"Oh, God, oh, God, my wife!"

"My father!"

"My precious!" [Tableau.]

Count Luigi bound his usurping brother hand and foot. The practiced knights from Palestine made holiday sport of carving the awkward men-at-arms into chops and steaks. The victory was complete. Happiness reigned. The knights all married the daughter. Joy! wassail! finis!

"But what did they do with the wicked brother?"

B.

" Oh, nothing — only hanged him on that iron hook I was speaking of.   By the chin."

" As how?"

" Passed it up through his gills into his mouth."

" Leave him there?"

" Couple of years."

" Ah — is — is he dead?"

" Six hundred and fifty years ago, or such a matter."

" Splendid legend — splendid lie — drive on."

We reached the quaint old fortified city of Bergamo, the renowed in history, some three-quarters of an hour before the train was ready to start.   The place has thirty or forty thousand inhabitants and is remarkable for being the birthplace of harlequin. When we discovered that, that legend of our driver took to itself a new interest in our eyes.

Rested and refreshed, we took the rail happy and contented.   I shall not tarry to speak of the handsome Lago di Garda; its stately castle that holds in its stony bosom the secrets of an age so remote that even tradition goeth not back to it; the imposing mountain scenery that ennobles the landscape thereabouts; nor yet of ancient Padua or haughty Verona; nor of their Montagues and Capulets, their famous balconies and tombs of Juliet and Romeo *et al.*, but hurry straight to the ancient city of the sea, the widowed bride of the Adriatic. It was a long, long ride.   But toward evening, as we sat silent and hardly conscious of where we were —

subdued into that meditative calm that comes so surely after a conversational storm — some one shouted:

"VENICE!"

And sure enough, afloat on the placid sea a league away, lay a great city, with its towers and domes and steeples drowsing in a golden mist of sunset.

CHAPTER XXII.

THIS Venice, which was a haughty, invincible, magnificent Republic for nearly fourteen hundred years; whose armies compelled the world's applause whenever and wherever they battled; whose navies well nigh held dominion of the seas, and whose merchant fleets whitened the remotest oceans with their sails and loaded these piers with the products of every clime, is fallen a prey to poverty, neglect and melancholy decay. Six hundred years ago, Venice was the Autocrat of Commerce; her mart was the great commercial center, the distributing house from whence the enormous trade of the Orient was spread abroad over the Western world. To-day her piers are deserted, her warehouses are empty, her merchant fleets are vanished, her armies and her navies are but memories. Her glory is departed, and with her crumbling grandeur of wharves and palaces about her she sits among her stagnant lagoons, forlorn and beggared, forgotten of the world. She, that in her palmy days commanded the commerce of a hemisphere and made the weal or woe of nations with a beck of her puissant finger, is become the humblest among the peoples of the earth,— a peddler of glass beads for women, and trifling toys and trinkets for school-girls and children.

The venerable Mother of the Republics is scarce a fit subject for flippant speech or the idle gossiping of tourists. It seems a sort of sacrilege to disturb the glamour of old romance that pictures her to us softly from afar off as through a tinted mist, and curtains her ruin and her desolation from our view. One ought, indeed, to turn away from her rags, her poverty, and her humiliation, and think of her only as she was when she sunk the fleets of Charlemagne; when she humbled Frederick Barbarossa or waved her victorious banners above the battlements of Constantinople.

We reached Venice at eight in the evening, and entered a hearse belonging to the Grand Hotel d'Europe. At any rate, it was more like a hearse than anything else, though, to speak by the card, it was a gondola. And this was the storied gondola of Venice! — the fairy boat in which the princely cavaliers of the olden time were wont to cleave the waters of the moonlit canals and look the eloquence of love into the soft eyes of patrician beauties, while the gay gondolier in silken doublet touched his guitar and sang as only gondoliers can sing! This the famed gondola and this the gorgeous gondolier! — the one an inky, rusty old canoe with a sable hearse-body clapped on to the middle of it, and the other a mangy, barefooted gutter-snipe with a portion of his raiment on exhibition which should have been sacred from public scrutiny. Presently, as he turned a corner and shot his hearse into a dismal ditch between two long rows of towering, untenanted buildings, the gay gondolier began to sing, true to the traditions of his race. I stood it a little while. Then I said:

" Now, here, Roderigo Gonzales Michael Angelo, I'm a pilgrim, and I'm a stranger, but I am not going to have my feelings lacerated by any such caterwauling as that. If that goes on, one of us has got to take water. It is enough that my cherished dreams of Venice have been blighted forever as to the romantic gondola and the gorgeous gondolier; this system of destruction shall go no farther; I will accept the hearse, under protest, and you may fly your flag of truce in peace, but here I register a dark and bloody oath that you shan't sing. Another yelp, and overboard you go."

I began to feel that the old Venice of song and story had departed forever. But I was too hasty. In a few minutes we swept gracefully out into the Grand Canal, and under the mellow moonlight the Venice of poetry and romance stood revealed. Right from the water's edge rose long lines of stately palaces of marble; gondolas were gliding swiftly hither and thither and disappearing suddenly through unsuspected gates and alleys; ponderous stone bridges threw their shadows athwart the glittering waves. There was life and motion every-

where, and yet everywhere there was a hush, a
stealthy sort of stillness, that was suggestive of secret
enterprises of bravoes and of lovers; and, clad half
in moonbeams and half in mysterious shadows, the
grim old mansions of the Republic seemed to have
an expression about them of having an eye out for
just such enterprises as these at that same moment.
Music came floating over the waters — Venice was
complete.

It was a beautiful picture — very soft and dreamy
and beautiful. But what was this Venice to compare with the Venice of midnight? Nothing. There
was a fête — a grand fête in honor of some saint
who had been instrumental in checking the cholera
three hundred years ago, and all Venice was abroad
on the water. It was no common affair, for the
Venetians did not know how soon they might need
the saint's services again, now that the cholera was
spreading everywhere. So in one vast space — say
a third of a mile wide and two miles long — were
collected two thousand gondolas, and every one of
them had from two to ten, twenty, and even thirty
colored lanterns suspended about it, and from four
to a dozen occupants. Just as far as the eye could
reach, these painted lights were massed together —
like a vast garden of many-colored flowers, except
that these blossoms were never still; they were
ceaselessly gliding in and out, and mingling together, and seducing you into bewildering attempts
to follow their mazy evolutions. Here and there a

strong red, green, or blue glare from a rocket that
was struggling to get away splendidly illuminated all
the boats around it.   Every gondola that swam by
us, with its crescents and pyramids and circles of
colored lamps hung aloft, and lighting up the faces
of the young and the sweet-scented and lovely
below, was a picture; and the reflections of those
lights, so long, so slender, so numberless, so many-
colored and so distorted and wrinkled by the waves,
was a picture likewise, and one that was enchantingly
beautiful.   Many and many a party of young ladies
and gentlemen had their state gondolas handsomely
decorated, and ate supper on board, bringing their
swallow-tailed, white-cravated varlets to wait upon
them, and having their tables tricked out as if for a
bridal supper.   They had brought along the costly
globe lamps from their drawing-rooms, and the lace
and silken curtains from the same places, I suppose.
And they had also brought pianos and guitars, and
they played and sang operas, while the plebeian
paper-lanterned gondolas from the suburbs and the
back alleys crowded around to stare and listen.

There was music everywhere — choruses, string
bands, brass bands, flutes, everything.   I was so
surrounded, walled in with music, magnificence, and
loveliness, that I became inspired with the spirit of
the scene, and sang one tune myself.   However,
when I observed that the other gondolas had sailed
away, and my gondolier was preparing to go overboard, I stopped.

The fête was magnificent. They kept it up the whole night long, and I never enjoyed myself better than I did while it lasted.

What a funny old city this Queen of the Adriatic is! Narrow streets, vast, gloomy marble palaces, black with the corroding damps of centuries, and all partly submerged; no dry land visible anywhere, and no sidewalks worth mentioning; if you want to go to church, to the theater, or to the restaurant, you must call a gondola. It must be a paradise for cripples, for verily a man has no use for legs here.

For a day or two the place looked so like an overflowed Arkansas town, because of its currentless waters laving the very doorsteps of all the houses, and the cluster of boats made fast under the windows, or skimming in and out of the alleys and byways, that I could not get rid of the impression that there was nothing the matter here but a spring freshet, and that the river would fall in a few weeks and leave a dirty high-water mark on the houses, and the streets full of mud and rubbish.

In the glare of day, there is little poetry about Venice, but under the charitable moon her stained palaces are white again, their battered sculptures are hidden in shadows, and the old city seems crowned once more with the grandeur that was hers five hundred years ago. It is easy, then, in fancy, to people these silent canals with plumed gallants and fair ladies — with Shylocks in gaberdine and sandals, venturing loans upon the rich argosies of Venetian commerce — with Othellos and Desdemonas, with Iagos and Roderigos — with noble fleets and victorious legions returning from the wars. In the treacherous sunlight we see Venice decayed, forlorn, poverty-stricken, and commerceless — forgotten and utterly insignificant. But in the moonlight, her fourteen centuries of greatness fling their glories about her, and once more is she the princeliest among the nations of the earth.

> "There is a glorious city in the sea;
> The sea is in the broad, the narrow streets,
> Ebbing and flowing; and the salt sea-weed
> Clings to the marble of her palaces.
> No track of men, no footsteps to and fro,
> Lead to her gates! The path lies o'er the sea,
> Invisible: and from the land we went,
> As to a floating city — steering in,
> And gliding up her streets, as in a dream,
> So smoothly, silently — by many a dome,
> Mosque-like, and many a stately portico,
> The statues ranged along an azure sky;
> By many a pile, in more than Eastern pride,
> Of old the residence of merchant kings;
> The fronts of some, tho' time had shatter'd them,
> Still glowing with the richest hues of art,
> As tho' the wealth within them had run o'er."

What would one naturally wish to see first in Venice? The Bridge of Sighs, of course — and next the Church and the Great Square of St. Mark, the Bronze Horses, and the famous Lion of St. Mark.

We intended to go to the Bridge of Sighs, but happened into the Ducal Palace first — a building which necessarily figures largely in Venetian poetry and tradition. In the Senate Chamber of the ancient Republic we wearied our eyes with staring at acres of historical paintings by Tintoretto and Paul Veronese, but nothing struck us forcibly except the one thing that strikes *all* strangers forcibly — a black square in the midst of a gallery of portraits. In one long row, around the great hall, were painted the portraits of the doges of Venice (venerable fellows, with flowing white beards, for of the three hundred Senators eligible to the office, the oldest was usually chosen doge), and each had its complimentary inscription attached — till you came to the place that should have had Marino Faliero's picture in it, and that was blank and black — blank, except that it bore a terse inscription, saying that the conspirator had died for his crime. It seemed cruel to keep that pitiless inscription still staring from the walls after the unhappy wretch had been in his grave five hundred years.

At the head of the Giant's Staircase, where Marino Faliero was beheaded, and where the doges were crowned in ancient times, two small slits in the stone wall were pointed out — two harmless, insignificant orifices that would never attract a stranger's attention — yet these were the terrible Lions' Mouths! The heads were gone (knocked off by the French during their occupation of Venice), but these were the throats, down which went the anonymous accusation, thrust in secretly at dead of night by an

19

enemy, that doomed many an innocent man to walk
the Bridge of Sighs and descend into the dungeon
which none entered and hoped to see the sun again.
This was in the old days when the Patricians alone
governed Venice — the common herd had no vote
and no voice. There were one thousand five hundred Patricians; from these, three hundred Senators
were chosen; from the Senators a Doge and a
Council of Ten were selected, and by secret ballot
the Ten chose from their own number a Council of
Three. All these were government spies, then, and
every spy was under surveillance himself — men
spoke in whispers in Venice, and no man trusted his
neighbor — not always his own brother. No man
knew who the Council of Three were — not even
the Senate, not even the Doge; the members of
that dread tribunal met at night in a chamber to
themselves, masked, and robed from head to foot in
scarlet cloaks, and did not even know each other,
unless by voice. It was their duty to judge heinous
political crimes, and from their sentence there was
no appeal. A nod to the executioner was sufficient.
The doomed man was marched down a hall and out
at a doorway into the covered Bridge of Sighs,
through it and into the dungeon and unto his death.
At no time in his transit was he visible to any save
his conductor. If a man had an enemy in those old
days, the cleverest thing he could do was to slip a
note for the Council of Three into the Lion's mouth,
saying "This man is plotting against the govern-

ment." If the awful Three found no proof, ten to one they would drown him anyhow, because he was a deep rascal, since his plots were unsolvable. Masked judges and masked executioners, with unlimited power, and no appeal from their judgments, in that hard, cruel age, were not likely to be lenient with men they suspected yet could not convict.

We walked through the hall of the Council of Ten, and presently entered the infernal den of the Council of Three.

The table around which they had sat was there still, and likewise the stations where the masked inquisitors and executioners formerly stood, frozen, upright and silent, till they received a bloody order, and then, without a word, moved off, like the inexorable machines they were, to carry it out. The frescoes on the walls were startlingly suited to the place. In all the other saloons, the halls, the great state chambers of the palace, the walls and ceilings were bright with gilding, rich with elaborate carving, and resplendent with gallant pictures of Venetian victories in war, and Venetian display in foreign courts, and hallowed with portraits of the Virgin, the Saviour of men, and the holy saints that preached the Gospel of Peace upon earth — but here, in dismal contrast, were none but pictures of death and dreadful suffering! — not a living figure but was writhing in torture, not a dead one but was smeared with blood, gashed with wounds, and distorted with the agonies that had taken away its life!

From the palace to the gloomy prison is but a
step — one might almost jump across the narrow
canal that intervenes. The ponderous stone Bridge
of Sighs crosses it at the second story — a bridge
that is a covered tunnel — you cannot be seen when
you walk in it. It is partitioned lengthwise, and
through one compartment walked such as bore light
sentences in ancient times, and through the other
marched sadly the wretches whom the Three had
doomed to lingering misery and utter oblivion in the
dungeons, or to sudden and mysterious death.
Down below the level of the water, by the light of
smoking torches, we were shown the damp, thick-
walled cells where many a proud patrician's life was
eaten away by the long-drawn miseries of solitary
imprisonment — without light, air, books; naked,
unshaven, uncombed, covered with vermin; his useless tongue forgetting its office, with none to speak
to; the days and nights of his life no longer marked,
but merged into one eternal eventless night; far
away from all cheerful sounds, buried in the silence
of a tomb; forgotten by his helpless friends, and
his fate a dark mystery to them forever; losing his
own memory at last, and knowing no more who he
was or how he came there; devouring the loaf of
bread and drinking the water that were thrust into
the cell by unseen hands, and troubling his worn
spirit no more with hopes and fears and doubts and
longings to be free; ceasing to scratch vain prayers
and complainings on walls where none, not even

himself, could see them, and resigning himself to
hopeless apathy, driveling childishness, lunacy!
Many and many a sorrowful story like this these
stony walls could tell if they could but speak.

In a little narrow corridor, near by, they showed
us where many a prisoner, after lying in the dungeons until he was forgotten by all save his perse-
cutors, was brought by masked executioners and
garroted, or sewed up in a sack, passed through a
little window to a boat, at dead of night, and taken
to some remote spot and drowned.

They used to show to visitors the implements of
torture wherewith the Three were wont to worm
secrets out of the accused — villainous machines for
crushing thumbs; the stocks where a prisoner sat
immovable while water fell drop by drop upon his
head till the torture was more than humanity could
bear; and a devilish contrivance of steel, which inclosed a prisoner's head like a shell, and crushed it
slowly by means of a screw. It bore the stains of
blood that had trickled through its joints long ago,
and on one side it had a projection whereon the tor-
turer rested his elbow comfortably and bent down
his ear to catch the moanings of the sufferer perishing within.

Of course, we went to see the venerable relic of
the ancient glory of Venice, with its pavements worn
and broken by the passing feet of a thousand years
of plebeians and patricians — The Cathedral of St.
Mark. It is built entirely of precious marbles,

19.

brought from the Orient — nothing in its composition is domestic. Its hoary traditions make it an object of absorbing interest to even the most careless stranger, and thus far it had interest for me; but no further. I could not go into ecstasies over its coarse mosaics, its unlovely Byzantine architecture, or its five hundred curious interior columns from as many distant quarries. Everything was worn out — every block of stone was smooth and almost shapeless with the polishing hands and shoulders of loungers who devoutly idled here in bygone centuries and have died and gone to the dev — no, simply died, I mean.

Under the altar repose the ashes of St. Mark — and Matthew, Luke, and John, too, for all I know. Venice reveres those relics above all things earthly. For fourteen hundred years St. Mark has been her patron saint. Everything about the city seems to be named after him or so named as to refer to him in some way — so named, or some purchase rigged in some way to scrape a sort of hurrahing acquaintance with him. That seems to be the idea. To be on good terms with St. Mark seems to be the very summit of Venetian ambition. They say St. Mark had a tame lion, and used to travel with him — and everywhere that St. Mark went, the lion was sure to go. It was his protector, his friend, his librarian. And so the Winged Lion of St. Mark, with the open Bible under his paw, is a favorite emblem in the grand old city. It casts its shadow from the most

ancient pillar in Venice, in the Grand Square of St.
Mark, upon the throngs of free citizens below, and
has so done for many a long century. The winged
lion is found everywhere — and doubtless here,
where the winged lion is, no harm can come.

St. Mark died at Alexandria, in Egypt. He was
martyred, I think. However, that has nothing to
do with my legend. About the founding of the city
of Venice — say four hundred and fifty years after
Christ (for Venice is much younger that any other
Italian city) — a priest dreamed that an angel told
him that until the remains of St. Mark were brought
to Venice, the city could never rise to high distinction among the nations; that the body must be
captured, brought to the city, and a magnificent
church built over it; and that if ever the Venetians
allowed the Saint to be removed from his new resting place, in that day Venice would perish from off
the face of the earth. The priest proclaimed his
dream, and forthwith Venice set about procuring the
corpse of St. Mark. One expedition after another
tried and failed, but the project was never abandoned
during four hundred years. At last it was secured
by stratagem, in the year eight hundred and something. The commander of a Venetian expedition
disguised himself, stole the bones, separated them,
and packed them in vessels filled with lard. The
religion of Mahomet causes its devotees to abhor
anything that is in the nature of pork, and so when
the Christian was stopped by the officers at the

8.

gates of the city, they only glanced once into his precious baskets, then turned up their noses at the unholy lard, and let him go. The bones were buried in the vaults of the grand cathedral, which had been waiting long years to receive them, and thus the safety and the greatness of Venice were secured. And to this day there be those in Venice who believe that if those holy ashes were stolen away, the ancient city would vanish like a dream, and its foundations be buried forever in the unremembering sea.

CHAPTER XXIII.

THE Venetian gondola is as free and graceful, in its gliding movement, as a serpent. It is twenty or thirty feet long, and is narrow and deep, like a canoe; its sharp bow and stern sweep upward from the water like the horns of a crescent with the abruptness of the curve slightly modified.

The bow is ornamented with a steel comb with a battle-axe attachment which threatens to cut passing boats in two occasionally, but never does. The gondola is painted black because in the zenith of Venetian magnificence the gondolas became too gorgeous altogether, and the Senate decreed that all such display must cease, and a solemn, unembellished black be substituted. If the truth were known, it would doubtless appear that rich plebeians grew too prominent in their affectation of patrician show on the Grand Canal, and required a wholesome snubbing. Reverence for the hallowed Past and its traditions keeps the dismal fashion in force now that the compulsion exists no longer. So let it remain. It is the color of mourning. Venice mourns. The stern of the boat is decked over and the gondolier

(293)

stands there. He uses a single oar — a long blade,
of course, for he stands nearly erect. A wooden
peg, a foot and a half high, with two slight crooks
or curves in one side of it and one in the other,
projects above the starboard gunwale. Against that
peg the gondolier takes a purchase with his oar,
changing it at intervals to the other side of the peg
or dropping it into another of the crooks, as the
steering of the craft may demand — and how in the
world he can back and fill, shoot straight ahead, or
flirt suddenly around a corner, and make the oar
stay in those insignificant notches, is a problem to
me and a never-diminishing matter of interest. I
am afraid I study the gondolier's marvelous skill
more than I do the sculptured palaces we glide
among. He cuts a corner so closely, now and then,
or misses another gondola by such an imperceptible
hair-breadth, that I feel myself " scrooching," as the
children say, just as one does when a buggy wheel
grazes his elbow. But he makes all his calculations
with the nicest precision, and goes darting in and
out among a Broadway confusion of busy craft with
the easy confidence of the educated hackman. He
never makes a mistake.

Sometimes we go flying down the great canals at
such a gait that we can get only the merest glimpses
into front doors, and again, in obscure alleys in the
suburbs, we put on a solemnity suited to the silence,
the mildew, the stagnant waters, the clinging weeds,
the deserted houses, and the general lifelessness

of the place, and move to the spirit of grave meditation.

The gondolier *is* a picturesque rascal for all he wears no satin harness, no plumed bonnet, no silken tights. His attitude is stately; he is lithe and supple; all his movements are full of grace. When his long canoe, and his fine figure, towering from its high perch on the stern, are cut against the evening sky, they make a picture that is very novel and striking to a foreign eye.

We sit in the cushioned carriage-body of a cabin, with the curtains drawn, and smoke, or read, or look out upon the passing boats, the houses, the bridges, the people, and enjoy ourselves much more than we could in a buggy jolting over our cobblestone pavements at home. This is the gentlest, pleasantest locomotion we have ever known.

But it seems queer — ever so queer — to see a boat doing duty as a private carriage. We see business men come to the front door, step into a gondola, instead of a street car, and go off down town to the counting-room.

We see visiting young ladies stand on the stoop, and laugh, and kiss good-bye, and flirt their fans and say " Come soon — now *do* — you've been just as mean as ever you can be — mother's dying to see you — and we've moved into the new house, oh, such a love of a place ! — so convenient to the post-office and the church, and the Young Men's Christian Association; and we do have such fishing, and

such carrying on, and *such* swimming-matches in
the back yard — Oh, you *must* come — no distance
at all, and if you go down through by St. Mark's
and the Bridge of Sighs, and cut through the alley
and come up by the church of Santa Maria dei
Frari, and into the Grand Canal, there isn't a *bit* of
current — now *do* come, Sally Maria — by-bye!"
and then the little humbug trips down the steps,
jumps into the gondola, says, under her breath,
"Disagreeable old thing, I hope she *won't!*"
goes skimming away, round the corner; and the
other girl slams the street door and says, "Well,
that infliction's over, anyway, — but I suppose I've
got to go and see her — tiresome, stuck-up thing!"
Human nature appears to be just the same, all over
the world. We see the diffident young man, mild
of moustache, affluent of hair, indigent of brain,
elegant of costume, drive up to *her* father's mansion, tell his hackman to bail out and wait, start
fearfully up the steps and meet "the old gentleman" right on the threshold! — hear him ask what
street the new British Bank is in — as if *that* were
what he came for — and then bounce into his boat
and skurry away with his coward heart in his boots!
— see him come sneaking around the corner again,
directly, with a crack of the curtain open toward the
old gentleman's disappearing gondola, and out
scampers his Susan with a flock of little Italian en-
dearments fluttering from her lips, and goes to drive
with him in the watery avenues down toward the Rialto.

We see the ladies go out shopping, in the most natural way, and flit from street to street and from store to store, just in the good old fashion, except that they leave the gondola, instead of a private carriage, waiting at the curbstone a couple of hours for them,— waiting while they make the nice young clerks pull down tons and tons of silks and velvets and moire antiques and those things; and then they buy a paper of pins and go paddling away to confer the rest of their disastrous patronage on some other firm. And they always have their purchases sent home just in the good old way. Human nature is *very* much the same all over the world; and it is *so* like my dear native home to see a Venetian lady go into a store and buy ten cents' worth of blue ribbon and have it sent home in a scow. Ah, it is these little touches of nature that move one to tears in these far-off foreign lands.

We see little girls and boys go out in gondolas with their nurses, for an airing. We see staid families, with prayer book and beads, enter the gondola dressed in their Sunday best, and float away to church. And at midnight we see the theater break up and discharge its swarm of hilarious youth and beauty; we hear the cries of the hackman-gondoliers, and behold the struggling crowd jump aboard, and the black multitude of boats go skimming down the moonlit avenues; we see them separate here and there, and disappear up divergent streets; we hear the faint sounds of laughter and of

shouted farewells floating up out of the distance;
and then, the strange pageant being gone, we have
lonely stretches of glittering water — of stately
buildings — of blotting shadows — of weird stone
faces creeping into the moonlight — of deserted
bridges — of motionless boats at anchor. And
over all broods that mysterious stillness, that
stealthy quiet, that befits so well this old dreaming
Venice.

We have been pretty much everywhere in our
gondola. We have bought beads and photographs
in the stores, and wax matches in the Great Square
of St. Mark. The last remark suggests a digression.
Everybody goes to this vast square in the evening.
The military bands play in the center of it and
countless couples of ladies and gentlemen promenade
up and down on either side, and platoons of them
are constantly drifting away toward the old cathedral, and by the venerable column with the Winged
Lion of St. Mark on its top, and out to where the
boats lie moored; and other platoons are as constantly arriving from the gondolas and joining the
great throng. Between the promenaders and the
sidewalks are seated hundreds and hundreds of people at small tables, smoking and taking *granita* (a
first cousin to ice-cream); on the sidewalks are
more employing themselves in the same way. The
shops in the first floor of the tall rows of buildings that
wall in three sides of the square are brilliantly lighted,
the air is filled with music and merry voices, and

altogether the scene is as bright and spirited and full of cheerfulness as any man could desire. We enjoy it thoroughly. Very many of the young women are exceedingly pretty and dress with rare good taste. We are gradually and laboriously learning the ill-manners of staring them unflinchingly in the face — not because such conduct is agreeable to us, but because it is the custom of the country and they say the girls like it. We wish to learn all the curious, outlandish ways of all the different countries, so that we can " show off " and astonish people when we get home. We wish to excite the envy of our untraveled friends with our strange foreign fashions which we can't shake off. All our passengers are paying strict attention to this thing, with the end in view which I have mentioned. The gentle reader will never, never know what a consummate ass he can become until he goes abroad. I speak now, of course, in the supposition that the gentle reader has not been abroad, and therefore is not already a consummate ass. If the case be otherwise, I beg his pardon and extend to him the cordial hand of fellowship and call him brother. I shall always delight to meet an ass after my own heart when I shall have finished my travels.

On this subject let me remark that there are Americans abroad in Italy who have actually forgotten their mother tongue in three months — forgot it in France. They cannot even write their address in English in a hotel register. I append these evidences, which I copied *verbatim* from the register of a hotel in a certain Italian city:

> " John P. Whitcomb, *États Unis.*
> " William L. Ainsworth, *travailleur* (he meant traveler, I suppose),
> *États Unis.*
> " George P. Morton *et fils, d'Amerique.*
> " Lloyd B. Williams, *et trois amis, ville de* Boston, *Amerique.*
> " J. Ellsworth Baker, *tout de suite de France, place de naissance
> Amerique, destination la Grande Bretagne.*"

I love this sort of people. A lady passenger of ours tells of a fellow-citizen of hers who spent eight weeks in Paris and then returned home and addressed his dearest old bosom friend Herbert as Mr. "Er-bare!" He apologized, though, and said, " 'Pon my soul it is aggravating, but I cahn't help it — I have got so used to speaking nothing but French, my dear Erbare — damme there it goes again! — got so used to French pronunciation that I cahn't get rid of it — it is positively annoying, I assure you." This entertaining idiot, whose name was Gordon, allowed himself to be hailed three times in the street before he paid any attention, and then begged a thousand pardons and said he had grown so accustomed to hearing himself addressed as M'sieu Gor-r-*dong*," with a roll to the r, that he had forgotten the legitimate sound of his name! He wore a rose in his buttonhole; he gave the French salutation — two flips of the hand in front of the face; he called Paris *Pairree* in ordinary English conversation; he carried envelopes bearing foreign postmarks protruding from his breast pocket; he cultivated a moustache and imperial, and did what else he could to suggest to the beholder his pet fancy that he resembled Louis Napoleon — and in a spirit of thankfulness which is entirely unaccountable, considering the slim foundation there was for it, he praised his Maker that he was *as* he was, and went on enjoying his little life just the same as if he really *had* been deliberately designed and erected by the great Architect of the Universe.

Think of our Whitcombs and our Ainsworths and our Williamses writing themselves down in dilapidated French in a foreign hotel register! We laugh at Englishmen, when we are at home, for sticking so sturdily to their national ways and customs, but we look back upon it from abroad very forgivingly. It is not pleasant to see an American thrusting his nationality forward *obtrusively* in a foreign land, but oh, it is pitiable to see him making of himself a thing that is neither male nor female, neither fish, flesh, nor fowl — a poor, miserable, hermaphrodite Frenchman!

Among a long list of churches, art galleries, and such things, visited by us in Venice, I shall mention only one — the Church of Santa Maria dei Frari. It is about five hundred years old, I believe, and stands on twelve hundred thousand piles. In it lie the body of Canova and the heart of Titian, under magnificent monuments. Titian died at the age of almost one hundred years. A plague which swept away fifty thousand lives was raging at the time, and there is notable evidence of the reverence in which the great painter was held, in the fact that to him alone the state permitted a public funeral in all that season of terror and death.

In this church, also, is a monument to the doge Foscari, whose name a once resident of Venice, Lord Byron, has made permanently famous.

The monument to the doge Giovanni Pesaro, in this church, is a curiosity in the way of mortuary adornment. It is eighty feet high and is fronted like some fantastic pagan temple. Against it stand four colossal Nubians, as black as night, dressed in white marble garments. The black legs are bare, and through rents in sleeves and breeches, the skin, of shiny black marble, shows. The artist was as ingenious as his funeral designs were absurd. There are two bronze skeletons bearing scrolls, and two great dragons uphold the sarcophagus. On high, amid all this grotesqueness, sits the departed doge.

In the conventual buildings attached to this church are the state archives of Venice. We did not see them, but they are said to number millions of documents. "They are the records of centuries of the most watchful, observant, and suspicious government that ever existed — in which everything was written down and nothing spoken out." They fill nearly three hundred rooms. Among them are manuscripts from the archives of nearly two thousand families, monasteries, and convents. The secret history of Venice for a thousand years is here — its plots, its

hidden trials, its assassinations, its commissions of
hireling spies and masked bravoes — food, ready to
hand, for a world of dark and mysterious romances.

Yes, I think we have seen all of Venice. We
have seen, in these old churches, a profusion of
costly and elaborate sepulchre ornamentation such
as we never dreamt of before. We have stood in
the dim religious light of these hoary sanctuaries, in
the midst of long ranks of dusty monuments and
effigies of the great dead of Venice, until we seemed
drifting back, back, back, into the solemn past, and
looking upon the scenes and mingling with the peoples of a remote antiquity. We have been in a
half-waking sort of dream all the time. I do not
know how else to describe the feeling. A part of
our being has remained still in the nineteenth century, while another part of it has seemed in some
unaccountable way walking among the phantoms of
the tenth.

We have seen famous pictures until our eyes are
weary with looking at them and refuse to find interest in them any longer. And what wonder, when
there are twelve hundred pictures by Palma the
Younger in Venice and fifteen hundred by Tintoretto? And behold, there are Titians and the works
of other artists in proportion. We have seen
Titian's celebrated Cain and Abel, his David and
Goliah, his Abraham's Sacrifice. We have seen
Tintoretto's monster picture, which is seventy-four
feet long and I do not know how many feet high,

and thought it a very commodious picture. We have seen pictures of martyrs enough, and saints enough, to regenerate the world. I ought not to confess it, but still, since one has no opportunity in America to acquire a critical judgment in art, and since I could not hope to become educated in it in Europe in a few short weeks, I may therefore as well acknowledge with such apologies as may be due, that to me it seemed that when I had seen one of these martyrs I had seen them all. They all have a marked family resemblance to each other, they dress alike, in coarse monkish robes and sandals, they are all bald-headed, they all stand in about the same attitude, and without exception they are gazing heavenward with countenances which the Ainsworths, the Mortons, and the Williamses, *et fils*, inform me are full of "expression." To me there is nothing tangible about these imaginary portraits, nothing that I can grasp and take a living interest in. If great Titian had only been gifted with prophecy, and had skipped a martyr, and gone over to England and painted a portrait of Shakespeare, even as a youth, which we could all have confidence in now, the world down to the latest generations would have forgiven him the lost martyr in the rescued seer. I think posterity could have spared one more martyr for the sake of a great historical picture of Titian's time and painted by his brush — such as Columbus returning in chains from the discovery of a world, for instance. The old

masters did paint some Venetian historical pictures,
and these we did not tire of looking at, notwithstanding representations of the formal introduction of
defunct Doges to the Virgin Mary in regions beyond
the clouds clashed rather harshly with the proprieties,
it seemed to us.

But, humble as we are, and unpretending, in the
matter of art, our researches among the painted
monks and martyrs have not been wholly in vain.
We have striven hard to learn. We have had some
success. We have mastered some things, possibly
of trifling import in the eyes of the learned, but to
us they give pleasure, and we take as much pride in
our little acquirements as do others who have learned
far more, and we love to display them full as well.
When we see a monk going about with a lion and
looking tranquilly up to heaven, we know that that
is St. Mark. When we see a monk with a book
and a pen, looking tranquilly up to heaven, trying
to think of a word, we know that that is St. Matthew.
When we see a monk sitting on a rock, looking tranquilly up to heaven, with a human skull beside him,
and without other baggage, we know that that is St.
Jerome. Because we know that he always went
flying light in the matter of baggage. When we see
a party looking tranquilly up to heaven, unconscious
that his body is shot through and through with
arrows, we know that that is St. Sebastian. When
we see other monks looking tranquilly up to heaven,
but having no trademark, we always ask who those

20*

parties are. We do this because we humbly wish to learn. We have seen thirteen thousand St. Jeromes, and twenty-two thousand St. Marks, and sixteen thousand St. Matthews, and sixty thousand St. Sebastians, and four millions of assorted monks, undesignated, and we feel encouraged to believe that when we have seen some more of these various pictures, and had a larger experience, we shall begin to take an absorbing interest in them like our cultivated countrymen from *Amerique*.

Now it does give me real pain to speak in this almost unappreciative way of the old masters and their martyrs, because good friends of mine in the ship — friends who do thoroughly and conscientiously appreciate them and are in every way competent to discriminate between good pictures and inferior ones — have urged me for my own sake not to make public the fact that I lack this appreciation and this critical discrimination myself. I believe that what I have written and may still write about pictures will give them pain, and I am honestly sorry for it. I even promised that I would hide my uncouth sentiments in my own breast. But alas! I never could keep a promise. I do not blame myself for this weakness, because the fault must lie in my physical organization. It is likely that such a very liberal amount of space was given to the organ which enables me to *make* promises, that the organ which should enable me to keep them was crowded out. But I grieve not. I like no half-way things. I had rather have one faculty nobly developed than two faculties of mere ordinary capacity. I certainly meant to keep that promise, but I find I cannot do it. It is impossible to travel through Italy without speaking of pictures, and can I see them through others' eyes?

If I did not so delight in the grand pictures that are spread before me every day of my life by that monarch of all the old masters, Nature, I should come to believe, sometimes, that I had in me no appreciation of the beautiful, whatsoever.

It seems to me that whenever I glory to think that for once I have discovered an ancient painting that is beautiful and worthy of all praise, the pleasure it gives me is an infallible proof that it is *not* a beautiful picture and not in any wise worthy of commendation. This very thing has occurred more times than I can mention, in Venice. In every single instance the guide has crushed out my swelling enthusiasm with the remark:

" It is nothing — it is of the *Renaissance*."

I did not know what in the mischief the Renaissance was, and so always I had to simply say:

" Ah! so it is — I had not observed it before."

I could not bear to be ignorant before a cultivated negro, the offspring of a South Carolina slave. But it occurred too often for even my self-complacency, did that exasperating " It is nothing — it is of the *Renaissance*." I said at last:

" *Who* is this Renaissance? Where did he come

T.

from? Who gave him permission to cram the Republic with his execrable daubs?"

We learned, then, that Renaissance was not a man; that *renaissance* was a term used to signify what was at best but an imperfect rejuvenation of art. The guide said that after Titian's time and the time of the other great names we had grown so familiar with, high art declined; then it partially rose again — an inferior sort of painters sprang up, and these shabby pictures were the work of their hands. Then I said, in my heat, that I "wished to goodness high art had declined five hundred years sooner." The Renaissance pictures suit me very well, though sooth to say its school were too much given to painting real men and did not indulge enough in martyrs.

The guide I have spoken of is the only one we have had yet who knew anything. He was born in South Carolina, of slave parents. They came to Venice while he was an infant. He has grown up here. He is well educated. He reads, writes, and speaks English, Italian, Spanish, and French, with perfect facility; is a worshiper of art and thoroughly conversant with it; knows the history of Venice by heart and never tires of talking of her illustrious career. He dresses better than any of us, I think, and is daintily polite. Negroes are deemed as good as white people, in Venice, and so this man feels no desire to go back to his native land. His judgment is correct.

I have had another shave. I was writing in our front room this afternoon and trying hard to keep my attention on my work and refrain from looking out upon the canal. I was resisting the soft influences of the climate as well as I could, and endeavoring to overcome the desire to be indolent and happy. The boys sent for a barber. They asked me if I would be shaved. I reminded them of my tortures in Genoa, Milan, Como; of my declaration that I would suffer no more on Italian soil. I said: "Not any for me, if you please."

I wrote on. The barber began on the doctor. I heard him say:

"Dan, this is the easiest shave I have had since we left the ship."

He said again, presently:

"Why, Dan, a man could go to sleep with this man shaving him."

Dan took the chair. Then he said:

"Why, this is Titian. This is one of the old masters."

I wrote on. Directly Dan said:

"Doctor, it is perfect luxury. The ship's barber isn't anything to him."

My rough beard was distressing me beyond measure. The barber was rolling up his apparatus. The temptation was too strong. I said:

"Hold on, please. Shave me also."

I sat down in the chair and closed my eyes. The barber soaped my face, and then took his razor and

gave me a rake that well nigh threw me into convul-
sions. I jumped out of the chair: Dan and the
doctor were both wiping blood off their faces and
laughing.

I said it was a mean, disgraceful fraud.

They said that the misery of this shave had gone
so far beyond anything they had ever experienced
before, that they could not bear the idea of losing
such a chance of hearing a cordial opinion from me
on the subject.

It was shameful. But there was no help for it.
The skinning was begun and had to be finished.
The tears flowed with every rake, and so did the
fervent execrations. The barber grew confused,
and brought blood every time. I think the boys
enjoyed it better than anything they have seen or
heard since they left home.

We have seen the Campanile, and Byron's house,
and Balbi's the geographer, and the palaces of all
the ancient dukes and doges of Venice, and we have
seen their effeminate descendants airing their nobility
in fashionable French attire in the Grand Square of
St. Mark, and eating ices and drinking cheap wines,
instead of wearing gallant coats of mail and destroy-
ing fleets and armies as their great ancestors did in
the days of Venetian glory. We have seen no
bravoes with poisoned stilettoes, no masks, no wild
carnival; but we have seen the ancient pride of
Venice, the grim Bronze Horses that figure in a
thousand legends. Venice may well cherish them,

for they are the only horses she ever had. It is said there are hundreds of people in this curious city who never have seen a living horse in their lives. It is entirely true, no doubt.

And so, having satisfied ourselves, we depart to-morrow, and leave the venerable Queen of the Republics to summon her vanished ships, and marshal her shadowy armies, and know again in dreams the pride of her old renown.

CHAPTER XXIV.

SOME of the *Quaker City's* passengers had arrived in Venice from Switzerland and other lands before we left there, and others were expected every day. We heard of no casualties among them, and no sickness.

We were a little fatigued with sightseeing, and so we rattled through a good deal of country by rail without caring to stop. I took few notes. I find no mention of Bologna in my memorandum book, except that we arrived there in good season, but saw none of the sausages for which the place is so justly celebrated.

Pistoia awoke but a passing interest.

Florence pleased us for a while. I think we appreciated the great figure of David in the grand square, and the sculptured group they call the Rape of the Sabines. We wandered through the endless collections of paintings and statues of the Pitti and Uffizzi galleries, of course. I make that statement in self-defense; there let it stop. I could not rest under the imputation that I visited Florence and did not traverse its weary miles of picture galleries. We tried indolently to recollect something about the Guelphs and Ghibelines and the other historical cut-throats whose quarrels and assassinations make up so large a share of Florentine history, but the subject was not attractive. We had been robbed of all the fine mountain scenery on our little journey by a system of railroading that had three miles of tunnel to a hundred yards of daylight, and we were not inclined to be sociable with Florence. We had seen the spot, outside the city somewhere, where these people had allowed the bones of Galileo to rest in unconsecrated ground for an age because his great discovery that the world turned around was regarded as a damning heresy by the church; and we know that long after the world had accepted his theory and raised his name high in the list of its great men, they had still let him rot there. That we had lived to see his dust in honored sepulture in the Church of Santa Croce we owed to a society of *literati*, and not to Florence or her rulers. We saw Dante's tomb in that church, also, but we were glad to know that his body was not in it; that the ungrateful city that had exiled him and persecuted him would give much to have it there, but need not hope to ever secure that high honor to herself. Medicis are good enough for Florence. Let her plant Medicis and build grand monuments over them to testify how gratefully she was wont to lick the hand that scourged her.

Magnanimous Florence! Her jewelry marts are

filled with artists in mosaic. Florentine mosaics are the choicest in all the world. Florence loves to have that said. Florence is proud of it. Florence would foster this specialty of hers. She is grateful to the artists that bring to her this high credit and fill her coffers with foreign money, and so she encourages them with pensions. With pensions! Think of the lavishness of it. She knows that people who piece together the beautiful trifles die early, because the labor is so confining, and so exhausting to hand and brain, and so she has decreed that all these people who reach the age of sixty shall have a pension after that! I have not heard that any of them have called for their dividends yet. One man did fight along till he was sixty, and started after his pension, but it appeared that there had been a mistake of a year in his family record, and so he gave it up and died. These artists will take particles of stone or glass no larger than a mustard seed, and piece them together on a sleeve-button or a shirt-stud, so smoothly and with such nice adjustment of the delicate shades of color the pieces bear, as to form a pigmy rose with stem, thorn, leaves, petals complete, and all as softly and as truthfully tinted as though Nature had builded it herself. They will counterfeit a fly, or a high-toned bug, or the ruined Coliseum, within the cramped circle of a breastpin, and do it so deftly and so neatly that any man might think a master painted it.

I saw a little table in the great mosaic school in

Florence — a little trifle of a center-table — whose top was made of some sort of precious polished stone, and in the stone was inlaid the figure of a flute, with bell-mouth and a mazy complication of keys. No painting in the world could have been softer or richer; no shading out of one tint into another could have been more perfect; no work of art of any kind could have been more faultless than this flute, and yet to count the multitude of little fragments of stone of which they swore it was formed would bankrupt any man's arithmetic! I do not think one could have seen where two particles joined each other with eyes of ordinary shrewdness. Certainly *we* could detect no such blemish. This table top cost the labor of one man for ten long years, so they said, and it was for sale for thirty-five thousand dollars.

We went to the Church of Santa Croce, from time to time, in Florence, to weep over the tombs of Michael Angelo, Raphael, and Machiavelli (I suppose they are buried there, but it may be that they reside elsewhere and rent their tombs to other parties — such being the fashion in Italy), and between times we used to go and stand on the bridges and admire the Arno. It is popular to admire the Arno. It is a great historical creek with four feet in the channel and some scows floating around. It would be a very plausible river if they would pump some water into it. They all call it a river, and they honestly think it *is* a river, do these dark and

bloody Florentines. They even help out the delusion by building bridges over it. I do not see why
they are too good to wade.

How the fatigues and annoyances of travel fill one
with bitter prejudices sometimes! I might enter
Florence under happier auspices a month hence and
find it all beautiful, all attractive. But I do not
care to think of it now, at all, nor of its roomy
shops filled to the ceiling with snowy marble and
alabaster copies of all the celebrated sculptures in
Europe — copies so enchanting to the eye that I
wonder how they can really be shaped like the dingy
petrified nightmares they are the portraits of. I
got lost in Florence at nine o'clock, one night, and
stayed lost in that labyrinth of narrow streets and
long rows of vast buildings that look all alike, until
toward three o'clock in the morning. It was a
pleasant night and at first there were a good many
people abroad, and there were cheerful lights about.
Later, I grew accustomed to prowling about mysterious drifts and tunnels and astonishing and interesting myself with com ng around corners expecting
to find the hotel staring me in the face, and not finding it doing anything of the kind. Later still, I felt
tired. I soon felt remarkably tired. But there was
no one abroad, now — not even a policeman. I
walked till I was out of all patience, and very hot
and thirsty. At last, somewhere after one o'clock,
I came unexpectedly to one of the city gates. I
knew then that I was very far from the hotel. The

soldiers thought I wanted to leave the city, and they sprang up and barred the way with their muskets. I said:

" Hotel d'Europe!"

It was all the Italian I knew, and I was not certain whether that was Italian or French. The soldiers looked stupidly at each other and at me, and shook their heads and took me into custody. I said I wanted to go home. They did not understand me. They took me into the guard-house and searched me, but they found no sedition on me. They found a small piece of soap (we carry soap with us now), and I made them a present of it, seeing that they regarded it as a curiosity. I continued to say Hotel d'Europe, and they continued to shake their heads, until at last a young soldier nodding in the corner roused up and said something. He said ne knew where the hotel was, I suppose, for the officer of the guard sent him away with me. We walked a hundred or a hundred and fifty miles, it appeared to me, and then *he* got lost. He turned this way and that, and finally gave it up and signified that he was going to spend the remainder of the morning trying to find the city gate again. At that moment it struck me that there was something familiar about the house over the way. It was the hotel!

It was a happy thing for me that there happened to be a soldier there that knew even as much as he did; for they say that the policy of the government is to change the soldiery from one place to another constantly and from country to city, so that they cannot become acquainted with the people and grow lax in their duties and enter into plots and conspiracies with friends. My experiences of Florence were chiefly unpleasant. I will change the subject.

At Pisa we climbed up to the top of the strangest structure the world has any knowledge of — the Leaning Tower. As every one knows, it is in the neighborhood of one hundred and eighty feet high — and I beg to observe that one hundred and eighty feet reach to about the height of four ordinary three-story buildings piled one on top of the other, and is a very considerable altitude for a tower of uniform thickness to aspire to, even when it stands upright — yet this one leans more than thirteen feet out of the perpendicular. It is seven hundred years old, but neither history nor tradition say whether it was built as it is, purposely, or whether one of its sides has settled. There is no record that it ever stood straight up. It is built of marble. It is an airy and a beautiful structure, and each of its eight stories is encircled by fluted columns, some of marble and some of granite, with Corinthian capitals that were handsome when they were new. It is a bell tower, and in its top hangs a chime of ancient bells. The winding staircase within is dark, but one always knows which side of the tower he is on because of his naturally gravitating from one side to the other of the staircase with the rise or dip of the

tower. Some of the stone steps are foot-worn only
on one end; others only on the other end; others
only in the middle. To look down into the tower
from the top is like looking down into a tilted well.
A rope that hangs from the center of the top
touches the wall before it reaches the bottom.
Standing on the summit, one does not feel altogether
comfortable when he looks down from the high
side; but to crawl on your breast to the verge on
the lower side and try to stretch your neck out far
enough to see the base of the tower, makes your
flesh creep, and convinces you for a single moment,
in spite of all your philosophy, that the building is
falling. You handle yourself very carefully, all the
time, under the silly impression that if it is *not* falling your trifling weight will start it unless you are
particular not to " bear down " on it.

The Duomo, close at hand, is one of the finest
cathedrals in Europe. It is eight hundred years
old. Its grandeur has outlived the high commercial
prosperity and the political importance that made it
a necessity, or rather a possibility. Surrounded by
poverty, decay, and ruin, it conveys to us a more
tangible impression of the former greatness of Pisa
than books could give us.

The Baptistery, which is a few years older than
the Leaning Tower, is a stately rotunda of huge
dimensions, and was a costly structure. In it hangs
the lamp whose measured swing suggested to Galileo
the pendulum. It looked an insignificant thing to

have conferred upon the world of science and
mechanics such a mighty extension of their dominions as it has. Pondering, in its suggestive presence, I seemed to see a crazy universe of swinging
disks, the toiling children of this sedate parent. He
appeared to have an intelligent expression about him
of knowing that he was not a lamp at all; that he
was a Pendulum; a pendulum disguised, for prodigious and inscrutable purposes of his own deep
devising, and not a common pendulum either, but
the old original patriarchal Pendulum — the Abraham
Pendulum of the world.

This Baptistery is endowed with the most pleasing
echo of all the echoes we have read of. The guide
sounded two sonorous notes, about half an octave
apart; the echo answered with the most enchanting,
the most melodious, the richest blending of sweet
sounds that one can imagine. It was like a long-
drawn chord of a church organ, infinitely softened
by distance. I may be extravagant in this matter,
but if this be the case my ear is to blame — not my
pen. I am describing a memory — and one that will
remain long with me.

The peculiar devotional spirit of the olden time,
which placed a higher confidence in outward forms
of worship than in the watchful guarding of the
heart against sinful thoughts and the hands against
sinful deeds, and which believed in the protecting
virtues of inanimate objects made holy by contact
with holy things, is illustrated in a striking manner

in one of the cemeteries of Pisa. The tombs are set in soil brought in ships from the Holy Land ages ago. To be buried in such ground was regarded by the ancient Pisans as being more potent for salvation than many masses purchased of the church and the vowing of many candles to the Virgin.

Pisa is believed to be about three thousand years old. It was one of the twelve great cities of ancient Etruria, that commonwealth which has left so many monuments in testimony of its extraordinary advancement, and so little history of itself that is tangible and comprehensible. A Pisan antiquarian gave me an ancient tear-jug which he averred was full four thousand years old. It was found among the ruins of one of the oldest of the Etruscan cities. He said it came from a tomb, and was used by some bereaved family in that remote age when even the Pyramids of Egypt were young, Damascus a village, Abraham a prattling infant and ancient Troy not yet dreamt of, to receive the tears wept for some lost idol of a household. It spoke to us in a language of its own; and with a pathos more tender than any words might bring, its mute eloquence swept down the long roll of the centuries with its tale of a vacant chair, a familiar footstep missed from the threshold, a pleasant voice gone from the chorus, a vanished form! — a tale which is always so new to us, so startling, so terrible, so benumbing to the senses, and behold how threadbare and old it is! No shrewdly-worded history could have brought the

21.

myths and shadows of that old dreamy age before us clothed with human flesh and warmed with human sympathies so vividly as did this poor little unsentient vessel of pottery.

Pisa was a republic in the Middle Ages, with a government of her own, armies and navies of her own, and a great commerce. She was a warlike power, and inscribed upon her banners many a brilliant fight with Genoese and Turks. It is said that the city once numbered a population of four hundred thousand; but her scepter has passed from her grasp now, her ships and her armies are gone, her commerce is dead. Her battle-flags bear the mold and the dust of centuries, her marts are deserted, she has shrunken far within her crumbling walls, and her great population has diminished to twenty thousand souls. She has but one thing left to boast of, and that is not much; viz., she is the second city of Tuscany.

We reached Leghorn in time to see all we wished to see of it long before the city gates were closed for the evening, and then came on board the ship.

We felt as though we had been away from home an age. We never entirely appreciated, before, what a very pleasant den our state-room is; nor how jolly it is to sit at dinner in one's own seat in one's own cabin, and hold familiar conversation with friends in one's own language. Oh, the rare happiness of comprehending every single word that is said, and knowing that every word one says in return will be understood as well! We would talk ourselves to death now, only there are only about ten passengers out of the sixty-five to talk to. The others are wandering, we hardly know where. We shall not go ashore in Leghorn. We are surfeited with Italian cities for the present, and much prefer to walk the familiar quarter-deck and view this one from a distance.

The stupid magnates of this Leghorn government cannot understand that so large a steamer as ours could cross the broad Atlantic with no other purpose than to indulge a party of ladies and gentlemen in a pleasure excursion. It looks too improbable. It is suspicious, they think. Something more important must be hidden behind it all. They cannot under-stand it, and they scorn the evidence of the ship's papers. They have decided at last that we are a battalion of incendiary, blood-thirsty Garibaldians in disguise! And in all seriousness they have set a gunboat to watch the vessel night and day, with orders to close down on any revolutionary movement in a twinkling! Police-boats are on patrol duty about us all the time, and it is as much as a sailor's liberty is worth to show himself in a red shirt. These policemen follow the executive officer's boat from shore to ship and from ship to shore, and watch his dark maneuvers with a vigilant eye. They will arrest him yet unless he assumes an expression of countenance that shall have less of carnage, insur-rection, and sedition in it. A visit paid in a friendly

U*

way to General Garibaldi yesterday (by cordial invitation) by some of our passengers, has gone far to confirm the dread suspicions the government harbors toward us. It is thought the friendly visit was only the cloak of a bloody conspiracy. These people draw near and watch us when we bathe in the sea from the ship's side. Do they think we are communing with a reserve force of rascals at the bottom?

It is said that we shall probably be quarantined at Naples. Two or three of us prefer not to run this risk. Therefore, when we are rested, we propose to go in a French steamer to Civita Vecchia, and from thence to Rome, and by rail to Naples. They do not quarantine the cars, no matter where they got their passengers from.

CHAPTER XXV.

THERE are a good many things about this Italy which I do not understand — and more especially I cannot understand how a bankrupt government can have such palatial railroad depots and such marvels of turnpikes. Why, these latter are as hard as adamant, as straight as a line, as smooth as a floor, and as white as snow. When it is too dark to see any other object, one can still see the white turnpikes of France and Italy; and they are clean enough to eat from, without a table-cloth. And yet no tolls are charged.

As for the railways — we have none like them. The cars slide as smoothly along as if they were on runners. The depots are vast palaces of cut marble, with stately colonnades of the same royal stone traversing them from end to end, and with ample walls and ceilings richly decorated with frescoes. The lofty gateways are graced with statues, and the broad floors are all laid in polished flags of marble.

These things win me more than Italy's hundred galleries of priceless art treasures, because I can understand the one and am not competent to appre-

ciate the other. In the turnpikes, the railways, the
depots, and the new boulevards of uniform houses
in Florence and other cities here, I see the genius of
Louis Napoleon, or rather, I see the works of that
statesman imitated. But Louis has taken care that
in France there shall be a foundation for these im-
provements — money. He has always the where-
withal to back up his projects; they strengthen
France and never weaken her. Her material prosperity is genuine. But here the case is different.
This country is bankrupt. There is no real foundation for these great works. The prosperity they
would seem to indicate is a pretense. There is no
money in the treasury, and so they enfeeble her
instead of strengthening. Italy has achieved the
dearest wish of her heart and become an independent
state — and in so doing she has drawn an elephant
in the political lottery. She has nothing to feed it
on. Inexperienced in government, she plunged into
all manner of useless expenditure, and swamped her
treasury almost in a day. She squandered millions
of francs on a navy which she did not need, and the
first time she took her new toy into action she got
it knocked higher than Gilderoy's kite — to use the
language of the Pilgrims.

But it is an ill-wind that blows nobody good. A
year ago, when Italy saw utter ruin staring her in
the face and her greenbacks hardly worth the paper
they were printed on, her Parliament ventured upon
a *coup de main* that would have appalled the stoutest

of her statesmen under less desperate circumstances.
They, in a manner, confiscated the domains of the
Church! This in priest-ridden Italy! This in a
land which has groped in the midnight of priestly
superstition for sixteen hundred years! It was a
rare good fortune for Italy, the stress of weather
that drove her to break from this prison-house.

They do not call it *confiscating* the church property. That would sound too harshly yet. But it
amounts to that. There are thousands of churches
in Italy, each with untold millions of treasures stored
away in its closets, and each with its battalion of
priests to be supported. And then there are the
estates of the Church — league on league of the
richest lands and the noblest forests in all Italy — all
yielding immense revenues to the Church, and none
paying a cent in taxes to the state. In some great
districts the Church owns *all* the property — lands,
water-courses, woods, mills and factories. They buy,
they sell, they manufacture, and since they pay no
taxes, who can hope to compete with them!

Well, the government has seized all this in effect,
and will yet seize it in rigid and unpoetical reality,
no doubt. Something must be done to feed a
starving treasury, and there is no other resource in
all Italy — none but the riches of the Church. So the
government intends to take to itself a great portion
of the revenues arising from priestly farms, factories,
etc., and also intends to take possession of the
churches and carry them on, after its own fashion

and upon its own responsibility. In a few instances
it will leave the establishments of great pet churches
undisturbed, but in all others only a handful of
priests will be retained to preach and pray, a few will
be pensioned, and the balance turned adrift.

Pray glance at some of these churches and their
embellishments, and see whether the government is
doing a righteous thing or not. In Venice, to-day,
a city of a hundred thousand inhabitants, there are
twelve hundred priests. Heaven only knows how
many there were before the Parliament reduced their
numbers. There was the great Jesuit Church.
Under the old régime it required sixty priests to
engineer it — the government does it with five now,
and the others are discharged from service. All
about that church wretchedness and poverty abound.
At its door a dozen hats and bonnets were doffed to
us, as many heads were humbly bowed, and as many
hands extended, appealing for pennies — appealing
with foreign words we could not understand, but
appealing mutely, with sad eyes, and sunken cheeks,
and ragged raiment, that no words were needed to
translate. Then we passed within the great doors,
and it seemed that the riches of the world were
before us! Huge columns carved out of single
masses of marble, and inlaid from top to bottom
with a hundred intricate figures wrought in costly
verde antique; pulpits of the same rich materials,
whose draperies hung down in many a pictured fold,
the stony fabric counterfeiting the delicate work of

the loom; the grand altar brilliant with polished
facings and balustrades of oriental agate, jasper,
verde antique, and other precious stones, whose
names, even, we seldom hear — and slabs of priceless lapis lazuli lavished everywhere as recklessly as
if the church had owned a quarry of it. In the
midst of all this magnificence, the solid gold and
silver furniture of the altar seemed cheap and trivial.
Even the floors and ceilings cost a princely fortune.

Now, where is the use of allowing all those riches
to lie idle, while half of that community hardly
know, from day to day, how they are going to keep
body and soul together? And, where is the wisdom
in permitting hundreds upon hundreds of millions of
francs to be locked up in the useless trumpery of
churches all over Italy, and the people ground to
death with taxation to uphold a perishing government?

As far as I can see, Italy, for fifteen hundred
years, has turned all her energies, all her finances,
and all her industry to the building up of a vast
array of wonderful church edifices, and starving half
her citizens to accomplish it. She is to-day one vast
museum of magnificence and misery. All the
churches in an ordinary American city put together
could hardly buy the jeweled frippery in one of her
hundred cathedrals. And for every beggar in
America, Italy can show a hundred — and rags and
vermin to match. It is the wretchedest, princeliest
land on earth.

Look at the grand Duomo of Florence — a vast
pile that has been sapping the purses of her citizens
for five hundred years, and is not nearly finished
yet. Like all other men, I fell down and worshiped it, but when the filthy beggars swarmed
around me the contrast was too striking, too suggestive, and I said, "Oh, sons of classic Italy, *is*
the spirit of enterprise, of self-reliance, of noble
endeavor, utterly dead within ye? Curse your
indolent worthlessness, why don't you rob your
church?"

Three hundred happy, comfortable priests are
employed in that cathedral.

And now that my temper is up, I may as well go
on and abuse everybody I can think of. They have
a grand mausol um in Florence, which they built to
bury our Lord and Saviour and the Medici family
in. It sounds blasphemous, but it is true, and here
they *act* blasphemy. The dead and damned Medicis
who cruelly tyrannized over Florence and were her
curse for over two hundred years, are salted away in
a circle of costly vaults, and in their midst the Holy
Sepulchre was to have been set up. The expedition
sent to Jerusalem to seize it got into trouble and
could not accompiish the burglary, and so the center
of the mausoleum is vacant now. They say the
entire mausoleum was intended for the Holy Sepulchre, and was only turned into a family burying
place after the Jerusalem expedition failed — but
you will excuse me. Some of those Medicis would

have smuggled themselves in sure. What *they* had not the effrontery to do, was not worth doing. Why, they had their trivial, forgotten exploits on land and sea pictured out in grand frescoes (as did also the ancient doges of Venice) with the Saviour and the Virgin throwing bouquets to them out of the clouds, and the Deity himself applauding from his throne in Heaven! And who painted these things? Why, Titian, Tintoretto, Paul Veronese, Raphael — none other than the world's idols, the " old masters."

Andrea del Sarto glorified his princes in pictures that must save them forever from the oblivion they merited, and they let him starve. Served him right. Raphael pictured such infernal villains as Catherine and Marie de Medici seated in heaven and conversing familiarly with the Virgin Mary and the angels (to say nothing of higher personages), and yet my friends abuse me because I am a little prejudiced against the old masters — because I fail sometimes to see the beauty that is in their productions. I cannot help but see it, now and then, but I keep on protesting against the groveling spirit that could persuade those masters to prostitute their noble talents to the adulation of such monsters as the French, Venetian, and Florentine princes of two and three hundred years ago, all the same.

I am told that the old masters had to do these shameful things for bread, the princes and potentates being the only patrons of art. If a grandly gifted man may drag his pride and his manhood in the dirt for bread rather than starve with the nobility that is in him untainted, the excuse is a valid one. It would excuse theft in Washingtons and Wellingtons, and unchastity in women as well.

But, somehow, I cannot keep that Medici mausoleum out of my memory. It is as large as a church; its pavement is rich enough for the pavement of a king's palace; its great dome is gorgeous with frescoes; its walls are made of — what? Marble? — plaster? — wood? — paper?—No. Red porphyry— verde antique — jasper — oriental agate — alabaster — mother-of-pearl — chalcedony — red coral — lapis lazuli! All the vast walls are made wholly of these precious stones, worked in and in and in together in elaborate patterns and figures, and polished till they glow like great mirrors with the pictured splendors reflected from the dome overhead. And before a statue of one of those dead Medicis reposes a crown that blazes with diamonds and emeralds enough to buy a ship-of-the-line, almost. These are the things the government has its evil eye upon, and a happy thing it will be for Italy when they melt away in the public treasury.

And now —. However, another beggar approaches. I will go out and destroy him, and then come back and write another chapter of vituperation.

Having eaten the friendless orphan — having driven away his comrades — having grown calm and reflective at length — I now feel in a kindlier mood.

I feel that after talking so freely about the priests and the churches, justice demands that if I know anything good about either I ought to say it. I *have* heard of many things that redound to the credit of the priesthood, but the most notable matter that occurs to me now is the devotion one of the mendicant orders showed during the prevalence of the cholera last year. I speak of the Dominican friars — men who wear a coarse, heavy brown robe and a cowl, in this hot climate, and go barefoot. They live on alms altogether, I believe. They must unquestionably love their religion, to suffer so much for it. When the cholera was raging in Naples; when the people were dying by hundreds and hundreds every day; when every concern for the public welfare was swallowed up in selfish private interest, and every citizen made the taking care of himself his sole object, these men banded themselves together and went about nursing the sick and burying the dead. Their noble efforts cost many of them their lives. They laid them down cheerfully, and well they might. Creeds mathematically precise, and hair-splitting niceties of doctrine, are absolutely necessary for the salvation of some kinds of souls, but surely the charity, the purity, the unselfishness that are in the hearts of men like these would save their souls though they were bankrupt in the true religion — which is ours.

One of these fat barefooted rascals came here to Civita Vecchia with us in the little French steamer.

22

There were only half a dozen of us in the cabin. He belonged in the steerage. He was the life of the ship, the bloody-minded son of the Inquisition! He and the leader of the marine band of a French man-of-war played on the piano and sang opera turn about; they sang duets together; they rigged impromptu theatrical costumes and gave us extravagant farces and pantomimes. We got along first-rate with the friar, and were excessively conversational, albeit he could not understand what we said, and certainly he never uttered a word that we could guess the meaning of.

This Civita Vecchia is the finest nest of dirt, vermin, and ignorance we have found yet, except that African perdition they call Tangier, which is just like it. The people here live in alleys two yards wide, which have a smell about them which is peculiar but not entertaining. It is well the alleys are not wider, because they hold as much smell now as a person can stand, and, of course, if they were wider they would hold more, and then the people would die. These alleys are paved with stone, and carpeted with deceased cats, and decayed rags, and decomposed vegetable tops, and remnants of old boots, all soaked with dish-water, and the people sit around on stools and enjoy it. They are indolent, as a general thing, and yet have few pastimes. They work two or three hours at a time, but not hard, and then they knock off and catch flies. This does not require any talent, because they only have to grab — if they do not get the one they are after, they get another. It is all the same to them. They have no partialities. Whichever one they get is the one they want.

They have other kinds of insects, but it does not make them arrogant. They are very quiet, unpretending people. They have more of these kind of things than other communities, but they do not boast.

They are very uncleanly — these people — in face, in person, and dress. When they see anybody with a clean shirt on, it arouses their scorn. The women wash clothes, half the day, at the public tanks in the streets, but they are probably somebody else's. Or may be they keep one set to wear and another to wash; because they never put on any that have ever been washed. When they get done washing, they sit in the alleys and nurse their cubs. They nurse one ash-cat at a time, and the others scratch their backs against the door-post and are happy.

All this country belongs to the Papal states. They do not appear to have any schools here, and only one billiard table. Their education is at a very low stage. One portion of the men go into the military, another into the priesthood, and the rest into the shoemaking business.

They keep up the passport system here, but so they do in Turkey. This shows that the Papal states are as far advanced as Turkey. This fact will be alone sufficient to silence the tongues of malignant calumniators. I had to get my passport *viséd* for Rome in Florence, and then they would not let me come ashore here until a policeman had examined it on the wharf and sent me a permit. They did not even dare to let me take my passport in my hands for twelve hours, I looked so formidable. They judged it best to let me cool down. They thought I wanted to take the town, likely. Little did they know me. I wouldn't have it. They examined my baggage at the depot. They took one of my ablest jokes and read it over carefully twice and then read it backwards. But it was too deep for them. They passed it around, and everybody speculated on it awhile, but it mastered them all.

It was no common joke. At length a veteran officer spelled it over deliberately and shook his head three or four times and said that, in his opinion, it was seditious. That was the first time I felt alarmed. I immediately said I would explain the document, and they crowded around. And so I explained and explained and explained, and they took notes of all I said, but the more I explained the more they could not understand it, and when they desisted at last, I could not even understand it myself. They said they believed it was an incendiary document, leveled at the government. I declared solemnly that it was not, but they only shook their heads and would not be satisfied. Then they consulted a good while; and finally they confiscated

it. I was very sorry for this, because I had worked
a long time on that joke, and took a good deal of
pride in it, and now I suppose I shall never see it
any more. I suppose it will be sent up and filed
away among the criminal archives of Rome, and
will always be regarded as a mysterious infernal
machine which would have blown up like a mine and
scattered the good Pope all around, but for a
miraculous providential interference. And I suppose that all the time I am in Rome the police will
dog me about from place to place because they
think I am a dangerous character.

It is fearfully hot in Civita Vecchia. The streets
are made very narrow and the houses built very
solid and heavy and high, as a protection against
the heat. This is the first Italian town I have seen
which does not appear to have a patron saint. I
suppose no saint but the one that went up in the
chariot of fire could stand the climate.

There is nothing here to see. They have not
even a cathedral, with eleven tons of solid silver
archbishops in the back room; and they do not
show you any moldy buildings that are seven thousand years old; nor any smoke-dried old fire-screens
which are *chef d'œuvres* of Rubens or Simpson, or
Titian or Ferguson, or any of those parties; and
they haven't any bottled fragments of saints, and
not even a nail from the true cross. We are going
to Rome. There is nothing to see here.

22 *

CHAPTER XXVI.

WHAT is it that confers the noblest delight?
What is that which swells a man's breast with
pride above that which any other experience can
bring to him? Discovery! To know that you are
walking where none others have walked; that you
are beholding what human eye has not seen before;
that you are breathing a virgin atmosphere. To
give birth to an idea — to discover a great thought
— an intellectual nugget, right under the dust of a
field that many a brain-plow had gone over before.
To find a new planet, to invent a new hinge, to find
the way to make the lightnings carry your messages.
To be the *first* — that is the idea. To do something, say something, see something, before *anybody*
else — these are the things that confer a pleasure
compared with which other pleasures are tame and
commonplace, other ecstasies cheap and trivial.
Morse, with his first message, brought by his
servant, the lightning; Fulton, in that long-drawn
century of suspense, when he placed his hand upon
the throttle-valve, and lo, the steamboat moved;
Jenner, when his patient with the cow's virus in his

blood, walked through the small-pox hospitals un-
scathed; Howe, when the idea shot through his
brain that for a hundred and twenty generations the
eye had been bored through the wrong end of the
needle; the nameless lord of art who laid down his
chisel in some old age that is forgotten now, and
gloated upon the finished Laocoön; Daguerre, when
he commanded the sun, riding in the zenith, to print
the landscape upon his insignificant silvered plate,
and he obeyed; Columbus, in the Pinta's shrouds,
when he swung his hat above a fabled sea and gazed
abroad upon an unknown world! These are the
men who have really *lived* — who have actually
comprehended what pleasure is — who have crowded
long lifetimes of ecstasy into a single moment.

What is there in Rome for me to see that others
have not seen before me? What is there for me to
touch that others have not touched? What is there
for me to feel, to learn, to hear, to know, that shall
thrill me before it pass to others? What can I discover? Nothing. Nothing whatsoever. One charm
of travel dies here. But if I were only a Roman!
If, added to my own I could be gifted with modern
Roman sloth, modern Roman superstition, and
modern Roman boundlessness of ignorance, what
bewildering worlds of unsuspected wonders I would
discover! Ah, if I were only a habitant of the
Campagna five and twenty miles from Rome!
Then I would travel.

I would go to America, and see, and learn, and

return to the Campagna and stand before my countrymen an illustrious discoverer. I would say:

" I saw there a country which has no overshadowing Mother Church, and yet the people survive. I saw a government which never was protected by foreign soldiers at a cost greater than that required to carry on the government itself. I saw common men and common women who could read; I even saw small children of common country people reading from books; if I dared think you would believe it, I would say they could write, also. In the cities I saw people drinking a delicious beverage made of chalk and water, but never once saw goats driven through their Broadway or their Pennsylvania avenue or their Montgomery street and milked at the doors of the houses. I saw real glass windows in the houses of even the commonest people. Some of the houses are not of stone, nor yet of bricks; I solemnly swear they are made of wood. Houses there will take fire and burn, sometimes — actually burn entirely down, and not leave a single vestige behind. I could state that for a truth, upon my death-bed. And as a proof that the circumstance is not rare, I aver that they have a thing which they call a fire-engine, which vomits forth great streams of water, and is kept always in readiness, by night and by day, to rush to houses that are burning. You would think one engine would be sufficient, but some great cities have a hundred; they keep men hired, and pay them by the month to do nothing

but put out fires. For a certain sum of money other
men will insure that your house shall not burn
down; and if it burns they will pay you for it.
There are hundreds and thousands of schools, and
anybody may go and learn to be wise, like a priest.
In that singular country, if a rich man dies a sinner,
he is damned; he cannot buy salvation with money
for masses. There is really not much use in being
rich, there. Not much use as far as the other world
is concerned, but much, very much use, as concerns
this; because there, if a man be rich, he is very
greatly honored, and can become a legislator, a
governor, a general, a senator, no matter how ignorant an ass he is — just as in our beloved Italy the
nobles hold all the great places, even though sometimes they are born noble idiots. There, if a man
be rich, they give him costly presents, they ask him
to feasts, they invite him to drink complicated
beverages; but if he be poor and in debt, they require him to do that which they term to ‘settle.’
The women put on a different dress almost every
day; the dress is usually fine, but absurd in shape;
the very shape and fashion of it changes twice in a
hundred years; and did I but covet to be called an
extravagant falsifier, I would say it changed even
oftener. Hair does not grow upon the American
women’s heads; it is made for them by cunning
workmen in the shops, and is curled and frizzled
into scandalous and ungodly forms. Some persons
wear eyes of glass which they see through with

facility perhaps, else they would not use them; and in the mouths of some are teeth made by the sacrilegious hand of man. The dress of the men is laughably grotesque. They carry no musket in ordinary life, nor no long-pointed pole; they wear no wide green-lined cloak; they wear no peaked black felt hat, no leathern gaiters reaching to the knee, no goatskin breeches with the hair side out, no hob-nailed shoes, no prodigious spurs. They wear a conical hat termed a 'nail-kag'; a coat of saddest black; a shirt which shows dirt so easily that it has to be changed every month, and is very troublesome; things called pantaloons, which are held up by shoulderstraps, and on their feet they wear boots which are ridiculous in pattern and can stand no wear. Yet dressed in this fantastic garb, these people laughed at *my* costume. In that country, books are so common that it is really no curiosity to see one. Newspapers also. They have a great machine which prints such things by thousands every hour.

"I saw common men there — men who were neither priests nor princes — who yet absolutely owned the land they tilled. It was not rented from the church, nor from the nobles. I am ready to take my oath of this. In that country you might fall from a third-story window three several times, and not mash either a soldier or a priest. The scarcity of such people is astonishing. In the cities you will see a dozen civilians for every soldier, and as many for every priest or preacher. Jews, there, are treated just like human beings, instead of dogs. They can work at any business they please; they can sell brand new goods if they want to; they can keep drugstores; they can practice medicine among Christians; they can even shake hands with Christians if they choose; they can associate with them, just the same as one human being does with another human being; they don't have to stay shut up in one corner of the towns; they can live in any part of a town they like best; it is said they even have the privilege of buying land and houses, and owning them themselves, though I doubt that myself; they never have had to run races naked through the public streets, against jackasses, to please the people in carnival time; there they never have been driven by the soldiers into a church every Sunday for hundreds of years to hear themselves and their religion especially and particularly cursed; at this very day, in that curious country, a Jew is allowed to vote, hold office, yea, get up on a rostrum in the public street and express his opinion of the government if the government don't suit him! Ah, it is wonderful. The common people there know a great deal; they even have the effrontery to complain if they are not properly governed, and to take hold and help conduct the government themselves; if they had laws like ours, which give one dollar of every three a crop produces to the government for taxes, they would have that law altered; instead of paying thirty-three dollars in taxes, out of every one hundred they receive, they complain if they have to pay seven. They are curious people. They do not know when they are well off. Mendicant priests do not prowl among them with baskets begging for the church and eating up their substance. One hardly ever sees a minister of the Gospel going around there in his bare feet, with a basket, begging for subsistence. In that country the preachers are not like our mendicant orders of friars — they have two or three suits of clothing, and they wash sometimes. In that land are mountains far higher than the Alban mountains; the vast Roman Campagna, a hundred miles long and full forty broad, is really small compared to the United States of America; the Tiber, that celebrated river of ours, which stretches its mighty course almost two hundred miles, and which a lad can scarcely throw a stone across at Rome, is not so long, nor yet so wide, as the American Mississippi — nor yet the Ohio, nor even the Hudson. In America the people are absolutely wiser and know much more than their grandfathers did. *They* do not plow with a sharpened stick, nor yet with a three-cornered block of wood that merely scratches the top of the ground. We do that because our fathers did, three thousand years ago, I suppose. But those people have no holy reverence for their ancestors. They plow with a plow that is a sharp, curved blade of iron, and it cuts into the earth full five inches. And this is not all. They cut their grain with a horrid machine that mows down whole fields in a day. If I dared, I would say that sometimes they use a blasphemous plow that works by fire and vapor and tears up an acre of ground in a single hour — but — but — I see by your looks that you do not believe the things I am telling you. Alas, my character is ruined, and I am a branded speaker of untruths."

Of course we have been to the monster Church of St. Peter, frequently. I knew its dimensions. I knew it was a prodigious structure. I knew it was just about the length of the capitol at Washington — say seven hundred and thirty feet. I knew it was three hundred and sixty-four feet wide, and consequently wider than the capitol. I knew that the cross on the top of the dome of the church was four hundred and thirty-eight feet above the ground, and therefore about a hundred or may be a hundred and twenty-five feet higher than the dome of the capitol. Thus I had one gauge. I wished to come as near forming a correct idea of how it was going to look as possible; I had a curiosity to see how much I would err. I erred considerably. St. Peter's did not look nearly so large as the capitol, and certainly not a twentieth part as beautiful, from the outside.

When we reached the door, and stood fairly within the church, it was impossible to comprehend that it was a *very* large building. I had to *cipher* a comprehension of it. I had to ransack my memory for some more similes. St. Peter's is bulky. Its height

and size would represent two of the Washington
capitol set one on top of the other — if the capitol
were wider; or two blocks or two blocks and a half
of ordinary buildings set one on top of the other.
St. Peter's *was* that large, but it could and would
not look so. The trouble was that everything in it
and about it was on such a scale of uniform vastness
that there were no contrasts to judge by — none but
the people, and I had not noticed them. They
were insects. The statues of children holding vases
of holy water were immense, according to the tables
of figures, but so was everything else around them.
The mosaic pictures in the dome were huge, and
were made of thousands and thousands of cubes of
glass as large as the end of my little finger, but
those pictures looked smooth, and gaudy of color,
and in good proportion to the dome. Evidently
they would not answer to measure by. Away down
toward the far end of the church (I thought it was
really clear at the far end, but discovered afterward
that it was in the center, under the dome) stood the
thing they call the *baldacchino* — a great bronze
pyramidal frame-work like that which upholds a
mosquito-bar. It only looked like a considerably
magnified bedstead — nothing more. Yet I knew it
was a good deal more than half as high as Niagara
Falls. It was overshadowed by a dome so mighty
that its own height was snubbed. The four great
square piers or pillars that stand equidistant from
each other in the church, and support the roof, I

could not work up to their real dimensions by any method of comparison. I knew that the faces of each were about the width of a very large dwelling-house front (fifty or sixty feet), and that they were twice as high as an ordinary three-story dwelling, but still they looked small. I tried all the different ways I could think of to compel myself to understand how large St. Peter's was, but with small success. The mosaic portrait of an Apostle who was writing with a pen six feet long seemed only an ordinary Apostle.

But the people attracted my attention after a while. To stand in the door of St. Peter's and look at men down toward its further extremity, two blocks away, has a diminishing effect on them; surrounded by the prodigious pictures and statues, and lost in the vast spaces, they look very much smaller than they would if they stood two blocks away in the open air. I "averaged" a man as he passed me and watched him as he drifted far down by the *baldacchino* and beyond — watched him dwindle to an insignificant school-boy, and then, in the midst of the silent throng of human pigmies gliding about him, I lost him. The church had lately been decorated, on the occasion of a great ceremony in honor of St. Peter, and men were engaged now in removing the flowers and gilt paper from the walls and pillars. As no ladders could reach the great heights, the men swung themselves down from balustrades and the capitals of pilasters by ropes, to do this work. The upper gallery which encircles the inner sweep of the dome is two hundred and forty feet above the floor of the church — very few steeples in America could reach up to it. Visitors always go up there to look down into the church because one gets the best idea of some of the heights and distances from that point. While we stood on the floor one of the workmen swung loose from that gallery at the end of a long rope. I had not supposed, before, that a man *could* look so much like a spider. He was insignificant in size, and his rope seemed only a thread. Seeing that he took up so little space, I could believe the story, then, that ten thousand troops went to St. Peter's once to hear mass, and their commanding officer came afterward, and not finding them, supposed they had not yet arrived. But they were in the church, nevertheless — they were in one of the transepts. Nearly fifty thousand persons assembled in St. Peter's to hear the publishing of the dogma of the Immaculate Conception. It is estimated that the floor of the church affords standing room for — for a large number of people; I have forgotten the exact figures. But it is no matter — it is near enough.

They have twelve small pillars, in St. Peter's, which came from Solomon's Temple. They have, also — which was far more interesting to me — a piece of the true cross, and some nails, and a part of the crown of thorns.

Of course, we ascended to the summit of the

dome, and, of course, we also went up into the gilt
copper ball which is above it. There was room
there for a dozen persons, with a little crowding, and
it was as close and hot as an oven. Some of those
people who are so fond of writing their names in
prominent places had been there before us—a
million or two, I should think. From the dome of
St. Peter's one can see every notable object in
Rome, from the Castle of St. Angelo to the
Coliseum. He can discern the seven hills upon
which Rome is built. He can see the Tiber, and
the locality of the bridge which Horatius kept "in
the brave days of old " when Lars Porsena attempted
to cross it with his invading host. He can see the
spot where the Horatii and the Curiatii fought their
famous battle. He can see the broad green Campagna, stretching away toward the mountains, with
its scattered arches and broken aqueducts of the
olden time, so picturesque in their gray ruin, and so
daintily festooned with vines. He can see the Alban
Mountains, the Apennines, the Sabine Hills, and
the blue Mediterranean. He can see a panorama
that is varied, extensive, beautiful to the eye, and
more illustrious in history than any other in Europe.
About his feet is spread the remnant of a city that
once had a population of four million souls; and
among its massed edifices stand the ruins of temples,
columns, and triumphal arches that knew the
Cæsars, and the noonday of Roman splendor; and
close by them, in unimpaired strength, is a drain of

23

arched and heavy masonry that belonged to that
older city which stood here before Romulus and
Remus were born or Rome thought of. The Appian
Way is here yet, and looking much as it did, perhaps, when the triumphal processions of the emperors moved over it in other days bringing fettered
princes from the confines of the earth. We cannot
see the long array of chariots and mail-clad men
laden with the spoils of conquest, but we can
imagine the pageant, after a fashion. We look out
upon many objects of interest from the dome of St.
Peter's; and last of all, almost at our feet, our eyes
rest upon the building which was once the Inquisition. How times changed, between the older ages
and the new! Some seventeen or eighteen centuries
ago, the ignorant men of Rome were wont to put
Christians in the arena of the Coliseum yonder, and
turn the wild beasts in upon them for a show. It
was for a lesson as well. It was to teach the people
to abhor and fear the new doctrine the followers of
Christ were teaching. The beasts tore the victims
limb from limb and made poor mangled corpses of
them in the twinkling of an eye. But when the
Christians came into power, when the holy Mother
Church became mistress of the barbarians, she
taught them the error of their ways by no such
means. No, she put them in this pleasant Inquisition and pointed to the Blessed Redeemer, who was
so gentle and so merciful toward all men, and they
urged the barbarians to love him; and they did all

they could to persuade them to love and honor him
— first by twisting their thumbs out of joint with a
screw; then by nipping their flesh with pincers —
red-hot ones, because they are the most comfortable
in cold weather; then by skinning them alive a
little, and finally by roasting them in public. They
always convinced those barbarians. The true religion, properly administered, as the good Mother
Church used to administer it, is very, very soothing.
It is wonderfully persuasive, also. There is a great
difference between feeding parties to wild beasts and
stirring up their finer feelings in an Inquisition.
One is the system of degraded barbarians, the other
of enlightened, civilized people. It is a great pity
the playful Inquisition is no more.

I prefer not to describe St. Peter's. It has been
done before. The ashes of Peter, the disciple of
the Saviour, repose in a crypt under the *baldacchino*.
We stood reverently in that place; so did we also in
the Mamertine Prison, where he was confined, where
he converted the soldiers, and where tradition says
he caused a spring of water to flow in order that he
might baptize them. But when they showed us the
print of Peter's face in the hard stone of the prison
wall and said he made that by falling up against it,
we doubted. And when, also, the monk at the
Church of San Sebastian showed us a paving stone
with two great footprints in it and said that Peter's
feet made those, we lacked confidence again. Such
things do not impress one. The monk said that

angels came and liberated Peter from prison by
night, and he started away from Rome by the Appian Way. The Saviour met him and told him to
go back, which he did. Peter left those footprints
in the stone upon which he stood at the time. It
was not stated how it was ever discovered whose
footprints they were, seeing the interview occurred
secretly and at night. The print of the face in the
prison was that of a man of common size; the footprints were those of a man ten or twelve feet high.
The discrepancy confirmed our unbelief.

We necessarily visited the Forum, where Cæsar
was assassinated, and also the Tarpeian Rock. We
saw the Dying Gladiator at the Capitol, and I think
that even we appreciated that wonder of art; as
much, perhaps, as we did that fearful story wrought
in marble, in the Vatican — the Laocoön. And
then the Coliseum.

Everybody knows the picture of the Coliseum;
everybody recognizes at once that "looped and
windowed" band-box with a side bitten out. Being
rather isolated, it shows to better advantage than
any other of the monuments of ancient Rome.
Even the beautiful Pantheon, whose pagan altars
uphold the cross now, and whose Venus, tricked out
in consecrated gimcracks, does reluctant duty as a
Virgin Mary to-day, is built about with shabby
houses and its stateliness sadly marred. But the
monarch of all European ruins, the Coliseum,
maintains that reserve and that royal seclusion which

is proper to majesty. Weeds and flowers spring from its massy arches and its circling seats, and vines hang their fringes from its lofty walls. An impressive silence broods over the monstrous structure where such multitudes of men and women were wont to assemble in other days. The butterflies have taken the places of the queens of fashion and beauty of eighteen centuries ago, and the lizards sun themselves in the sacred seat of the emperor. More vividly than all the written histories, the Coliseum tells the story of Rome's grandeur and Rome's decay. It is the worthiest type of both that exists. Moving about the Rome of to-day, we might find it hard to believe in her old magnificence and her millions of population; but with this stubborn evidence before us that she was obliged to have a theater with sitting room for eighty thousand persons and standing room for twenty thousand more, to accommodate such of her citizens as required amusement, we find belief less difficult. The Coliseum is over one thousand six hundred feet long, seven hundred and fifty wide, and one hundred and sixty-five high. Its shape is oval.

In America we make convicts useful at the same time that we punish them for their crimes. We farm them out and compel them to earn money for the state by making barrels and building roads. Thus we combine business with retribution, and all things are lovely. But in ancient Rome they combined religious duty with pleasure. Since it was

23.

necessary that the new sect called Christians should be exterminated, the people judged it wise to make this work profitable to the state at the same time, and entertaining to the public. In addition to the gladiatorial combats and other shows, they sometimes threw members of the hated sect into the arena of the Coliseum and turned wild beasts in upon them. It is estimated that seventy thousand Christians suffered martyrdom in this place. This has made the Coliseum holy ground, in the eyes of the followers of the Saviour. And well it might; for if the chain that bound a saint, and the footprints a saint has left upon a stone he chanced to stand upon, be holy, surely the spot where a man gave up his life for his faith is holy.

Seventeen or eighteen centuries ago this Coliseum was *the* theater of Rome, and Rome was mistress of the world. Splendid pageants were exhibited here, in presence of the emperor, the great ministers of state, the nobles, and vast audiences of citizens of smaller consequence. Gladiators fought with gladiators and at times with warrior prisoners from many a distant land. It was *the* theater of Rome — of the world — and the man of fashion who could not let fall in a casual and unintentional manner something about "my private box at the Coliseum" could not move in the first circles. When the clothing-store merchant wished to consume the corner-grocery man with envy, he bought secured seats in the front row and let the thing be known. When the irre-

sistible drygoods clerk wished to blight and destroy,
according to his native instinct, he got himself up
regardless of expense and took some other fellow's
young lady to the Coliseum, and then accented the
affront by cramming her with ice-cream between the
acts, or by approaching the cage and stirring up the
martyrs with his whalebone cane for her edification.
The Roman swell was in his true element only when
he stood up against a pillar and fingered his moustache unconscious of the ladies; when he viewed the
bloody combats through an opera-glass two inches
long; when he excited the envy of provincials by
criticisms which showed that he had been to the
Coliseum many and many a time and was long ago
over the novelty of it; when he turned away with a
yawn at last and said:

"*He* a star! handles his sword like an apprentice
brigand! he'll do for the country, maybe, but he
don't answer for the metropolis!"

Glad was the contraband that had a seat in the pit
at the Saturday matinee, and happy the Roman
street boy who ate his peanuts and guyed the gladiators from the dizzy gallery.

For me was reserved the high honor of discover-
ing among the rubbish of the ruined Coliseum the
only playbill of that establishment now extant.
There was a suggestive smell of mint drops about it
still, a corner of it had evidently been chewed, and
on the margin, in choice Latin, these words were
written in a delicate female hand:

W*

"Meet me on the Tarpeian Rock to-morrow evening, dear, @ sharp seven. Mother will be absent on a visit to her friends in the Sabine Hills.   CLAUDIA."

Ah, where is that lucky youth to-day, and where the little hand that wrote those dainty lines? Dust and ashes these seventeen hundred years!

Thus reads the bill:

ROMAN COLISEUM.

UNPARALLELED ATTRACTION!

NEW PROPERTIES! NEW LIONS! NEW GLADIATORS!

Engagement of the renowned

MARCUS MARCELLUS VALERIAN!

FOR SIX NIGHTS ONLY!

The management beg leave to offer to the public an entertainment surpassing in magnificence anything that has heretofore been attempted on any stage. No expense has been spared to make the opening season one which shall be worthy the generous patronage which the management feel sure will crown their efforts. The management beg leave to state that they have succeeded in securing the services of a

GALAXY OF TALENT!

such as has not been beheld in Rome before.

The performance will commence this evening with a

GRAND BROADSWORD COMBAT!

between two young and promising amateurs and a celebrated Parthian gladiator who has just arrived a prisoner from the Camp of Verus.

This will be followed by a grand moral

BATTLE-AX ENGAGEMENT!

between the renowned Valerian (with one hand tied behind him) and two gigantic savages from Britain.

After which the renowned Valerian (if he survive) will fight with the broadsword,

LEFT HANDED!

against six Sophomores and a Freshman from the Gladiatorial College!

A long series of brilliant engagements will follow, in which the finest talent of the Empire will take part.

After which the celebrated Infant Prodigy known as

"THE YOUNG ACHILLES,"

will engage four tiger whelps in combat, armed with no other weapon than his little spear!

The whole to conclude with a chaste and elegant

GENERAL SLAUGHTER!

In which thirteen African Lions and twenty-two Barbarian Prisoners will war with each other until all are exterminated.

BOX OFFICE NOW OPEN.

Dress Circle One Dollar; Children and Servants half price.

An efficient police force will be on hand to preserve order and keep the wild beasts from leaping the railings and discommoding the audience.

Doors open at 7; performance begins at 8.

POSITIVELY NO FREE LIST.

Diodorus Job Press.

It was as singular as it was gratifying that I was also so fortunate as to find among the rubbish of the arena a stained and mutilated copy of the *Roman Daily Battle-Axe*, containing a critique upon this very performance. It comes to hand too late by many centuries to rank as news, and therefore I translate and publish it simply to show how very little the general style and phraseology of dramatic criticism has altered in the ages that have dragged their slow length along since the carriers laid this one damp and fresh before their Roman patrons:

"THE OPENING SEASON. — COLISEUM. — Notwithstanding the inclemency of the weather, quite a respectable number of the rank and fashion of the city assembled last night to witness the debut upon metropolitan boards of the young tragedian who has of late been winning such golden opinions in the amphitheaters of the provinces. Some sixty thousand persons were present, and but for the fact that the streets were almost impassable, it is fair to presume that the house would have been full. His august Majesty, the Emperor Aurelius, occupied the imperial box, and was the cynosure of all eyes. Many illustrious nobles and generals of the Empire graced the occasion with their presence, and not the least among them was the young patrician lieutenant whose laurels, won in the ranks of the 'Thundering Legion,' are still so green upon his brow. The cheer which greeted his entrance was heard beyond the Tiber!

"The late repairs and decorations add both to the comeliness and the comfort of the Coliseum. The new cushions are a great improvement upon the hard marble seats we have been so long accustomed to. The present management deserve well of the public. They have restored to the Coliseum the gilding, the rich upholstery, and the uniform magnificence which old Coliseum frequenters tell us Rome was so proud of fifty years ago.

"The opening scene last night — the broadsword combat between two young amateurs and a famous Parthian gladiator who was sent here a prisoner — was very fine. The elder of the two young gentlemen handled his weapon with a grace that marked the possession of extraordinary talent. His feint of thrusting, followed instantly by a happily delivered blow which unhelmeted the Parthian, was received with hearty applause. He was not thoroughly up in the backhanded stroke, but it was very gratifying to his numerous friends to know that, in time, practice would have overcome this defect. However, he was killed. His sisters, who were present, expressed considerable regret. His mother left the Coliseum. The other youth maintained the contest with such spirit as to call forth enthusiastic bursts of applause. When at last he fell a corpse, his aged mother ran screaming, with hair disheveled and tears streaming from her eyes, and swooned away just as her hands were clutching at the railings of the arena. She was promptly removed by the police. Under the circumstances the woman's conduct was pardonable, perhaps, but we suggest that such exhibitions interfere with the decorum which should be preserved during the performances, and are highly improper in the presence of the Emperor. The Parthian prisoner fought bravely and well; and well he might, for he was fighting for both life and liberty. His wife and children were there to nerve his arm with their love, and to remind him of the old home he should see again if he conquered. When his second assailant fell, the woman clasped her children to her breast and wept for joy. But it was only a transient happiness. The captive staggered toward her and she saw that the liberty he had earned was earned too late. He was wounded unto death. Thus the first act closed in a manner which was entirely satisfactory. The manager was called before the curtain and returned his thanks for the honor done him, in a speech which was replete with wit and humor, and closed by hoping that his humble efforts to afford cheerful and instructive entertainment would continue to meet with the approbation of the Roman public.

"The star now appeared, and was received with vociferous applause and the simultaneous waving of sixty thousand handkerchiefs. Marcus Marcellus Valerian (stage name — his real name is Smith) is a splendid specimen of physical development, and an artist of rare merit. His management of the battle-axe is wonderful. His gayety and his playfulness are irresistible, in his comic parts, and yet they are inferior to his sublime conceptions in the grave realm of tragedy. When his axe was describing fiery circles about the heads of the bewildered barbarians, in exact time with his springing body and his prancing legs, the audience gave way to uncontrollable bursts of laughter; but when the back of his weapon broke the skull of one and almost in the same instant its edge clove the other's body in twain, the howl of enthusiastic applause that shook the building was the acknowledgment of a critical assemblage that he was a master of the noblest department of his profession. If he has a fault (and we are sorry to even intimate that he has), it is that of glancing at the audience, in the midst of the most exciting moments of the performance, as if seeking admiration. The pausing in a fight to bow when bouquets are thrown to him is also in bad taste. In the great left-handed combat he appeared to be looking at the audience half the time, instead of carving his adversaries; and when he had slain all the sophomores and was dallying with the freshmen, he stooped and snatched a bouquet as it fell, and offered it to his adversary at a time when a blow was descending which promised favorably to be his death-warrant. Such levity is proper enough in the provinces, we make no doubt, but it ill suits the dignity of the metropolis. We trust our young friend will take these remarks in good part, for we mean them solely for his benefit. All who know us are aware that although we are at times justly severe upon tigers and martyrs, we never intentionally offend gladiators.

"The Infant Prodigy performed wonders. He overcame his four tiger whelps with ease, and with no other hurt than the loss of a portion of his scalp. The General Slaughter was rendered with a faithfulness to details which reflects the highest credit upon the late participants in it.

"Upon the whole, last night's performances shed honor not only upon the management but upon the city that encourages and sustains such wholesome and instructive entertainments. We would simply suggest that the practice of vulgar young boys in the gallery of shying peanuts and paper pellets at the tigers, and saying 'Hi-yi!' and manifesting approbation or dissatisfaction by such observations as 'Bully for the lion!' 'Go it, Gladdy!' 'Boots!' 'Speech!' 'Take a walk round the block!' and so on, are extremely reprehensible, when the Emperor is present, and ought to be stopped by the police. Several times last night, when the supernumeraries entered the arena to drag out the bodies, the young ruffians in the gallery shouted, 'Supe! supe!' and also, 'Oh, what a coat!' and 'Why don't you pad them shanks?' and made use of various other remarks expressive of derision. These things are very annoying to the audience.

"A matinée for the little folks is promised for this afternoon, on which occasion several martyrs will be eaten by the tigers. The regular performance will continue every night till further notice. Material change of programme every evening. Benefit of Valerian, Tuesday, 29th, if he lives."

I have been a dramatic critic myself, in my time, and I was often surprised to notice how much more I knew about Hamlet than Forrest did; and it gratifies me to observe, now, how much better my brethren of ancient times knew how a broadsword battle ought to be fought than the gladiators.

CHAPTER XXVII.

SO far, good. If any man has a right to feel proud of himself, and satisfied, surely it is I. For I have written about the Coliseum and the gladiators, the martyrs and the lions, and yet have never once used the phrase " butchered to make a Roman holiday." I am the only free white man of mature age who has accomplished this since Byron originated the expression.

Butchered to make a Roman holiday sounds well for the first seventeen or eighteen hundred thousand times one sees it in print, but after that it begins to grow tiresome. I find it in all the books concerning Rome — and here latterly it reminds me of Judge Oliver. Oliver was a young lawyer, fresh from the schools, who had gone out to the deserts of Nevada to begin life. He found that country, and our ways of life there, in those early days, different from life in New England or Paris. But he put on a woolen shirt and strapped a navy revolver to his person, took to the bacon and beans of the country, and determined to do in Nevada as Nevada did. Oliver accepted the situation so completely that

although he must have sorrowed over many of his
trials, he never complained — that is, he never complained but once. He, two others, and myself,
started to the new silver mines in the Humboldt
mountains — he to be Probate Judge of Humboldt
county, and we to mine. The distance was two
hundred miles. It was dead of winter. We bought
a two-horse wagon and put eighteen hundred pounds
of bacon, flour, beans, blasting powder, picks, and
shovels in it; we bought two sorry-looking Mexican
" plugs," with the hair turned the wrong way and
more corners on their bodies than there are on the
mosque of Omar; we hitched up and started. It
was a dreadful trip. But Oliver did not complain.
The horses dragged the wagon two miles from town
and then gave out. Then we three pushed the
wagon seven miles, and Oliver moved ahead and
pulled the horses after him by the bits. We complained, but Oliver did not. The ground was frozen,
and it froze our backs while we slept; the wind
swept across our faces and froze our noses. Oliver
did not complain. Five days of pushing the wagon
by day and freezing by night brought us to the bad
part of the journey — the Forty Mile Desert, or the
Great American Desert, if you please. Still, this
mildest-mannered man that ever was had not complained. We started across at eight in the morning,
pushing through sand that had no bottom; toiling
all day long by the wrecks of a thousand wagons,
the skeletons of ten thousand oxen; by wagon-tires

enough to hoop the Washington Monument to the top, and ox-chains enough to girdle Long Island; by human graves; with our throats parched always with thirst; lips bleeding from the alkali dust; hungry, perspiring, and very, very weary — so weary that when we dropped in the sand every fifty yards to rest the horses, we could hardly keep from going to sleep — no complaints from Oliver; none the next morning at three o'clock, when we got across, tired to death. Awakened two or three nights afterward at midnight, in a narrow cañon, by the snow falling on our faces, and appalled at the imminent danger of being " snowed in," we harnessed up and pushed on till eight in the morning, passed the " Divide " and knew we were saved. No complaints. Fifteen days of hardship and fatigue brought us to the end of the two hundred miles, and the judge had not complained. We wondered if anything *could* exasperate him. We built a Humboldt house. It is done in this way. You dig a square in the steep base of the mountain, and set up two uprights and top them with two joists. Then you stretch a great sheet of " cotton domestic " from the point where the joists join the hillside down over the joists to the ground; this makes the roof and the front of the mansion; the sides and back are the dirt walls your digging has left. A chimney is easily made by turning up one corner of the roof. Oliver was sitting alone in this dismal den, one night, by a sagebrush fire, writing poetry; he was very fond of

digging poetry out of himself — or blasting it out
when it came hard. He heard an animal's footsteps
close to the roof; a stone or two and some dirt
came through and fell by him. He grew uneasy
and said: "Hi! — clear out from there, can't
you!" — from time to time. But by and by he
fell asleep where he sat, and pretty soon a mule fell
down the chimney! The fire flew in every direction, and Oliver went over backwards. About ten
nights after that he recovered confidence enough to
go to writing poetry again. Again he dozed off to
sleep, and again a mule fell down the chimney.
This time, about half of that side of the house came
in with the mule. Struggling to get up, the mule
kicked the candle out and smashed most of the
kitchen furniture, and raised considerable dust.
These violent awakenings must have been annoying
to Oliver, but he never complained. He moved to
a mansion on the opposite side of the cañon, because he had noticed the mules did not go there.
One night about eight o'clock he was endeavoring to
finish his poem, when a stone rolled in — then a
hoof appeared below the canvas — then part of a
cow — the after part. He leaned back in dread,
and shouted "Hooy! hooy! get out of this!" and
the cow struggled manfully — lost ground steadily —
dirt and dust streamed down, and before Oliver
could get well away, the entire cow crashed through
on to the table and made a shapeless wreck of everything!

Then, for the first time in his life, I think, Oliver complained. He said:

" *This thing is growing monotonous !*"

Then he resigned his judgeship and left Humboldt county. "Butchered to make a Roman holiday" has grown monotonous to me.

In this connection I wish to say one word about Michael Angelo Buonarotti. I used to worship the mighty genius of Michael Angelo — that man who was great in poetry, painting, sculpture, architecture — great in everything he undertook. But I do not want Michael Angelo for breakfast — for luncheon — for dinner — for tea — for supper — for between meals. I like a change, occasionally. In Genoa, he designed everything; in Milan he or his pupils designed everything; he designed the Lake of Como; in Padua, Verona, Venice, Bologna, who did we ever hear of, from guides, but Michael Angelo? In Florence, he painted everything, designed everything, nearly, and what he did not design he used to sit on a favorite stone and look at, and they showed us the stone. In Pisa he designed everything but the old shot-tower, and they would have attributed that to him if it had not been so awfully out of the perpendicular. He designed the piers of Leghorn and the custom-house regulations of Civita Vecchia. But, here — here it is frightful. He designed St. Peter's; he designed the Pope; he designed the Pantheon, the uniform of the Pope's soldiers, the Tiber, the Vatican, the Coliseum, the Capitol, the

Tarpeian Rock, the Barberini Palace, St. John Lateran, the Campagna, the Appian Way, the Seven Hills, the Baths of Caracalla, the Claudian Aqueduct, the Cloaca Maxima — the eternal bore designed the Eternal City, and unless all men and books do lie, he painted everything in it! Dan said the other day to the guide, "Enough, enough, enough! Say no more! Lump the whole thing! say that the Creator made Italy from designs by Michael Angelo!"

I never felt so fervently thankful, so soothed, so tranquil, so filled with a blessed peace, as I did yesterday when I learned that Michael Angelo was dead.

But we have taken it out of this guide. He has marched us through miles of pictures and sculpture in the vast corridors of the Vatican; and through miles of pictures and sculpture in twenty other palaces; he has shown us the great picture in the Sistine Chapel, and frescoes enough to fresco the heavens — pretty much all done by Michael Angelo. So with him we have played that game which has vanquished so many guides for us — imbecility and idiotic questions. These creatures never suspect — they have no idea of a sarcasm.

He shows us a figure and says: "Statoo brunzo." (Bronze statue.)

We look at it indifferently and the doctor asks: "By Michael Angelo?"

"No — not know who."

Then he shows us the ancient Roman Forum. The doctor asks: "Michael Angelo?"

A stare from the guide. "No — a thousan' year before he is born."

Then an Egyptian obelisk. Again: "Michael Angelo?"

"Oh, *mon dieu*, genteelmen! Zis is *two* thousan' year before he is born!"

He grows so tired of that unceasing question sometimes, that he dreads to show us anything at all. The wretch has tried all the ways he can think of to make us comprehend that Michael Angelo is only responsible for the creation of a *part* of the world, but somehow he has not succeeded yet. Relief for overtasked eyes and brain from study and sightseeing is necessary, or we shall become idiotic sure enough. Therefore this guide must continue to suffer. If he does not enjoy it, so much the worse for him. We do.

In this place I may as well jot down a chapter concerning those necessary nuisances, European guides. Many a man has wished in his heart he could do without his guide; but knowing he could not, has wished he could get some amusement out of him as a remuneration for the affliction of his society. We accomplished this latter matter, and if our experience can be made useful to others they are welcome to it.

Guides know about enough English to tangle everything up so that a man can make neither head nor tail of it. They know their story by heart — the history of every statue, painting, cathedral, or other

wonder they show you. They know it and tell it as
a parrot would — and if you interrupt, and throw
them off the track, they have to go back and begin
over again. All their lives long, they are employed
in showing strange things to foreigners and listening
to their bursts of admiration. It is human nature
to take delight in exciting admiration. It is what
prompts children to say " smart " things, and do
absurd ones, and in other ways " show off " when
company is present. It is what makes gossips turn
out in rain and storm to go and be the first to tell a
startling bit of news. Think, then, what a passion
it becomes with a guide, whose privilege it is, every
day, to show to strangers wonders that throw them
into perfect ecstasies of admiration! He gets so
that he could not by any possibility live in a soberer
atmosphere. After we discovered this, we *never*
went into ecstasies any more — we never admired
anything — we never showed any but impassible
faces and stupid indifference in the presence of the
sublimest wonders a guide had to display. We had
found their weak point. We have made good use of
it ever since. We have made some of those people
savage, at times, but we have never lost our own
serenity.

The doctor asks the questions, generally, because
he can keep his countenance, and look more like an
inspired idiot, and throw more imbecility into the
tone of his voice than any man that lives. It comes
natural to him.

The guides in Genoa are delighted to secure an American party, because Americans so much wonder, and deal so much in sentiment and emotion before any relic of Columbus. Our guide there fidgeted about as if he had swallowed a spring mattress. He was full of animation — full of impatience. He said:

"Come wis me, genteelmen! — come! I show you ze letter writing by Christopher Colombo! — write it himself! — write it wis his own hand! — come!"

He took us to the municipal palace. After much impressive fumbling of keys and opening of locks, the stained and aged document was spread before us. The guide's eyes sparkled. He danced about us and tapped the parchment with his finger:

"What I tell you, genteelmen! Is it not so? See! handwriting Christopher Colombo! — write it himself!"

We looked indifferent — unconcerned. The doctor examined the document very deliberately, during a painful pause. Then he said, without any show of interest:

"Ah — Ferguson — what — what did you say was the name of the party who wrote this?"

"Christopher Colombo! ze great Christopher Colombo!"

Another deliberate examination.

"Ah — did he write it himself, or — or how?"

"He write it himself! — Christopher Colombo! he's own handwriting, write by himself!"

24*

Then the doctor laid the document down and said:

"Why, I have seen boys in America only fourteen years old that could write better than that."

"But zis is ze great Christo——"

"I don't care who it is! It's the worst writing I ever saw. Now you mustn't think you can impose on us because we are strangers. We are not fools, by a good deal. If you have got any specimens of penmanship of real merit, trot them out!—and if you haven't, drive on!"

We drove on. The guide was considerably shaken up, but he made one more venture. He had something which he thought would overcome us. He said:

"Ah, genteelmen, you come wis me! I show you beautiful, oh, magnificent bust Christopher Colombo!—splendid, grand, magnificent!"

He brought us before the beautiful bust—for it *was* beautiful—and sprang back and struck an attitude:

"Ah, look, genteelmen!—beautiful, grand,—bust Christopher Colombo!—beautiful bust, beautiful pedestal!"

The doctor put up his eyeglass—procured for such occasions:

"Ah—what did you say this gentleman's name was?"

"Christopher Colombo!—ze great Christopher Colombo!"

"Christopher Colombo—the great Christopher Colombo. Well, what did *he* do?"

"Discover America! — discover America, oh, ze devil!"

"Discover America. No — that statement will hardly wash. We are just from America ourselves. We heard nothing about it. Christopher Colombo — pleasant name — is — is he dead?"

"Oh, corpo di Baccho! — three hundred year!"

"What did he die of?"

"I do not know! — I cannot tell."

"Small-pox, think?"

"I do not know, genteelmen! — I do not know *what* he die of!"

"Measles, likely?"

"May be — may be — I do *not* know — I think he die of somethings."

"Parents living?"

"Im-posseeble!"

"Ah — which is the bust and which is the pedestal?"

"Santa Maria! — *zis* ze bust! — *zis* ze pedestal!"

"Ah, I see, I see — happy combination — very happy combination, indeed. Is — is this the first time this gentleman was ever on a bust?"

That joke was lost on the foreigner — guides cannot master the subtleties of the American joke.

We have made it interesting for this Roman guide. Yesterday we spent three or four hours in the Vatican again, that wonderful world of curiosities. We came very near expressing interest, sometimes — even admiration — it was very hard to keep from it.

x*

We succeeded though. Nobody else ever did, in the Vatican museums. The guide was bewildered — nonplussed. He walked his legs off, nearly, hunting up extraordinary things, and exhausted all his ingenuity on us, but it was a failure; we never showed any interest in anything. He had reserved what he considered to be his greatest wonder till the last — a royal Egyptian mummy, the best-preserved in the world, perhaps. He took us there. He felt so sure, this time, that some of his old enthusiasm came back to him:

"See, genteelmen! — Mummy! Mummy!"

The eyeglass came up as calmly, as deliberately as ever.

"Ah, — Ferguson — what did I understand you to say the gentleman's name was?"

"Name? — he got no name! — Mummy! — 'Gyptian mummy!"

"Yes, yes. Born here?"

"No! *Gyptian* mummy!"

"Ah, just so. Frenchman, I presume?"

"No! — *not* Frenchman, not Roman! — born in Egypta!"

"Born in Egypta. Never heard of Egypta before. Foreign locality, likely. Mummy — mummy. How calm he is — how self-possessed. Is, ah — is he dead?"

"Oh, *sacré bleu*, been dead three thousan' year!"

The doctor turned on him savagely:

"Here, now, what do you mean by such conduct

"IS HE DEAD?"

as this! Playing us for Chinamen because we are strangers and trying to learn! Trying to impose your vile second-hand carcasses on *us!* — thunder and lightning, I've a notion to — to — if you've got a nice *fresh* corpse, fetch him out! — or, by George, we'll brain you!"

We make it exceedingly interesting for this Frenchman. However, he has paid us back, partly, without knowing it. He came to the hotel this morning to ask if we were up, and he endeavored as well as he could to describe us, so that the landlord would know which persons he meant. He finished with the casual remark that we were lunatics. The observation was so innocent and so honest that it amounted to a very good thing for a guide to say.

There is one remark (already mentioned) which never yet has failed to disgust these guides. We use it always, when we can think of nothing else to say. After they have exhausted their enthusiasm pointing out to us and praising the beauties of some ancient bronze image or broken-legged statue, we look at it stupidly and in silence for five, ten, fifteen minutes — as long as we can hold out, in fact — and then ask:

" Is — is he dead?"

That conquers the serenest of them. It is not what they are looking for — especially a new guide. Our Roman Ferguson is the most patient, unsuspecting, long-suffering subject we have had yet. We shall be sorry to part with him. We have enjoyed his society very much. We trust he has enjoyed ours, but we are harassed with doubts.

We have been in the catacombs. It was like going down into a very deep cellar, only it was a cellar which had no end to it. The narrow passages are roughly hewn in the rock, and on each hand, as you pass along, the hollowed shelves are carved out, from three to fourteen deep; each held a corpse once. There are names, and Christian symbols, and prayers, or sentences expressive of Christian hopes, carved upon nearly every sarcophagus. The dates belong away back in the dawn of the Christian era, of course. Here, in these holes in the ground, the first Christians sometimes burrowed to escape persecution. They crawled out at night to get food, but remained under cover in the daytime. The priest told us that St. Sebastian lived under ground for some time while he was being hunted; he went out one day, and the soldiery discovered and shot him to death with arrows. Five or six of the early Popes — those who reigned about sixteen hundred years ago — held their papal courts and advised with their clergy in the bowels of the earth. During seventeen years — from A. D. 235 to A. D. 252 — the Popes did not appear above ground. Four were raised to the great office during that period. Four years apiece, or thereabouts. It is very suggestive of the unhealthiness of underground graveyards as places of residence. One Pope afterward spent his entire pontificate in the catacombs — eight years.

Another was discovered in them and murdered in the episcopal chair. There was no satisfaction in being a Pope in those days. There were too many annoyances. There are one hundred and sixty catacombs under Rome, each with its maze of narrow passages crossing and recrossing each other and each passage walled to the top with scooped graves its entire length. A careful estimate makes the length of the passages of all the catacombs com bined foot up nine hundred miles, and their graves number seven millions. We did not go through all the passages of all the catacombs. We were very anxious to do it, and made the necessary arrangements, but our too limited time obliged us to give up the idea. So we only groped through the dismal labyrinth of St. Calixtus, under the Church of St. Sebastian. In the various catacombs are small chapels rudely hewn in the stones, and here the early Christians often held their religious services by dim, ghostly lights. Think of mass and a sermon away down in those tangled caverns under ground!

In the catacombs were buried St. Cecilia, St. Agnes, and several other of the most celebrated of the saints. In the catacomb of St. Calixtus, St. Bridget used to remain long hours in holy contemplation, and St. Charles Borromeo was wont to spend whole nights in prayer there. It was also the scene of a very marvelous thing.

"Here the heart of St. Philip Neri was so inflamed with divine love as to burst his ribs."

I find that grave statement in a book published in New York in 1858, and written by " Rev. William H. Neligan, LL.D., M.A., Trinity College, Dublin; Member of the Archæological Society of Great Britain." Therefore, I believe it. Otherwise, I could not. Under other circumstances I should have felt a curiosity to know what Philip had for dinner.

This author puts my credulity on its mettle every now and then. He tells of one St. Joseph Calasanctius whose house in Rome he visited; he visited only the house — the priest has been dead two hundred years. He says the Virgin Mary appeared to this saint. Then he continues:

"His tongue and his heart, which were found after nearly a century to be whole, when the body was disinterred before his canonization, are still preserved in a glass case, and after two centuries the heart is still whole. When the French troops came to Rome, and when Pius VII. was carried away prisoner, blood dropped from it."

To read that in a book written by a monk far back in the Middle Ages, would surprise no one; it would sound natural and proper; but when it is seriously stated in the middle of the nineteenth century, by a man of finished education, an LL.D., M.A., and an archæological magnate, it sounds strangely enough. Still, I would gladly change my unbelief for Neligan's faith, and let him make the conditions as hard as he pleased.

The old gentleman's undoubting, unquestioning simplicity has a rare freshness about it in these matter-of-fact railroading and telegraphing days. Hear him, concerning the Church of Ara Cœli:

"In the roof of the church, directly above the high altar, is engraved, '*Regina Cœli lætare Alleluia*.' In the sixth century Rome was visited by a fearful pestilence. Gregory the Great urged the people to do penance, and a general procession was formed. It was to proceed from Ara Cœli to St. Peter's. As it passed before the mole of Adrian, now the Castle of St. Angelo, the sound of heavenly voices was heard singing (it was Easter morn)—'*Regina Cœli, lætare! alleluia! quia quem meruisti portare, alleluia! resurrexit sicut dixit; alleluia!*' The Pontiff, carrying in his hands the portrait of the Virgin (which is over the high altar and is said to have been painted by St. Luke), answered, with the astonished people, '*Ora pro nobis Deum, alleluia!*' At the same time an angel was seen to put up a sword in a scabbard, and the pestilence ceased on the same day. There are four circumstances which *confirm** this miracle: the annual procession which takes place in the western church on the feast of St. Mark: the statue of St. Michael, placed on the mole of Adrian, which has since that time been called the Castle of St. Angelo ; the antiphon Regina Cœli, which the Catholic church sings during paschal time ; and the inscription in the church."

* The italics are mine—M. T.